DATE DUE

Returning to Eden

Also by Michael W. Fox

CANINE BEHAVIOR
CANINE PEDIATRICS
INTEGRATIVE DEVELOPMENT OF BRAIN AND BEHAVIOR IN THE DOG
BEHAVIOR OF WOLVES, DOGS AND RELATED CANIDS
UNDERSTANDING YOUR DOG
UNDERSTANDING YOUR CAT
CONCEPTS IN ETHOLOGY, ANIMAL AND HUMAN BEHAVIOR
BETWEEN ANIMAL AND MAN: THE KEY TO THE KINGDOM
THE DOG: ITS DOMESTICATION AND BEHAVIOR
UNDERSTANDING YOUR PET
ONE EARTH, ONE MIND
THE SOUL OF THE WOLF

Editor

ABNORMAL BEHAVIOR IN ANIMALS
READINGS IN ETHOLOGY AND COMPARATIVE PSYCHOLOGY
THE WILD CANIDS
ON THE FIFTH DAY: ANIMAL RIGHTS AND HUMAN OBLIGATIONS

Children's Books

THE WOLF
VIXIE, THE STORY OF A LITTLE FOX
SUNDANCE COYOTE
RAMU AND CHENNAI
WHAT IS YOUR DOG SAYING?
WILD DOGS THREE
WHITEPAWS: A COYOTE-DOG

Returning to Eden
Animal Rights and Human Responsibility

Michael W. Fox

ROBERT E. KRIEGER PUBLISHING COMPANY
MALABAR, FLORIDA
1986

Original Edition 1980
Reprint Edition 1986

Printed and Published by
ROBERT E. KRIEGER PUBLISHING COMPANY, INC.
KRIEGER DRIVE
MALABAR, FLORIDA 32950

Printed in the United States of America

Library of Congress Cataloging in Publication Data

Fox, Michael W., 1937-
    Returning to Eden.

    Reprint. Originally published: New York : Viking Press, 1980.
    Bibliography: p.
    Includes index.
    1. Animals, Treatment of.   I. Title   II. Title: Animal rights and human responsibility.
(HV4708.F72   1986)   179.3   85-23695
ISBN 0-89874-934-4

10 9 8 7 6 5 4 3 2

First, it was necessary to civilize man in relation to man. Now it is necessary to civilize man in relation to nature and the animals.
—Victor Hugo, 1802–1885

Acknowledgments

The author wishes to express his gratitude for the support and encouragement of friends and colleagues and the Humane Society of the United States and is especially appreciative of the inspiration and encouragement of the society's president, John Hoyt. The author also wishes to express his thanks to Darlene Gehley for secretarial assistance and to Barbara Burn, senior editor for The Viking Press.

Contents

Introduction

This book is about the relationships, good and bad, between humans and other animals. It explores and exposes many of the contemporary human attitudes and values which together make us the most dangerous, destructive, selfish, and unethical animal on earth. It also reveals how we and the other animals are so closely interrelated that we all are kin in a biological, if not spiritual, sense; we all exist under the same benevolent star whose sunlight gives us life.

Yet in the sunlight we walk in the darkness of ignorance and indifference to the plight and future of the other creatures that share this earth and time with us. Few of us feel or act consciously—with conscience—knowing that humanity and nature are interdependent. The reasons why we and our social institutions act without fellow feeling toward the rest of creation are detailed, often with painful clarity, in the pages that follow. It is distrubing for me to hold up this mirror, but I do so because I am concerned over the suffering of wild and domestic animals; I am equally concerned, however, for the future of my own species, since the values and actions that destroy nonhuman life and cause untold suffering do no less to humans. In the diversity of relationships between people, animals, and nature, I have discovered a single unifying thread. It bridges time through the continuum of evolution, and it binds all life within ecological systems. This same thread can give human life both significance and fulfillment; it can lead us to a new awareness. It is expressed as empathy and vivified in a humane attitude toward animals and the natural world.

Mankind has severed itself from this thread and, in so doing, has become an alien on earth. Our detachment from nature, our lack of a sense of kinship and continuity with all life underlie the inhumane uses and abuses of animals and the havoc that is being wrought on the natural world. Freeing the world and our fellow creatures from such dominionism, suffering, and exploitation is one of the most urgent imperatives today, for our own survival depends upon it.

Human salvation is wholly dependent upon the liberation of nature from our selfish treatment and on humane consideration. Human liberation will begin when we understand that our evolution and fulfillment are contingent on the recognition of animal rights and on a compassionate and responsible stewardship of nature. The dawning of a new Eden is to come.

Returning to Eden

1

Animals Are Almost Humans

One major factor that separates us from animals and breaks the thread of kinship is the widespread belief that animals are very different from human beings. For example, many people think that animals have no emotional needs comparable to our own. It is also commonly believed that all nonhuman animals are governed by inborn instincts and lack the ability to reason, that they possess none of the "higher" human qualities, such as compassion, empathy, and a sense of morality.

Much has been written about the animal nature of humans in such popular but often misleading books as *The Naked Ape, The Territorial Imperative,* and *On Aggression* Even since Darwin, whose classic treatise *The Expression of the Emotions in Man and the Animals* created a stir, especially in religious circles (in which the supremacy and uniqueness of man over beast were upheld as divine gifts), people have been fascinated by and curious about the animal in man.

But what of the converse situation—the humanlike qualities of animals? Such considerations are generally judged as unsound, unscientific, or sentimental nonsense. To entertain the possibility that any animal other than a human one may think or feel as we do, have similar needs, and even develop anxiety states, phobias, and other emotional problems is to invite a skeptical reaction, if not ridicule.

1

One would be judged as being anthropomorphic, a term used when an animal is given humanlike attributes. Anthropomorphism is generally interpreted as oversentimental behavior, certainly as the biased perceptions of some people who are emotionally involved with their pets as though they were four-legged people. Ironically, anthropomorphism is criticized to a far greater extent today than the converse—zoomorphism. It seems to be easier for people to see animallike qualities in humans than it is to recognize the fact that many animals possess a variety of humanlike qualities. We accept the evidence of evolution insofar as man has evolved from the "lower" animals, but we firmly believe ourselves to be superior to any other living creature on earth. Perhaps we reject anthropomorphism as a travesty of human superiority over all other creatures.

Today, however, it should be considered unscientific *not* to take seriously the possibility that many animals do have certain qualities that have hitherto been thought to be exclusively human. There is a good deal of scientific evidence to support this contention, and once these facts become more widely known, they should change our regard for nonhuman animals in ways that will be good for both them and us.

Sentimental anthropomorphizing about animals can be improved upon through informed and empathic understanding. A deeper reverence for animals—for all life—may be encouraged not, as it generally is today, on purely emotional grounds, but on the more objective basis of scientific proof (as I have presented in my books, particularly in *The Soul of the Wolf* and *Between Animal and Man*). I have often overheard well-educated people arguing about whether or not animals feel pain to any degree, whether they can actually think, conceptualize, or experience emotions. Other people, no better informed, will often abuse the animals in their charge, perhaps holding onto the outmoded idea that animals can't suffer in order to allay their own guilt. The belief that animals are little more than unfeeling machines operated by reflexes and controlled by instincts is a long-standing and widely held view. The following observations are evidence to the contrary and should help dispel such erroneous beliefs.

ANIMAL AND HUMAN EMOTIONS

It is no anthropomorphism to assume that animals feel humanlike emotions such as pain, fear, anxiety, pleasure, and satisfaction. The proof lies in the brain. The brains of both man and dog (which I compared in my Ph.D. thesis entitled *Integrative Development of Brain and Behavior in the Dog*) have the same nerve centers (the limbic system) which modulate these emotional reactions. Stimulation of these centers via implanted electrodes in humans and animals produce almost identical physiological and behavior changes. Other emotional reactions thought to be exclusively human include jealousy, guilt, embarrassment, sadness/depression, love/devotion, and altruism. Research by ethologists and psychologists and a number of well-documented reports from owners of household pets show that this is far from the truth. These emotions are seen more frequently in relatively sociable and dependent animals such as dogs and rhesus monkeys than in the more solitary and independent species such as cats and foxes.

An infant monkey separated from its mother will show the same kind of anaclitic depression as a human infant does when separated, as for hospitalization. A black Labrador retriever in England became so depressed when it was left in a veterinary boarding kennel that it refused to eat food and was almost dead by the time its owners returned from a long vacation. But as soon as they returned, it began to eat again and quickly recovered.

One of the most remarkable examples of devotion concerns a Skye terrier dog in Scotland. After his master was buried in a small graveyard in Edinburgh, Bobby went and lay on his master's grave every night for no less than fourteen years. A statue in Greyfriar's Square was erected by local citizens in memory of this little dog. A similar case was told to me by a farmer in the midwestern United States. After his son's sudden death, the boy's border collie visited the grave every day for many months.

We might ask how a pet conceptualizes death, if it can. Certainly it experiences the emotional loss of a loved one, but is there any understanding of the actuality of death itself? A psychic mechanism may operate in some cases. I have six cases on record of pet dogs and cats becoming depressed and calling mournfully when a companion animal in the same house has been taken away to be put to sleep because of some incurable disease. In all cases, at about the same time that the companion pet was being destroyed, the surviving animal showed a sudden and obvious change in behavior. In one case the owner did not know that the vet had put the other pet to sleep until he called an hour later, and for an hour before, her cat had been calling frantically and showing distress.

But what of empathy, compassion, and altruism, the highest of human attributes? While the defense of one's offspring may be governed principally by instincts and hormones, a mechanistic explanation is inadequate to account for the following examples of animal compassion and altruism.

A field observer was recently amazed after closely watching two wild chimpanzees huddled close together while one poked around inside the other's mouth. An abscessed molar tooth was extracted, and after a little more surgery, another one was also removed!

Highly sociable wild animals, such as elephants and dolphins, will collectively defend an injured companion and will try to help it stand up or keep above water in order to breathe.

There are many stories of animal heroism—not of the dog or cat that coincidentally "wakes up" the family and saves them from a house on fire because it was terrified, but rather those pets that show clear insight and altruism. Until help came, one German shepherd held a little boy up by his coat after he fell through the ice; a Saint Bernard placed itself in front of its master's two unattended little children and refused to let them go near a busy highway in front of their house (the dog had never been trained to do this).

Although these are just a few examples, I think it is safe to say that the owner of a cat or dog who says that his pet is jealous, possessive, or embarrassed is not always being anthropomorphic. A socially dependent but emotionally insecure animal can, in a given situation (such as when rivalry erupts with a companion), react jealously or possessively. As for embarrassment, I recall feeling quite guilty once when I laughed at a friend's poodle after it had been shorn of its thick natural coat. It shrank away and hid under a table while the owner rightly chastised me for embarrassing her pet.

Guilt is easier to instill in a dependent, willing-to-please dog than in a relatively independent and self-confident cat. Every owner of a dog can tell if his pet has done something it shouldn't have during an absence. Instead of giving a friendly greeting, the pet may crouch submissively, anxiously lick its lips, or slink away to hide in anticipation of punishment. Some may choose to call this simple conditioning, but it is not simple, although it is a conditioned (learned) response. A dog and a child both learn what is socially acceptable behavior and, in knowing the difference between right and wrong, develop the sense of conscience and guilt.

ANIMAL SENSE AND CONSCIOUSNESS

To have a conscience implies that one experiences consciousness; thus, if an animal has a conscience and a sense of self in relation to others, does it not have consciousness? Animals are very much like children in this regard, tending to be stimulus-oriented, seeking immediate gratification, and by and large living for the moment. Adult people are more future-oriented and conditioned by habits developed in the past. It is easier to understand what is going on in animals and children because they naturally lack inhibitions about expressing what they want and how they feel. But with increasing maturity, this openness and here-and-now attitude undergo inhibition or repression as the adult learns to adapt himself to social norms.

In spite of these insights, we are still a long way from knowing just what an animal is thinking. The evidence seems to indicate that because of the stimulus-bound nature of animals' lives, they have little use for such abilities as reasoning and insight. Certainly in creatures with very simple nervous systems, such as insects, behavior is characteristically automatic, and no reasoning is ever needed to construct a complex hive or termite "city." Working together like a collective brain, such creatures shape their environments from an innate blueprint rather than on the basis of a concept.

An animal doesn't normally have to reason and conceptualize in its everyday existence, even if it were capable of doing so, for the environment doesn't necessarily develop or challenge such potentialities. One of the best examples of this is in the chimpanzee. As Ann Premack has shown in her book *Why Chimps Can Read*, with intensive training, they have been taught to communicate in American sign language and to read, and they can construct sentences and spontaneously make correct associations. They can do this because they use a language of gestures in communicating among themselves, but probably not to the degree of subtlety and complexity they manifest when taught deaf-mute sign language. Presumably under natural conditions they could get along just fine with what they have already developed as a means of communication.

But the communication of *ideas* is a different matter. Whereas animals easily communicate their *intentions* (playful, sexual, and so on), do and can they ever communicate concepts or ideas to each other? Certain alarm signals in monkeys evoke different reactions according to the type of signal, be it a warning of an aerial predator (eagle) or ground predator (panther). Is this simple conditioning, or does the animal have a concept about what each signal means? We can never know—or can we? Sometimes pets closely attuned to their owners seem capable of expressing concepts. For example, one of my graduate students has a poodle who loves cheese. She was having a cheese snack one day and said no to her dog. The animal went into the kitchen, brought out a large dog-bone biscuit, and placed it at her feet; it looked beseechingly at her and then at the cheese just to make the point crystal clear.

A male mongrel dog in St. Louis was tested by his owner, a dog trainer. She put on her coat, and the dog got excited, expecting to go out for a walk. Then the woman took off her coat and sat down. She repeated this performance four times, curious to see what her dog would do. He seemed somewhat confused, but when she finally put on her coat and took him out, he seemed overjoyed. Then suddenly the dog began to limp painfully on one leg. She took him back indoors to examine him, and while carefully feeling his foot, she looked up and caught his eye. He had a big panting grin on his face and, wagging his tail, leaped up and ran outdoors. He had turned the tables on his mistress and beat her at her own game.

A third remarkable anecdote concerns a German shepherd guide dog whose blind mistress told me this story. She was working in the kitchen when her dog grabbed her arm and insisted that she follow. He took her out into the backyard where her children were playing. The woman asked them what they were doing. They were playing with matches—a forbidden activity. Her dog, not trained to know this, had sensed that something was wrong and told his mistress the best way that he could.

TOUCH IS LOVE

Dogs and cats enjoy being stroked, and many a dog will work hard for its master just for the reward of a mere pat or two. Petting an animal produces an astonishing change not only in its behavior (it relaxes and solicits more petting) but also in its physiology, which I have detailed in my book *The Dog: Its Domestication and Behavior.* The heart rate slows down dramatically, indicating that the so-called parasympathetic system, which is part of the autonomic nervous system, has been activated. Petting an infant animal or human baby stimulates this system so that muscular relaxation also occurs and the flow of digestive juices and peristalsis are stimulated. These physiological changes not only are associated with contact comfort but also help consolidate the social bond between mother and infant. Many adult animals will also groom each other (an activity which produces the same effect as petting); the grooming can be observed during courtship in foxes and cats and as part of everyday social behavior in monkeys—in which it serves as a pleasurable, socially bonding activity.

A human infant, monkey, or puppy deprived of this "mother love" or tender contact will not thrive. Abnormal behavior, especially self-clutching and sucking—comfort actions that serve as a substitute for loving contact—usually develops. Without this stimulation, as Ashley Montagu describes in his book *Touching*, growth may also be retarded because the digestive processes are not adequately stimulated. Contentment noises in animals, such as purring in cats, may be a form of "auditory stroking" (i.e., grooming sounds) since, like stroking and licking, they evoke a sense of well-being and relaxation in both the sender and the receiver. Cats are especially instructive in this regard; since the petting phenomenon develops in infancy, many a well-socialized adult cat, as I discuss in *Understanding Your Cat*, will "regress" and behave like a kitten when it is being stroked by its owner; it will knead with its forepaws and sometimes salivate and nuzzle as though it were trying to nurse. If an animal doesn't like contact and is touch-shy (people are like this, too), one may suspect a lack of adequate gentle contact early in life, which greatly limits the social capacities of the adult.

Although there are great cultural differences in humans as to the amount and kind of touching that is socially acceptable, we all need some kind of physical contact, especially in infancy. Touch and love are synonymous, for both animals and people.

CRITICAL ATTACHMENT TIME

If a puppy is raised without human contact until it is three or four months of age, it will be wild and unapproachable. There is a critical period early in life—between five and ten weeks of age—when it can be most readily socialized or emotionally attached. Similarly, in human infants there is a critical period between three and seven months when the child develops its primary social bond with its mother. If this bond is not properly established, the child, like the dog, will have difficulties later in life in social relationships with people. The best time to adopt a puppy and a child is around six weeks and three to four months, respectively, since both animals and humans in their development have this same critical period in early life. Deprivation or inadequate socialization will be detrimental to the adult animal and human, and both will have difficulties establishing close bonds and adjusting to social relationships when they are mature.

PET NEUROSES

Dogs especially, because of their great social dependence, often develop a variety of neurotic and psychosomatic disorders if the close bond with their owners is threatened in some way. Many of the symptoms they develop are like those that emotionally disturbed and insecure children sometimes show—because their brains are similar (the emotional centers described earlier), because they also have a critical period for socialization, and because owners, like parents, can be overpermissive, inconsistent, overindulgent, and so on, inadvertently reinforcing dependency, which is at the root of so many emotional problems in both animal and man.

Psychosomatic hives, itching, seizures, bronchiospasms and asthmatic attacks, gastrointestinal disorders, anorexia nervosa (refusal to eat food), and compulsive eating occur as a result of your dog's being emotionally disturbed. Paranoid reactions to sudden noises (especially thunder) and to strangers or people in uniform and even psychoticlike symptoms have also been reported. The most astounding case is one of an overdependent dog that suddenly developed a classic conversion hysteria; both hind legs were paralyzed. Alone at the veterinary hospital it made spontaneous recovery, but when it was returned home, a relapse occurred. The cause? Its "mother" mistress had just given birth to her first child and no longer gave the dog her undivided attention. The cure? The dog was given to another childless couple.

I often hear the phrase "If only animals could talk" from people who do not understand how clearly they do communicate. Understanding animals, which is what I have attempted to explain in my books *Understanding Your Cat* and *Understanding Your Dog*, can open up an entirely new world for many people—the world of animals, whom we can learn to treat with the respect and reverence we generally reserve for humans. Even if animals aren't quite people, there is far more human in them than we might dare believe.

OUR ANIMAL ROOTS

One proof of our kinship with animals can be seen in studies of the human brain. Comparing its structure and function with the brains of other mammals, we find that we differ in fewer ways than we may think; surprisingly, the similarities are greater than the differences. For example, the human brain goes through stages of development very similar to the developing nervous system of a lizard, chicken, or dog. In fact, the human brain is a composite accumulation of earlier brains, brought along with us from past lives or evolutionary epochs and encoded in our genes. As Professor Paul MacLean has shown, the human brain has three distinct regions. One, the brain stem or core, is termed the old brain, which differs little from the brain of a reptile or bird. An extended outgrowth of this is the middle brain, the emotional center or limbic system; this represents the final stage of development for primitive mammals, such as the kangaroo and opossum. The forebrain or neocortex is the latest evolutionary addition to the complex brains of placental mammals—herbivores, carnivores, and primates. In man, it is a relatively huge mushrooming outgrowth, which subtly regulates activities in the middle and lower brains; in addition, this portion of the brain, like a complex biocomputer, is a storage center for information and contains a well-developed speech center. This continuum of increasing complexity indicates a continuum of awareness or mental experience from the "lower" to the "higher" (most recently evolved) animal species. Man is not so different from other animals qualitatively, but rather in a quantitative sense, reflected in the great mass of new brain he has acquired (much of which, incidentally, he does not use). The subjective, inner, emotional world, however, is principally modulated by the forebrain or the neocortex, which regulates the middle brain.

Another striking similarity between the human and nonhuman mammalian brain is seen in the electrical activity patterns of electroencephalograph (EEG) recordings. A dog, for example, has the same states of activity as a man, its EEG patterns being almost identical in wakefulness, quiet sleep, dreaming, and daydreaming.

As for the chemistry of the central nervous and endocrine systems, we know that there is no difference in kind between humans and other animals. The biochemistry of physiological and emotional states (of stress and anxiety, for example) differ little between mice and men. Thus, it is not illogical to assume that associated emotional "mental" states are basically the same for people and their animal kin. The only major difference perhaps is that some may choose to interpret them differently.

ANIMAL AWARENESS

Dr. Donald Griffin, in his provocative book *The Question of Animal Awareness,* observes:

> ... behavioral scientists have grown highly uncomfortable at the very thought of mental states or subjective qualities in animals. When they intrude on our scientific discourse, many of us feel sheepish, and when we find ourselves using such words as fear, pain, pleasure, or the like, we tend to shield our reductionist egos behind a respectable blanket of quotation marks.

One must seriously question why behavioral and biomedical scientists think in the way Dr. Griffin describes. Perhaps they do so to absolve themselves from the burden of responsibility and guilt they should feel toward the animals they use and sacrifice for the sake of knowledge.

To doubt that an animal can experience pain, fear, anxiety, satisfaction, and pleasure is to doubt the very existence of our own consciousness. And to reject the very existence of our own consciousness. And to reject the possibility that our most recently evolved animal kin—the carnivores and primates—cannot or do not experience comparable states of joy, depression, guilt, remorse, and love is as illogical as denying that you or I have such experience.

There is a general consensus among scientists that instinctive or

innate actions are genetically predetermined, more or less automatic or "unconscious" behaviors. I would suggest, however, that
an animal, during and after an instinctual act, is acutely aware of
what it is doing, although it may not reach a human level of *reflective* consciousness at which it asks itself why it is doing what it is
doing.

It seems to me that a number of culturally acquired actions in
man—rituals and other habitual modes of behavior—are not unlike
instincts in that during their execution humans tend to act and react
without asking why. I sometimes get the impression that humans
are often far less aware of what they are doing, of what is going on
around them, than an alert dog or pig might be

Partially because of our own unthinking states of habitual action,
I believe that man projects this state of nonawareness upon the animal, presuming that the animal, too, is in a state of relative unconsciousness. In so doing, we demean the degree of awareness of
nonhuman sentient beings. Biological instincts are not the same as
unconscious cultural habits.

Another category of unconscious habits in man includes idiosyn-
cratic bodily movements, postures, and attitudes. In sensitivity and
body-awareness training a person learns to become aware of such
actions. The training is designed not to open up the instinctual unconscious, but to break the blocks of blind habits. What I am implying here is that the instinctual unconscious of Freud is not the
hidden id of blind animalistic instincts, but the blocks created by
cultural and personal habits that repress our thinking and behavior.
These must be removed before we can become fully awake, aware,
and sensitized to ourselves. Animals lacking such blocks may be far
more aware (and possibly more sentient) than we are. Man's highest
state of consciousness must integrate total instinctual awareness (the
existential here-and-now of the animal) with reflective consciousness, in which we are aware of each sensation and action.

One question still remains to be answered. When an animal acts
altruistically toward another, may we interpret this as true empathy, or is it an anthropomorphic projection of human behavior? If
an animal acts "instinctively" toward another to enhance its own
survival or the survival of its species, does it "know" what it is

doing, does it really care, or is the response purely reflexive? Here I would like to challenge the Cartesian mechanistic view of animals, for I believe that an animal *is* fully aware of what it does when it responds with fellow feeling and helps a companion in distress. One may ask if the animal *needs* to know. It may *need* to act in a particular way, but it may not need to know the purpose of its actions. Such reflective awareness is most likely shared by only a few mammalian species, but the sympathetic tuning, the sense of fellow feeling, may be shared by all sentient creatures. Animals that rely on instincts do not by definition or necessity lack sense or sensitivity. Perhaps man is the only animal that can ask itself why, but we may never be really sure of this.

Only a skeptic divorced from his own animal self would argue against the evidence of animal sentience and awareness and refuse to recognize in animals the existence of mental states akin to our own. Why would one argue against such evidence? Perhaps to avoid the revolutionary consequences of such evidence because it is easier to think of other animals as different, inferior, and unfeeling. To assume otherwise is to assume the enormous responsibilities of equitable benevolence to all life, of animal rights on a level of equal consideration with human rights.

2

Man and Nature: Biological and Cultural Perspectives

Because of the way life is organized on earth, we and all other creatures are biologically dependent on each other. In this chapter I will explore certain aspects of this complex relationship, using available scientific evidence as a basis to establish the existence of what I call a unifying biospiritual ethic.

ECOLOGY: THE HARMONY OF LIFE

Ecology is one branch of the natural sciences that serves as a bridge between science and philosophy. For example, the ecological fitness or adaptability of an animal in relation to its environment and the interdependence of different creatures is like the Zen Buddhist concept of the unity of all in one and the One in all. Such holistic thinking contrasts with the Aristotelian method of dividing in order to understand—of separating the observer from the observed, the mind from the body, the animal from its environment, and so on. Actually both views can be complementary, but in the Western world the latter view has predominated with unfortunate consequences, as we shall see. Historically this Western outlook of separateness and individuality is derived from or at least is reflected in the Judeo-Christian belief in man's supremacy over all creation, but in recent years the science of ecology has come to the forefront, offering us a more balanced and harmonizing world view, as exemplified in the writings of René Dubos (*A God Within*), Guy Murchie (*The Seven Mysteries of Life*), and Dolores La Chapelle (*Earth Wisdom*).

How might the findings of ecology influence us? For example, you as an individual, ecologically speaking, can be defined in terms of all your relationships—that is, in a social context—rather than as a separate being. You are as much a part of other people and of the world as a whole as you are an individual unto yourself. The fact that you seem to be the center of your universe is just a coincidence because of the egocentric nature of your nervous system. Molecular biology teaches us that we all are living communities—with amoebas in our bloodstreams, mitochondria in the cells of our bodies, bacteria on our skin and in our intestines. Destroy this organic menagerie or disturb its equilibrium in our bodies, as Lewis Thomas shows in *The Lives of a Cell*, and we would quickly sicken and die. The ecological balance of life in our bodies is like that anywhere else on earth. Imbalance means sickness for the individual human body or for the earth. The application of the ecological principle of holism to Western concepts of medicine is a much needed innovation today and will improve the effectiveness of current methods of medical diagnosis and treatment.

SELF-REGULATION

One of the most delicately balanced relationships in nature is that of prey and predator populations. All natural systems are self-regulating, and all wild animal populations have naturally evolved population-regulating controls. For example, quail and pheasant produce enormous numbers of eggs, and field mice and other rodents have many offspring. The production of many young is an evolved adaptation to ensure the survival of at least enough young to continue the species in the face of natural diseases and predators, such as foxes and bobcats, which in turn control bird and rodent overpopulation which could cause destruction of the habitat. The same system works also for the wolf's prey—the deer, moose, and caribou. To regulate their own populations, foxes, bobcats, and wolves are very territorial and keep others of their kind away, thus preventing the supply of prey from becoming exhausted in their hunting ranges. Destroy the quail, rodents, or deer, and there would be no foxes, bobcats, or wolves. Destroy foxes, bobcats, or wolves, and there would be an overabundance of prey, habitat destruction through overgrazing, and eventually a "crash" in the prey population. It follows, therefore, that any form of human intervention (by hunting or poisoning) may have disastrous consequences.

As R. L. Smith shows in *The Ecology of Man*, if modern man is to learn anything from ecology, it is this: He must act with the utmost caution because the balance of nature is extremely delicate and often unpredictable. Using specialized equipment and years of field data, a national body of scientists some years ago predicted a population explosion of lemmings in a particular area of Alaska. But during the summer of that predicted lemming high, hardly a lemming was to be seen on the tundra in the study area! Not even the best scientific minds can understand every aspect of this infinitely complex natural structure of life. Since this is so, we should exercise a measure of self-control before we attempt to control our surroundings and learn more of ecology before we interfere further with order or nature.

EVOLUTION: KINSHIP IN THE CONTINUITY OF DIVERSITY

An outstanding feature of animal and plant evolution is diversity. Within each major evolutionary branch—for example, the insect division—there are countless smaller branches leading from the main stem of the phylum to the millions of separate species.

We know that over many generations exposure of the same species to different environmental conditions can eventually lead to changes in structure and behavior. Through natural selection, the useful qualities of the species survive and are passed along genetically to future members of the population. The genetic diversity in species groups gives them their potential for survival and for further diversity.

But when a species is protected or "buffered" from the pressures of environmental and social selection so that there are no strong forces to shape structure and behavior in one direction, only then may even greater variation develop. Our domesticated dogs, for example (as I detail in *The Dog: Its Behavior and Domestication*), protected by man from natural selection to varying degrees, manifest wide variations in size and temperament; contrast a chihuahua and a great Dane, a beagle and a bulldog. Domestication, a special form of evolution, can increase diversity, and a comparable process in man—civilization or acculturation—can increase diversity in a comparable way. Highly civilized cultures can support many variants that might be physically or psychologically incapable of surviving off the land without the support of others.

Interestingly, superficial similarities between species can give a misleading impression of relatedness. In order to adapt to similar conditions, many diverse species evolve similar adaptive strategies in structure or behavior; compare the wings of flying birds and insects or the fins of fish and seals. Some types of structure and behavior do, however, help us identify kinship similarities in closely related species; compare the facial expressions of humans and rhesus monkeys or the similar behaviors of cats and foxes, who share recent common ancestors.

The human mind, in classifying human and nonhuman animals into "like" and "unlike," may be misled by apparent superficial differences and not appreciate the less obvious, deeper similarities. Superficial and often illusory differences have led to racist, sexist, "speciesist," and other separatist views which have divisive and alienating consequences. They contaminate our thinking with such notions as the superiority of man over animal, whites over blacks, men over women, and so on. Even today people still question whether blacks are less intelligent than whites or dogs superior to cats. If we look for differences, we can find them even within members of one family, race, or species.

But this apparent diversity is only a surface phenomenon which can distract us from the underlying truth of our kinship with all life.

When we go back in time, to study fossil records of past epochs, or when we compare the structure and components of our body cells with those of slime molds, fish, and prairie grass, we find that we all converge. As Lewis Thomas eloquently shows, at deeper levels there are more similarities than there are differences in both structure and function. All existing species come from common ancestral family roots which can easily be traced; for example, bears, raccoons, ferrets, cats, and wolves all share the same ancestors.

When Charles Darwin came forward with evidence to support his theory of evolution in *The Origin of Species* the continuity between species evolving toward greater mental abilities was accepted by very few. Most people chose to use Darwin's evidence to support their view of man's superiority and dominion over all creatures.

Although the theory of evolution is now widely accepted, some people continue to believe that human beings are a special form of divine creation, something separate from and above all other life forms—the only species with a "soul." There are no scientific grounds for assuming that we are the only earthbeings to have souls, immortal or otherwise, but it is clearly traditional for us to cling to the Judeo-Christian tradition of man's God-given dominion over all creation. Some people take this as the right to use nature as a convenient resource for their own self-centered gratification and to think of all creatures as theirs to harvest and dispose of at will. But if we interpret humanely, we can accept it as stewardship rather than as exploitation. We must, however, begin by establishing dominion over ourselves.

The evidence that there is kinship beneath the apparent diversity of all life is now irrefutable. Surely this fact is an injunction to mankind to think and act differently and to work toward a unity of all nations and races and of the rest of creation. Our survival and fulfillment depend on our knowledge of kinship with all life, and the ethical responsibilities that come with such knowledge are one of the most vital imperatives of the times.

"Kill or be killed" is one of the rules of nature, in which life is a struggle for survival. Each individual is devoured or otherwise utilized by another until we reach the top of the food chain. The jungle seems to expose the cruel realities of survival by violent combat, stealth and might, agility and wit, or so many would believe.

From behavioral studies of predator animals, such as the wolf, lion, and hyena (by David Mech, Michael Fox, George Schaller, Hans Kruuk, and other ethologists), there is no evidence of malicious intent. We readily misinterpret nature by projecting our own values and judgments on what we see. We mistakenly equate those destructive elements of nature with human destructiveness—ignorance, cruelty, and killing for killing's sake—as we also identify the "beastliness" of nature with the "beast" that surfaces when man acts inhumanely.

Nature is not cruel, however; it is merely impartial, with its own implicit laws that create an ecological harmony between species. The "laws" of nature have evolved so that the continuation of each species is ensured, in spite of the destructive forces that appear to be at work when, for example, a wolf pack tears a deer apart. It might seem inhumane to stand by and allow the wolves to kill the deer especially for someone who believes in ahimsa (the ethic of nonviolence). Yet to intervene would be ecologically and therefore ethically unsound; reverence for all life must include within it an awareness of natural laws. I call this the biospiritual ethic (see Chapter 11), in which sound and sensible biological knowledge and spiritual reverence for all life are combined.

Where, then, does compassionate action fit in, if one must ignore such an act of violence? I do not refer to the callous indifference of ignorance as when a person cannot empathize with an animal's suffering and rationalizes that animals don't feel pain as humans do. Nor do I refer to blind anthropomorphic sentimentalism, which can be equally disruptive both socially and ecologically, as when someone might actually try to prevent wolves from making their kill. This is simply a case of misplaced kindness, like a person who puts out food for stray cats and dogs and does nothing else to rectify the stray-pet problem—actually aggravating the problem in the process rather than the reverse.

Truly compassionate action may be superficially contrary to the code of ahimsa and to the humane, biospiritual ethic. Responsible intervention is the key, combining reverence for all life with sound social and ecological knowledge. For example, the deer population in a particular locale may be extremely low in proportion to the number of wolves—perhaps because of excessive human hunting of deer or improper forest management—so that there is inadequate browse for the deer. Some wolves may have to be killed, fewer deer hunting permits issued, and some acres of forest burned to encourage new growth. By the same token, several thousand stray cats and dogs may have to be humanely destroyed, neuter clinics run to help control the population problem, and educational programs and legislation set up to make people more responsible owners.

The biospiritual ethic can thus accept destruction sometimes as part of an essential act of compassion. This is not at variance with the humane code of conduct, although it may, like the wolves killing the deer, be misinterpreted as an act of violence. All forces of destruction in nature are regulated and balanced with the forces of creation and multiplication. Like the wolves, we must kill in order to live, but let us at least avoid unnecessary suffering and killing for selfish reasons of profit, or else we will simply live to kill. May we, instead, kill in order to live and only then with understanding and compassion.

It is through the humane movement, with people's active involvement in the concern for animal welfare and conservation, that we come face to face with many human values and attitudes. Blind reverence for all life without ecological awareness is something we must face up to realistically. We must discover the intrinsic truth and meaning in life and man's role therein as steward, as distinct from "manager" of his own vested emotional, financial, or recreational interests.

A healthy attitude toward what we judge as wrong and cruel in nature may help us become more ethically responsible in our human endeavors. It may also lead us to accept that as there is nothing fundamentally cruel or "beastly" in nature, so there is nothing fundamentally "beastly" about human nature. I believe that man is, by nature, a potentially humane and ethically responsible animal. To blame evolution or the animal within us for not realizing our potential is to abdicate the responsibility for our own shortcomings. We tend to blame nature for our "beastliness" because we still identify the inhumanity of mankind with the cruel and evil forces of nature. There is nothing wrong with nature or with human nature when it is allowed to develop normally, though it can become deformed and distorted by cultural values and attitudes.

MAN AND ENVIRONMENT

The human species possesses one trait unique in the animal kingdom. No other species can change its environment to any comparable degree. This trait sets man apart from other animals, the structure and behavior of which are primarily shaped by the environment. In humans, this relationship has been reversed so that, for technological man, almost any habitat can be changed to serve human interests, though usually at the expense of other species. This ability, combined with the ever-increasing mass of humanity, could so change the natural world that within only a few more generations there will be little of nature left.

While today we may glorify the scientific, technological, and cultural achievements of our species, many people still find greater satsifaction with the wonders of nature. Most human creations pale into insignificance before those of natural creation.

The two need not be mutually exclusive, although human building too often takes precedence over nature, at the expense of wildlife and habitat. We can surely incorporate nature—lakes, forests, rivers, open meadows, prairies, and such—into the total design of the human environment, as Ian McHarg urges in *Design with Nature.* By considering the immediate environment and the "rights" of its plant and animal residents, we can find solutions that would not jeopardize the natural world and that would at the same time satisfy those human needs for change. Land developers and real estate agents, for example, are finding that people prefer to live and work in surroundings that have a semblance, whether real or contrived, of naturalness. The jungles of potted plants in high-rise apartments and offices alone attest to this deep-seated human tendency.

This love of nature is not sufficient, however, to control the many ways in which we defile and destroy the natural world. Skeptics wonder now just what is left on earth that has not been changed in some way by mankind. Many desert areas in the world, for example, were created by our forefathers, just as we are creating others for our children, as Erik Eckholm recounts in *Losing Ground.*

We are becoming increasingly aware of our biologically unprecedented ability to change the environment in countless ways— through irrigation, introduction of domesticated plants and animals, deforestation, mining, and so forth—and we are slowly learning that we must temper our actions for our future survival. Natural biological controls are by and large inadequate, for humans work quickly, while nature generally has a delayed effect and works too slowly to be effective to control us. Hence the necessity for us to develop foresight and to devise social and legal controls and guidelines for our actions. It is here that conservation represents not a sentimental/aesthetic concern for nature, but rather a major effort to regulate our impact upon the natural world: self-dominion instead of global domination and self-destruction. Conservation is one of the most significant cultural advances that our species has made, and we can only hope that it has not come 10,000 years too late.

DIVERSITY AND EQUILIBRIUM:
THE PEACEABLE KINGDOM

Within a given habitat each plant and animal species occupies a particular niche and role in using available resources. Through the interplay of complex feedback-control systems, as demonstrated by Professor E. P. Odum, each individual in a species is restrained through competition and cooperation. Similar species (in their behavior, niche requirements, and so forth) will also compete with each other, while diverse species will cooperate in sharing the resources of a given habitat.

Competition within species can be reduced through evolutionary adaptations, leading to diverse forms and eventually to different species. A good example is the Galápagos finch, thirteen species of which presumably evolved from a common ancestor into different forms, each of which has a different means of feeding and thus fills a different niche in its habitat. Their diversity ensures that they will not overlap significantly in their food requirements and compete, nor will they exhaust any particular food source.

This natural order of life, of balanced diversity, makes a striking contrast with the condition of our own species. We are running out of resources, and the diversity of our specialist roles is becoming excessive, leading to a breakdown in communication and a disequilibrium in organization. Like the structural "inventions" of animals, which enable them to adapt to different niches, our technological inventions and specialized techniques have enabled us to fill increasingly varied niches throughout the world. But this has also led to competition with other species, resulting in the extinction of many, and to the destruction of local cultures and traditions even in our own species.

We should study and apply the theory of natural equilibrium if we are to control our disruptive proliferation not only in terms of population but also in terms of progressive diversity. There are limits to growth, but the limits to diversity (as discussed by J. H. Connell in relation to diversity in tropical rain forests and coral reefs) are not widely recognized. The study of nature shows that there is a finite set of niches in each ecosystem, and even though we may create artificial niches (as in the various hierarchical roles in a bureaucracy), the same natural laws that limit growth and diversity hold true. We must therefore regulate these forms of human "progress" since both of them, if unrestrained, will have biocidal consequences.

As we multiply and compete for living space and for resources with other living creatures, destruction escalates. We destroy forests and take more land for growing our food; by doing so, we reduce natural diversity and eliminate the niches as well as the associated species of countless creatures. Ironically, we also create new niches for pests and pestilence, which are natural consequences of man-induced disequilibrium. While we invade the niches of other species, as with our fishing fleet "factories," we also contaminate them with pesticides, pollutants, and other chemicals which enter the food chain and eventually reach us.

As we continue to develop our technology to exploit the earth's resources, we destroy even more species and niches and further disrupt natural equilibrium. Scientific studies of natural processes can help us avoid catastrophe, but scientific technology is still contaminated with materialism and egocentric human needs. Science has been abused in our preoccupation with mastering the material world. We need a science of humanity to balance the externally applied science of technology.

In the past, laws and ethics were related to regulating human societies, but they must now have a much broader relevance in terms of mankind and the world. We would do well to revise the old injunction and cease from the urge to prosper and multiply and cover the earth.

The so-called order of nature is not stable; it is always in a state of dynamic change as it achieves equilibrium through evolution, as one epoch succeeds another, as one species succeeds another. But we are increasing the rate of change, and by accelerating entropy (rate of energy consumed), we accelerate the rate and frequency of extinction. One of many dangers is that some new opportunistic species or mutant—like drug-resistant crop pests—can quickly evolve and predominate over others so that diversity is further reduced and stability cannot be restored.

This danger is compounded by the fact that natural selection for "fitness" is relaxed or undirected in our species; consequently we may become overdependent upon medical support with drugs, prosthetic devices, and so on, the genetic consequences of which only the future will tell. Worse still, perhaps, is that society tends to reinforce and reward undesirable types over others (such as megalomaniac status seekers, "workaholics," and competitive individualists). Our very unnatural selection criteria (in terms of ideologies and values if not of genes per se) for our own species may well add to our own demise.

Without control, it is highly likely that predictions of megacatastrophes and depletion of the earth will come true. Are we to look forward to a future of cloned and artificially propagated animal and plant species preserved as living museum specimens in carefully managed natural and artificial sanctuaries? Wildness will soon be something of the past, and we all will be diminished with its passing. Man-created "Edens," where formerly wild creatures are tamed or semidomesticated, may be all that remains when we have "civilized" the world. Safari parks and other wildlife preserves already point to this future probability. We must preserve what natural diversity there is, so that the "peaceable kingdom" to come will not be impoverished.

THE PATHOLOGY OF UNIFORMITY

"No one yet knows how many kinds of plants and animals are needed to stabilize natural systems enough for any given level of brain complexity." In this statement, Paul Shepard emphasizes the connection between environment and consciousness. If the environment degenerates and diversity is reduced, parallel degenerative changes may occur in human consciousness since it is a product of the environment. Already, according to Valerius Geist, our brain size is about one-sixth less than that of our Cro-Magnon ancestors. Many studies (which I reviewed in my book *Integrative Development of Brain and Behavior in the Dog*) have shown that domestication—developing in a simple, deprived environment—results in the reduction in brain size and complexity in animals, and civilization or acculturation in man may well result in comparable changes. The, apparent diversity and complexity of technology is an illusion hiding the conformity of values, needs, and attitudes. A technological "utopia" of uniformity, like the sterile suburbs of middle-class America, attests to the stimulus-deprivation effects of sameness.

Sameness is the pathology of a human-dominated world in which nature is sterilized, tamed, domesticated, and simplified to facilitate control. But humans themselves become like the natural world they have changed, and this affects (as well as reflects) their state of awareness. The totality and depth of one's self-identity are surely created through experience and involvement with diverse others, both people and animals. But when diversity is reduced and dominated by uniformity, self-identity will be shallow and poorly grounded. Sameness can therefore limit the realization of human potential and also reduce our capacity to relate and empathize with others who are not the same. The lack of challenge in a monotonous, all-providing utopia may also lead to physical and psychological deterioration. Symptoms of the pathology of sameness include identity crisis, boredom, escapism, subclinical autism, and xenophobia (fear of or indifference toward strangers, including unfamiliar races, classes, species, and environments).

The tension that exists between man and the natural world, especially between "primitive" man, the omnivore and hunter, and his swift and intelligent prey, and between man and his natural enemies was the impetus for the evolution of human intelligence. Today new challenges, such as the conquest of space and environmental crises, push us still further, not only to adapt but to acquire more knowledge as well. But there are many of us who, because of unequal opportunity or sheer contentment with the status quo of creature comforts, are deprived of the experience of challenge. This may mean that in spite of individual exceptions, the general level of intelligence of our culture and of the species itself may be now on the decline.

We may not be lacking for facts, thanks to our experts and our computers, but we may be losing our insight and wisdom. Overeducating the left, cerebral hemisphere of the brain (the objective, factual, and analytical side) and neglecting the right (associated with subjective, intuitive, and synthesizing functions) is the most serious flaw in modern education. Robots are produced, the fruits of scientific reductionism, serving not humanity and nature, but industry and technology. Such utilitarian rationalists are the new elite intelligentsia, but like the systems they create and serve, they are not entirely human. Their minds are programmed like the machines, technology, and organizations they serve; their environment mirrors their state of consciousness. This is not science-fiction speculation: Ronald Reagan, as governor of California, had a significant impact on state colleges when he reduced the "right-hemisphere" departments of the arts and humanities, proclaiming that "Society needs scientists and technologists." Graduate students at many universities now require classes in remedial English. (Let it not be interpreted, though, that I am against science or appropriate technology. What is needed is wholeness, a whole earth, with all its richness and diversity, and whole people to enrich and diversify our culture—not a technocracy.)

Words enable us to express our right-hemisphere functions, but when language degenerates to jargon, no matter how expedient or objectively efficient, poetic and inner imagery is lost. The sharing of "mind pictures" is superficial, adding to our sense of aloneness and alienation. Language is essential for the development of human intelligence. To reduce language to mechanistic and operational "isms," to the point where the individual cannot express his or her feelings or ideas is to encourage illiteracy.* The degeneration of language leads to the loss of culture and consciousness, and this loss is exacerbated by our growing detachment from and destruction of nature. Like all animals, we are a product of our environment. If we simplify or destroy it, we will simplify or destroy ourselves, and if we change it, we will be changed, for better or for worse.

HUMAN CONCEPTIONS OF NATURE

Pantheism and animism are two consistent characteristics of "primitive" human cultures in their relationship with nature. Still today, among relatively uncontaminated societies, the science of natural history is of a highly practical and pragmatic nature. Unlike Western science, these traditional conceptions of nature are now shorn of mythological beliefs and animistic fantasies. Fact and fantasy are interwoven in ways that are often judged by the Western mind as based upon ignorance and superstition. Yet it is somewhere between the extremes of science and myth that a balanced relationship may be established. The objective and logical orientation of science as a value system usually serves utilitarian ends, reducing nature to a "resource." It replaces animistic and vitalistic beliefs with a mechanistic regard for nature, thus setting man apart from nature. Alienation was aggravated first by the Judeo-Christian belief in a per-

---

* Ironically, many new therapies designed to help us "get in touch with our feelings" entail learning complex left-hemisphere jargon or "psychobabble," which can create even greater distance since few can understand the language!

sonalized god which came to take precedence over pantheistic beliefs, and consequently the monotheistic dogma of early missionaries and the later advent of Western science/technology had a major impact in changing primitive man's relationship with nature. The primitive mind was more at one with nature than the Western mind with its personalized god. By denaturing nature into a resource, an object of property, and by changing pantheism into monotheism, man placed himself in the center of creation. This essentially pre-Copernican view has done much to separate man from nature and has caused serious social and ecological chaos.

Human interpretations of nature and human nature, even by noted writers, are often biased because of the way in which the human mind functions. First, we observe; then, immediately, we interpret on the basis of personal, but not necessarily related, experiences and associations. Evaluation follows, and finally, we arrive at a wholly biased anthropocentric judgment. A major virtue of the scientific rule of objectivity is its strict adherence to describing only what is seen. This can lead to a highly mechanistic view of how animals behave and ecosystems work, which is only part of the whole picture. Worse still, if we are not objective, the words we use may lead us to make inaccurate evaluative or judgmental descriptions. For example, the competition within and between animal and plant species and the phenomenon of natural selection are often interpreted as the "struggle" for survival. Through such an inappropriate term, man projects his own values on nature and in this way has an erroneous understanding of reality. Nature is not simply "red in tooth and claw," nor is it a complex system of mechanical components.

For many people, the unresolved paradoxes of life amid death and of cooperation amid competition are projected onto nature. But in nature there are no paradoxes; they exist only in the minds of man as chaos and order, destruction and creation, purpose and meaning, purposelessness and meaninglessness.

Even Thoreau in his book *Walden* confused, like Freud and others, the destructive aspects of nature with the negative, "beastly" attributes of human nature when he said, "Nature is hard to overcome, but she must be overcome." And in yet another passage Thoreau says, "Shall I not have intelligence with the earth? Am I not partly leaves and vegetable mold myself?" He urges purification through simplicity (in one's life, needs, relations, and dependencies) and abhors the enslavement of humanity to conformity and to material things and values. He offers the aesthetic and spiritual promise of fulfillment through nature as the only viable alternative for the discontent and ills of humanity caught in its own snare—or becoming mummified in its own pyramid.

Although Thoreau's illumination of nature is through a prism of ascetic purity, such self-discipline and denial may help cast off the trappings of culturally biased perceptions and values and illusory purpose and meaning, but they do not necessarily lead one to a deeper empathy with nature. Thoreau's relationship to nature was both aesthetic and empathic, but the latter was qualified, as we can see in such statements as "He is blessed who is assured the animal is dying out in him day by day and the divine being established."

Thoreau perhaps never fully came to terms with humanity, nor was his relationship with nature completely freed from the culture within which he was raised. But he came to terms with himself and with his life, which, through his outward searching and inner scrutiny for meaning, had deep significance and fulfillment for him. His simplicity will elude many who may take more indirect or esoteric paths than those of nature to discover themselves. Thoreau's asceticism and empathy gave him his freedom, and the message that he brought back, even if limited by the words of his era and culture, conveyed the eternal truth and significance of nature for all men. He demonstrated the aesthetic and spiritual aspects of man's relationship with nature.

In order for man to rediscover and understand nature, our sense of wonder and our curiosity must be reawakened. An aesthetic approach to nature opens up the senses, and such was the goal of the nature mystics of Thoreau's era. To this we can now add the ecological dimension afforded by recent advances in the natural sciences. Man's responsibility must be tied into his aesthetic and empathic feelings toward nature—the biological and spiritual components of ethical living. But a scientific knowledge of ecological principles can improve our interactions with nature while the aesthetic approach to nature affects only the quality of our reactions, provided, of course, that aesthetics do not lead us to depreciate life forms that are ugly and that scientific knowledge is applied not solely to improve the world for mankind alone. A passive mode will not necessarily help us conserve nature or lead to active responsibility, which is necessary since our time is limited.

WILDNESS AND CIVILIZATION

Wildness is often misconstrued as total freedom, yet all the actions and needs of wild animals are regulated in order to ensure the continuation of each species. Wildness is better described as freedom constrained not necessarily by opposing wills to survive, as Schweitzer reasons, but by many complex mechanisms. For example, the quality of food available during pregnancy will influence the survival rate of the offspring; the presence of more than one male may have a measurable effect on the production of sexual hormones in females and in other males as well. An increase in the population of a given species may reach a critical point, even when food is abundant, so that individuals may fail to reproduce. Even more complex and as yet little understood are the feedback mechanisms between different species, as between parasite and host and prey and predator.

When man crossed the threshold from being a hunter-gatherer to develop agriculture and technology, he freed himself from many of these natural constraints. From wildness came civilization, with its own rules and constraints, as vital for survival and procreation as before. Civilization did not give man more freedom than he had before; rather, he had less freedom and more responsibility. His future was now in his own hands. Natural, biological constraints were replaced by laws, traditions, and rules of conduct in private and in public, agreements between tribes and, later, between nations. Anthropologists today, as reported in Richard Lee and Irven DeVore's *Man the Hunter,* are astonished to observe the harmony within and between the few remaining "primitive" hunter-gatherer tribes in South America, Australia, and New Guinea. Even so, many of their traditions and laws (especially of infanticide, gerontocide, and retribution) seem "uncivilized" to us, as does their often inhumane treatment of animals and people of alien tribes. What they seem to lack in empathy, modern technological man seems to lack ethically. It would astonish those simple tribal people that we must make rules and laws to protect both consumers and the environment from the unethical activities of companies and corporations. Even unethical conduct is justified in the highest levels of government if it is judged to be "in the best interests" of the party or the country.

While in nature the wild individual is biologically constrained, for civilized man the dilemma of personal freedom versus constraint (for the welfare and benefit of others) through social consensus has not yet been fully resolved. A collective ego may operate successfully in a primitive society, but in a larger, more diversified society, it is a failure; communism has historically repressed personal freedom and limited its own potentials by channeling diversity into conformity and uniformity. Biologically speaking, no species could evolve under such a regime, and for man as well it is no less restrictive. Another attempt to resolve this problem is Western capitalism, in which personal freedom is equated with free enterprise. But this in turn can lead to a lack of concern or empathy for others (both consumers and competitors) and for the environment. While competitive individualism may bring out the best under the free enterprise system, democracy fails when competition leads to powerful oligopolies and devalues cooperation and social responsibility. We cannot have freedom without responsibility, nor can we have socialistic unity without freedom for individuality.

These political influences on human behavior are as important as religious and philosophical beliefs, yet they all have failed to free man. They have failed to foster empathy and ethical conduct and to reunite man with nature. An internalized set of values is needed to end man's alienation from nature and from his own kind as well.

Each living thing is the center of its own universe—a complex system individuated in space and time but integrated with its environment and with others necessary for survival and procreation. As the system becomes increasingly complex, consciousness evolves—awareness of self, of one's role in society and relationships with others. Self-consciousness is reaching its ultimate point of evolutionary development in humans. The evolution of human consciousness must continue both inward and outward as an open but integrative system, but first it must be liberated. How? We each have the potential to create the right conditions for self-liberation and self-actualization. Politically we must seek a midpoint between free enterprise capitalism and collective socialism. Socially we need freedom and responsibility. Psychologically we must nurture, through education in right living, the normal, healthy state of human consciousness—the natural mind, in which man is at one and at peace with himself and the world as a whole.

Viktor E. Frankl, the existential psychotherapist, states, "Being human means being conscious and being responsible." He adds: "More than such faculties as the power of speech, conceptual thinking, or walking erect, the factor of doubting the significance of his own existence is what sets man apart from animals." He contends that *responsibility* and *freedom* constitute the spiritual domain of man. While animal activity is purposive, it lacks historical dimension and meaning, for while purpose, biologically, is related to survival and procreation, meaning is an essential human quality which contains the elements of personal freedom and responsibility that make us fully human. Reverence for life and for the living can give the deepest personal meaning.

"KNOW THYSELF"

Mankind's need to dominate and control nature may be based upon deep-rooted fears for survival and insecurities, which are projected as greed and selfishness. Our greatest perceptual flaw has been to regard nature as being something separate. Yet all of us are of the same essence, the same condensation of dust and gas. We all are part of a cosmic supraorganism which we cannot apprehend in our closeness to it, except in small, fragmented pieces that we are slowly coming to understand. If such understanding is applied not simply to regulate our lives and to monitor our effects on the biosphere, but to control, dominate, and exploit, then we will never truly understand. We will never, as the Delphic inscription urges, know ourselves. Truth is not pure when the quest for knowledge is overridden by selfish needs. Such knowledge is not wisdom, for wisdom resonates with the purity of truth and operates within ethical constraints, with humility and compassion and with regard for the rights of all creation. Wisdom cannot and does not serve selfish ends.

Science and technology cannot regulate and monitor themselves without our making a radical change in our values and needs. Factual knowledge must become integrated as wisdom. The Cartesian view that all except humans are insensitive "machines" correlates well with our insensitive use of our own bodies and technology. Of the two worlds, the natural-subjective and holistic and the mechanistic-objective and individuated, we have become so much a part of the latter that it seems to be the only reality. But it is not so. Trees and oceans can suffer in ways as similar and as different as we, and the other animals suffer. Lost in the world of mechanistic objectivity, the subjective world is treated as something already dead. Its component parts have become "things" or resources, and its dynamics have been reduced to mechanical processes.

Many Amerindians, relative aliens to Western man, have long contended that the white man does not respect the nonhuman spirit world and that he relates to the world as something separate from himself. He acts on the basis of his own laws, not within the framework of a broader ethic which includes all creation. As Black Elk observed, the white man treats nonhuman creations as "things," not as fellow beings. Seeing the rest of the world as dead, we deaden and dehumanize ourselves in the process. How else, without forethought or feeling, can we explain the desecration of rivers and oceans with millions of gallons of pollutants every day? If we felt the aliveness of the river, we could not abuse it in this way.

We cannot separate "what is good for man" from what is good for the rest of creation. But in our desire to control and use nature for our own exclusive good, we only increase human suffering as we run out of resources and destroy our own life-support systems. Understanding and mastery of ourselves, not of nature, are our most ur-

gent imperatives. "Know thyself" is neither a riddle nor an intellectual solipsism. It is the key to our survival and to the fulfillment of
life.

Given our kinship with animals and with earth as a whole (for the
earth is indeed our flesh), let us now turn to examine the uses and
abuses of animals under man's dominion. It will become apparent
that our misconceptions about them correlate with many of the
ways in which we have mistreated them.

3
Animal Uses and Abuses: A Historical Overview

Archaeologists and anthropologists estimate that since the evolution of our species, *Homo sapiens*, we have spent nine-tenths of our history as hunter-gatherers. Only recently, within the last 10,000 years, have we domesticated plants and animals and developed agricultural technologies. Our earliest relationships with animals were, therefore, very much like those of other predators, such as the wolf and lion: We had to kill certain prey species for food. Later, when we developed the skills, we utilized their remains for many purposes—hides and skins for clothing, sinews for thread and fishing lines, bones for tools and weapons.

From the pieces that can be fitted together from the long past, our hunting forefathers were not primitive savages, half hyena and half ape. Their consummate skills in living under often harsh conditions, equipped with the most rudimentary "technology" of bone, flint, and, later, metal instruments, attest to their intelligence and adaptability. Furthermore, their often elaborate cave paintings, carvings, burial sites, and astrological calendars indicate that they possessed a sensitivity toward nature and a wisdom about the earth and cosmos that may well surpass our own today.

Studies (cited in Lee and DeVore's *Man the Hunter*) of the few hunter-gatherer societies that are still in existence, such as the bushmen of Africa, aborigines of Australia, and the Arctic Eskimos, reveal three common attributes. First, they do not overkill or live (as we do today) beyond the capacity of their environment. They take only what they need, and the subsistence economy keeps them in ecological balance with their surroundings. Is it that they do not have the technology to take more or that they do not have the need or desire to do so? Considering the resistance to Western values and the absence of the "work ethic" in some tribes, anthropologists believe that the latter rather than the former may be the case. There are now several hunting societies that have been contaminated by Western values and technology to hunt for profit, and the result has been a destruction of both their culture and their environment. Today, for example, Eskimos use modern technology to hunt and kill whales, and some species such as the bowhead are now endangered. A century ago American Indians were encouraged to trap beaver and other furbearers for European traders, again with disastrous consequences both culturally and biologically.

The second attribute common to hunter-gatherer societies is the size of the population. As they do not overkill for profit and have a highly adaptive subsistence economy, so their population is held at a subsistence level—i.e., *below* the optimal carrying capacity of their habitat. Death from such natural causes as disease, physical injury, and periodic famine was *accepted as a normal event,* while the natural biological population controls were further influenced by such cultural traditions as seasonal migration, emigration, infanticide (especially of "surplus" females), and gerontocide (killing of old people). Today we combat these natural controls with medicine and other altruistic interventions, but in so doing, we must realize that we create an escalating ecological imbalance by increasing overpopulation and accelerating the rate of entropy.

The third common element in primitive societies is the absence of an adequate technology to store enough food to maintain a large population during lean seasons and poor years.

It is because of these three primary conditions that our ancestors, being subject to natural biological and ecological constraints, were able to live in harmony with nature. In fact, they could not do otherwise. The scattering of humanity over the earth was so thin that even destructive hunting practices such as burning grassland or forest to flush out game had very little impact on the environment.

This relationship, in spite of the hardships involved, was idyllic in many ways, if we can judge from the cultural traditions and attitudes of the few remaining hunting societies of today. But with uncanny synchrony throughout the world, some 10,000 to 12,000 years ago, possibly linked with the end of the last great ice age, the technology of agriculture emerged. Plants and animals were tamed, herded, corralled, and even selectively bred for desirable traits. Natural meadows were plowed up for crops, forests cleared, and swamps drained for raising more crops and livestock. The Garden of Eden was now being cultivated because man had become a gardener. With plenty of livestock and storage facilities for grains, roots, and other crops, the capacity of the environment was increased, and the human population began to expand and diversify into various specialized occupations.

As domesticated species and farming techniques were traded and spread throughout the world, more and more agrarian communities were established. Game and natural habitat were less available in heavily developed regions, except to wealthy landowners who could afford to keep some "game" on their estates for sport hunting. By the Middle Ages much of Europe was under the plow and ax. Hunting preserves, such as the deer parks of England, were set aside for the rich aristocracy, for hunting, once a subsistence activity for all, had become an exclusive luxury. The basic need to hunt obviously persisted, as game hunting (including falconry) was elevated to the "sport of kings."

During the transition from hunting to farming culture humans acquired the resources and the freedom to develop a rich diversity of cultural activities. Many of these recreational pastimes had elements of earlier hunting practices, such as coursing and bearbaiting. Others, such as bullfighting and chasing a fox on horseback with a pack of hounds, became highly ritualized cultural traditions, sometimes echoing even earlier rituals of sacrificial slaughter.

When there is plenty, there is time for recreation and enjoyment, and the affluence of an agrarian way of life brought with it a new epoch of animal exploitation for spectator and participant "sports."

The fate of wildlife was sealed because we did not temper our hunting urge; in fact, we found it necessary to exterminate many wild species that competed with or preyed upon our own stock. For with the domestication of animals we developed a new regard for them. The first species to be domesticated is thought to be the dog, most likely derived from a southern wolf or a dingolike wild dog. The Egyptians, according to F. E. Zeuner's *A History of Domesticated Animals*, were the first to experiment extensively with a wide variety of species, many of which proved to be of little use. While some animals were raised primarily for food or clothing, others, such as the ox, mule, and dog, were used as beasts of burden. Later on, selected species were raised and bred for specific purposes, including hunting and related sports (cock- and dogfighting) and war. Horses, mules, camels, dogs, and even elephants have played their role in man's conquest over his own kind as well as over nature.

While the underlying motives in domesticating animals were wholly utilitarian, other attitudes certainly influenced the relationships between man and his animal "creations." Because of the survival of man, the hunter depended on an intimate knowledge of the environment and of the major prey species that were killed for food. So, too, man the farmer had to acquire considerable knowledge about the land and animals under his dominion. It must have been realized very early on that sensitivity and empathy were an essential part of good animal husbandry. One who did not "know" his animals and care for them humanely could not be a successful horseman, shepherd, cowman, or whatever. As Calvin Schwabe describes, the Egyptians, for example, not only developed the basic scientific skills of veterinary medicine and animal husbandry but also had a deep reverence for the animals under their care, some of them even being revered as deities. Such animalistic and totemistic beliefs may well have originated from our earlier hunting-gathering stage, when pantheism and zoomorphic religions were linked with a deeply felt dependence on animals for one's survival. There must also have been a sense of deep personal investment and pride in the domesticated creations of the husbandryman. This endures today in country livestock shows, sheep- and gundog trials, horse shows and races, and dog shows.

As man became more adept in breeding and raising domesticated animals, techniques of animal husbandry and veterinary medicine evolved into sciences, replacing animistic beliefs and traditional superstitions. As a hunter man did not have to concern himself with knowing what and how to feed animals, but as a farmer he had to learn such things and more: He had to learn to recognize and treat plant and animal diseases, for his livelihood depended upon such knowledge. With greater freedom from the vicissitudes of nature (those were unavoidable for man the hunter) came the burden of greater responsibility. The more man changed the environment and developed domestic strains of plants and animals, the more he had to know in order to survive, and there was an ever-growing population to feed and additional nonsubsistence needs to be satisfied.

A vicious cycle developed as man learned to grow and reap more than he needed. Surplus crops, grains, and livestock could be bartered for nonessential consumables and raw materials. Civilizations grew and flourished, but at the expense of the land and of wildlife. Some groups were destroyed or assimilated by more powerful invaders, but others destroyed themselves by reducing the land to desert scrub. Few civilizations realized the negative impact of a sedentary, profit-oriented agrarian way of life. While small hunting bands could move on to more productive regions, large centralized communities were far more restrained, more vulnerable to natural disasters (such as drought) in spite of having adequate stores of food. They could not easily move on when the climate turned against them and when their land was exhausted.

The act of creating domestic species gave a new dimension to man's relationship with animals. Financial profit, pride of possession and status, aesthetic appreciation, the pleasure of companionship (with a horse or dog), and the satisfaction of producing highly prized specimens were some of the rewards reaped by the successful animal breeder. How different from the relatively simple relationship between man the hunter and his prey. No matter how profound early man's knowledge of animal behavior must have been in order to make him an effective hunter, a very different order of knowledge was a necessity for the new steward of nature. The human species was gradually evolving from being a part of nature to being separate from nature as an independent and autonomous species.

Nature became something to control and exploit, to understand and to alter according to our own needs. Regrettably for both man and nature, a spiraling sequence of events led to an increasing disequilibrium between humankind and the natural world, as natural biological controls on human population growth became increasingly ineffectual. More natural resources had to be utilized to support an expanding populace, causing further and often irreparable damage to the environment. With the advent of the Industrial Revolution, first in Europe and then on the American continent and elsewhere, the rate of extraction of natural resources had escalated together with the growth of the human population. The quality of human life was measured by a new set of nonsubsistence values: economic growth, power, progress, production, and wealth. It is ironic that as the "standard" of living increased materially, the quality of the environment and the diversity of nonhuman life declined.

This energy-consumptive and biocidal way of life became the new status quo for our species, for the Western world served as a model for other civilizations. Subsistence economies became "underdeveloped," and as we tried to help, we gave them poverty and famine along with our values and our misguided altruism (medicine, especially). Our "help" increased population growth, but it destroyed socially and ecologically stabilizing tribal traditions. And overpopulation combined with destructive, wasteful, and generally inappropriate technology and agri-industries created a situation that could be maintained only at the expense of (a) the environment, (b) other animals and less fortunate people, and (c) our own future.

At the present rate of consumption, most of the tropical rain forests will be gone within the next 50 to 100 years, and by the turn of the century an estimated 50,000 species of plants and animals will have become extinct, according to Lester Brown's *The Twenty-ninth Day*. Barring any major famines or epidemics, the human population will have doubled by then, and the amount of available arable land in the world, because of current destructive farming methods, will be half what it is today. And as we clear more forests, construct more dams, fill in more swampland, and pollute the earth, air, and seas, so we eliminate more and more natural habitat and the wild plants and animals that live there. Even now we compete for the same resources with many animals: whales, dolphins, wolves, lions. We will soon have eliminated all creatures that compete with us in the food chain.

The promise of a great "marriage" between man and nature, with mankind as the steward of the biosphere, was latent in our hunting stage. It began to blossom when we became farmers and husbanded parts of nature. But now this marriage between man and nature is being destroyed, as are our relationships with each other and with our fellow animals. We are becoming competitors and adversaries. Nations compete and go to war over vital minerals and other natural resources. We no longer lovingly husband the land or our livestock; instead, we manage "agribusinesses." Underlying the economic imperatives of productivity and profit is the basic drive to survive: Man must eat even if he must kill seals and whales, destroy a forest, pollute a river, or raise hogs or chickens inhumanely. The tragedy comes when we no longer have, or are capable of finding, a less destructive or more humane way of survival, of making a living at the expense of others. One who is secure in his life does not need to profit at the expense of others; hence the inference that the existential insecurity of mankind is what underlies greed, power, and profit motives (in the absence, that is, of starvation and abject poverty). The survival drive has also become distorted and misplaced, survival now being equated not with ensuring a near-subsistence life-style and national economy, but with maintaining a status quo of material affluence at the expense of others (including other nations, ecosystems, plants, and animals). We would, for example, survive without electricity, a car, or a beefsteak.

Unnecessary inhumane practices are now justified for the "good of humanity" (i.e., in order to ensure our survival). Farmers rationalize that in order to feed so many people, some abuse of the land and of animals is inevitable, but there is always a surplus. Scientists say that animals must suffer under various tests, but much of this suffering takes place so that people can have safe cosmetics and other nonessential luxuries.

Competitive and impersonal transactions—rather than cooperation—and the application of knowledge, not to understand and husband nature but to exploit it totally and exclusively for human purposes, have resulted in a gradual breakdown of society and of man's relationship with both domesticated and wild segments of nature. Modern man is as much an alien to himself as he is toward animals and nature, and with this growing alienation we see a breakdown of nation, tribe, community, family, and individual as well as of those ancient bonds between man, nature, and animals.

Like the early farmers who did not give up their hunting past but enjoyed it for recreation, many individuals today continue to enjoy a meaningful contact with animals and nature. Herein lies our only hope of overcoming the disastrous consequences of alienation. Efficiency of operation or organization does not necessarily lead to alienation. I have visited large farms and corporations where empathy, involvement, and responsibility were very much in evidence. We should not, therefore, blame automation, technology, or organizational complexity for creating alienation. For example, a farmer can still husband a thousand pigs well, even if he has a machine that feeds them a premixed diet. But when they are not his and, instead, belong to investors or some remote corporation, he may have less interest in them, even though he is well paid for his services. The problem here lies in the alienation that already exists between the hired hand and the investors and between the pigs and the corporation. What then of the seeming lack of concern of some scientists for the welfare of the animals they use in their studies, or of rodeo cowboys and others who often mistreat animals for sport and profit? Only one who is alien to himself could treat another living creature with indifference and a complete lack of compassion. There may be no intention to be deliberately cruel (true sadists are rare in my experience), but there is a lack of awareness of what one is actually doing—a symptom of alienation. It becomes easy to accept and even to instigate such abuses on animals when, through desensitization and habituation, we join the consensus and cease to feel and see. Such inability to feel (to empathize) and see (objectively and critically to evaluate one's and others' actions) increases our alienation from the rest of creation. This, I believe, is the present overall state of our relationship with animals.

While the Industrial Revolution certainly helped liberate draft animals from their lifelong work, it did not (but still may) liberate man and did, I believe, increase his alienation from animals and nature. The Baconian dream of a scientific-technological utopia became a reality for an affluent few. Instead of the rural population's being liberated from manual labor in the fields, rural farm workers were relocated to rapidly urbanizing industrial centers and became the victims of the Industrial Revolution—liberation indeed, in those "satanic mills."

Alienation from animals and nature was intensified, if not catalyzed, by the Industrial Revolution, in spite of the efforts of nature romanticists and mystics, such as Wordsworth and, of course, the antitechnology Luddites. Increasing urbanization reduced people's contact with animals and nature. But perhaps more significant than this was the belief that nature was the exclusive resource for science to explore and technology to exploit. Possibly in association with man's narcissistic reverence for his own creations, the mystery of and reverence for the creations of nature waned. As man created and understood the mechanics of the "things" he created, so natural creations were objectified as analogous "things," yet inferior if they were of no use (aesthetics aside). Scientific hubris and technological-industrial power helped create an increasingly human-centered world view. Animals, as natural creations, were seen as analogues of man's mechanical creations, a belief supported by the Cartesian philosophy that animals are unfeeling machines, mere automatons.

The Industrial Revolution in many ways set man back into a pre-Copernican state of perceiving himself egocentrically, as the center of the universe, a long way from universal consciousness and brotherhood or kinship with all life.

Today we have such groups as antitechnology neo-Luddites, antinukies, back-to-nature counterculturists, animal liberationists, and countless others who collectively create the climate and momentum for much-needed social reforms and changes in values and attitudes toward nature and animal and human life. But to be exclusively zoocentric or biocentric is as unbalanced, unrealistic, and ineffectual as being wholly technocentric, humanocentric, or religiously/mystically noocentric. We are reaching a critical and historical epoch of synthesis, synergy, and balance, a point in evolutionary time at which all the different value-centered groups must cooperate to restore, heal, and protect the biosphere.

In so doing, mankind will be liberated from those value-motivated systems which are both humanocidal and biocidal.

At this critical time in the history of our species, I believe we have a moment's grace to accomplish this monumental task of transformation of man from global parasite into earth steward and ultimately into co-creator, as the interlocutor between creator (or the evolutionary process) and creation. Today this latter conception is hubris, and it will continue to be until we have attained self-control, the wisdom of humility and compassion not only for all life but for all future life as well. Esoterically this is the evolutionary threshold at which the collective spirit of humanity begins to develop, what Teilhard de Chardin envisioned as the noosphere or Christogenesis (the second coming of Christ as spirit embodied in people; man becoming one with God as co-creator). Teilhard also proposed that the development of the noosphere can be potentiated not by abandoning technology, but by using it properly to effect "technoinvolution," as he called it. Properly utilized, the technological fruits of scientific and industrial progress can help us evolve not into egocentric technocrats, but into stewards and co-creators. It can become the matrix for global communication and world government for the good of all life on earth. At the interface between the humanosphere and the biosphere, this technosphere, like a protective membrane, could be developed to restore, protect, and monitor the entire biosphere and to satisfy the interests of people and at the same time maintain the health, integrity, and diversity of the natural world. First, the right ethics and values must be acquired (i.e., remove the ideological "pollutants" or contaminants of the noosphere which are the causes of the many biocidal symptoms that are at last being recognized, from lake-killing, crop-stunting acid rain created by fossil-fuel-burning industries to the exploitation and extinction of animal species and whole ecosystems). The ideological contaminants include those created by hubris, blind pride, arrogance and shortsighted indifference; greed and selfishness; ignorance and faith in often inadequate scientific data; lack of empathy and responsible compassion; lack of appreciation for the intrinsic "rights" of all creation; insecurity and dependence, financial or otherwise, on maintaining a pathogenic status quo; lack of faith in and commitment to work toward healing the earth; rationalization to justify potential or proved biocidal acts on the basis of cost/benefit assessments from a human-centered rather than eco-centered world view; unwillingness and laziness to make personal sacrifices to further the greater good; blind belief in outmoded and even destructive ideologies (political, religious, and scientific); fear and defensiveness; resistance to constructive criticism and to an open exchange of views; being judgmental of and hateful (even violent) to those whose ideologies are different or not conducive to furthering the greater good of all life; lack of faith and commitment and surrendering one's power and potential; alienation and dehumanization.

The above "contaminants" of the noosphere, the collective body of human feelings, perceptions, and values, have been presented in a very broad, earth-minded perspective, from the outside in, so to speak. A more personal perspective is given in the following beautiful and timeless lines, quoted in David Spangler's *Toward a Planetary Vision,* from the ancient Bhagavad-Gita:

> Who hateth nought
> Of all which lives, living himself benign,
> Compassionate, from arrogance exempt,
> Exempt from love of self, unchangeable
> By good or ill; patient, contented, firm
> In faith, mastering himself, true to his word,
> Seeking Me, heart and soul; vowed unto Me,—
> That man I love! Who troubleth not his kind,
> And is not troubled by them; clear of wrath,
> Living too high for gladness, grief, or fear,
> That man I love! Who, dwelling quiet-eyed,
> Stainless, serene, well-balanced, unperplexed,
> Working with Me, yet from all works detached,
> That man I love! Who, fixed in faith on Me,
> Dotes upon none, scorns none; rejoices not,
> And grieves not, letting good or evil hap
> Light when it will, and when it will depart,

That man I love! Who, unto friend and foe
Keeping an equal heart, with equal mind
Bears shame and glory; with an equal peace
Takes heat and cold, pleasure and pain; abides
Quit of desires, hears praise or calumny
In passionless restraint, unmoved by each;
Linked by no ties to earth, steadfast in Me,
That man I love! But most of all I love
Those happy ones to whom 'tis life to live
In single fervid faith and love unseeing,
Drinking and blessed Amrit of my Being!

In essence, as a man is, how he thinks, feels, perceives, so is his world. If the natural world seems wrong or is going to ruin, we cannot blame it or change it. We cannot "blame" nature or science or technology. We must accept the responsibility and change ourselves—how we think, feel, and act—and our sociopolitical and industrial institutions which today threaten our existence. We have no lack of resources to effect this transformation; we are our greatest resource, and love, empathy, humility, educability, science, and intuition are our finest tools and assets.

4

Wildlife: The Living Harvest

A major area of extensive animal use and abuse is in the hunting and commercial trapping of wild animals. In order to ensure enough animals for all to kill, the land is "managed" to various degrees by state and federal wildlife officers. Some of these wildlife managers are at last coming to realize (to quote one state wildlife department director) that "most wildlife management is wildlife mismanagement"—a reality exposed in V. B. Scheffer's *A Voice for Wildlife.* This is because management policies have not been primarily based upon a concept of whole ecosystems. Rather, management policies have focused selectively on certain species for particular interest groups (such as raising deer for hunters and nutrias for trappers). The consequences of such practices have been detrimental to much of the wildlife and wilderness in the United States.

Wildlife management at the federal and state levels performs two basic services not for the primary benefit of wildlife, but for the benefit of man: first, to ensure a ready "surplus" each year of one or more species that can be harvested for fun or profit by hunters or trappers; and secondly, to control certain species in order to protect domestic livestock and arable land from pests and predators such as the wolf and coyote.

In implementing the former, some ecosystems are actually

changed to encourage the proliferation of certain "feature" species, and other indigenous species are eliminated. One area may have turkey as the so-called featured species, and the vegetation has to be so modified that other species of bird, such as quail, cannot survive. Nutrias, water-living rodents from South America, have been introduced into many states for the fur trapper, and this, like the introduction of other foreign species, as Clive Roots has shown, has resulted in serious damage to swamp and freshwater ecosystems. In many areas, predators, such as the coyote and wolf, have been eliminated so that the hunters may have no other competitors for "their" deer or antelope. And many other natural habitats have been irrevocably changed in order to accommodate the needs of hunters and trappers. Optimal species diversity has been reduced, and with the consequent disruption of natural ecological balance, new problems have followed. Without the natural selection pressures created by the selective culling of sick adults and surplus infant deer by wolves, the vitality of many deer herds may be on the decline. The human hunter does not have the same selective hunting pattern that natural predators do. As a consequence of killing the prime animals and trophy heads, the social organization and reproductive potential of the herd may be adversely affected. Frequently at the end of a hunting season state wildlife officers have to go in and shoot any remaining surplus in order to prevent overgrazing, which is destruction of habitat and starvation. Little thought is ever given to reintroducing natural predators, which would surely do a more effective job (for the hunter) in maintaining the quality of game.

Many of the hunting, trapping, and fishing areas in the United States can no longer be regarded as natural habitats. They are more like wildlife "ranches," where certain species are selectively propagated for the enjoyment and profit of a few people. The rights of such people should be secondary to the rights of indigenous species to life and habitat.

In Alaska, under states' rights and in the presence of a strong hunting lobby, a wolf extermination program was instigated in 1976 in direct opposition to the views of many conservationists and ecologists. It was claimed that the decline in caribou and moose was due solely to the wolf and that the latter should be eliminated. The real motive was to eliminate all competition for the white hunter, and since Eskimo and Indian hunters could not be effectively controlled, the solution was obvious: Eliminate the wolf. I gave the following statement at a congressional hearing (September 20, 1976, before the Subcommittee on Fisheries, Wildlife Conservation and the Environment, Washington, D.C.):

> Irrespective of ethical considerations, the Alaska State Management Program of "Wolf Control" is illogical and unscientific. All natural systems are self-regulating, and all interspecies populations (as between moose and wolf, caribou and wolf) as well as social groups (wolf packs) have naturally evolved self-regulating systems. . . . Prey and predator species are essentially married together, and thousands of generations of evolution bind them in total dependence and harmony. We know, too, that a wolf pack will defend its hunting range from other packs and socially regulate pack size and birthrates. Kill out some pack areas, and wolves in adjacent packs will breed more and move into the vacated territory . . . thus restoring a balance once more. If prey are scarce, social dominance and conflict over food will inhibit breeding; also the wolf pack maintains a natural equilibrium in relation to its prey. Thus, the proposed wolf eradication program in selected areas of the tundra biome obviously contradicts an irrevocable scientific fact—namely, that natural populations are self-regulating.
>
> It may be contended that the natural regulating system has broken down between wolf and moose and caribou, but evidence must be presented to show that the wolf is the *cause* and not the *effect* or *consequence*, if it is to be the sole target to be affected. Present available field data do not allow any firm conclusions to be made; if, for example, the alleged wolf abundance is a consequence of population disequilibrium, a wolf eradication program could be ecologically disastrous—detrimental to both the wolves and the moose and caribou.
>
> The wolf *alone* cannot be the sole cause of the disequilibrium between predator and prey and held wholly responsible for the decline in moose and caribou. Some other factors, or *synergistic combination* of two or more, must be suspect, considering the evolved relationship established between wolves and caribou and moose, coadapted to live harmoniously for the past one to two million years

Considering the paucity of data in support of a large-scale wolf eradication program, any such actions would be premature and should be delayed until further data are available. Why the natural prey-predator regulation system has broken down (if it actually has; it may, in fact, be in an extreme point in its natural oscillatory pattern) remains to be determined.

Such factors as hunting and trapping by man, the impact of human activities directly and indirectly on the fragile tundra biome, the effect of disease and severe winters on moose and caribou may all play an important part and have an additive effect in the alleged imbalance between wolves and their prey, the latter toward which some hunters make claim to irrespective of the rights of the wolf and with total disregard for its intrinsic role as a natural manager of the ecosystem. This role of the wolf is recognized by most authorities, and to plan to exterminate it as the sole factor responsible for the ecological imbalance is premature, potentially disastrous, and inhumane.

Addendum. Alaska's Governor Hammond's suggestion to export "surplus" wolves from the state and reintroduce them into other states where they are rare or extinct is as illogical as the state's eradication program. Wolves evolve and adapt subtly, each individual and each successive generation, to the complex nexus of interacting variables in their particular hunting range. Such attunement takes millenia, and thus, a transplantation proposal, like the eradication program, does not accord with what is common knowledge to the scientific community.

We were successful in stopping the wolf eradication program. Two years later we learned of another similar program which was clearly designed to protect Alaska moose for local hunters by slaughtering more wolves. Since some of the wolves would be killed on so-called public land, the federal government should have immediately intervened to stop the wolf kill because it is illegal, under the Endangered Species Act, to kill an endangered species on public land. The Department of the Interior simply stood by and did nothing to protect the wolves. We had to take the department and its secretary, Cecil Andrus, to court to force them to uphold the law. Since this was the secretary's responsibility, why, you may wonder, did he not make any attempt to act on behalf of the wolves and uphold the law?

The hunting lobby is extremely influential in high places. A good example of how state and federal agencies still operate primarily for the sake of the hunter and not first for wildlife was recently exposed in the following incident. For many years now, a man named John Harris has traveled throughout the United States with one or more captive-born and -raised wolves, visiting thousands of schools and conservation groups to present a very effective wolf appreciation and conservation program. He had to apply for a permit to the state fish and game department in some states before he would be allowed to give his programs. For some reason, he had considerable problems obtaining a permit whenever he wanted to give programs in New York State. When receipt of the permit had been delayed so long that it was simply too late for him to do his programs, he obtained the file that was being kept on his activities from the state, under the Freedom of Information Act. The following two department memos seem to explain why he had such difficulties in obtaining the permit.

New York State Department of Environmental Conservation

MEMORANDUM

TO: Ned Holmes
FROM: Ronald L. Schroder, Senior Wildlife Biologist
SUBJECT: Wildlife Programs

DATE: November 8, 1976

> On Friday, I participated in the Environmental Symposium at the Klem Road South Elementary School in Webster and on Saturday I attended the Museum and Science Center's wildlife program entitled "Our Heritage—The Wilderness." Rocky—the wolf and John Harris were at both sessions. Harris did not personally participate in any of the "large group" sessions held. His presentations were given to the 2nd grades at the same time as mine.
>
> From past performances I know that John sticks basically with natural history of the wolf. He stresses that wildlife are not "pets." His only mention of not killing is used in connection with endangered species. The use

of a real wolf adds tremendously to the impact of the presentation. Use of slides, movies or even mounted specimens could not substitute.

The draw back of the use of a live wolf is that the wolf can be used by others as it was Friday and Saturday. Dr. Michael Fox, of the Humane Society of the United States, used Rocky on both days to drum up anti-kill emotions among the audience.

The Saturday "Anti-Kill" session was attended by about 80–100 people. The attached brochures will give you the participants and the general theme. Three of the four (John Harris did not talk) presentations were anti-kill, anti-government wildlife management (as it is presently practiced, i.e. Game species—prime management). The fourth presentation by Thelma Rodney concerned itself with a recently developed curriculum about wolves, being used by the Toronto Board of Education.

A side note from the session—a Rochester Chapter of the Fund for Animals will be started in the near future:

Please return the brochures.

New York State Department of Environmental Conservation

MEMORANDUM

TO: W. Hollister
FROM: S. Parker, Principal Clerk, Program Administration
SUBJECT: Permit for "Rocky" the wolf

DATE: 9 March 1977

Recently John Harris requested a permit to cover the transportation of "Rocky" the wolf in the state to include several lecture stops in several locations. As per procedure, John Hayward referred the request to the applicable supervisors for approval.

Ned Holmes called me on Tuesday and he has some reservations about issuance of a permit. One, which John can cover in writing the permit, is that the wolf is to be kept from all potential public contact. Ned said that the animal, while in Rochester last year, was paraded about a meeting hall in the Museum and that there was an episode in the school year when "Rocky" knocked a newspaper reporter off his feet. Ned feels strongly that any permit should spell out fairly rigid restraints.

Another concern was with the use of the animal to further the cause of anti-hunt and anti-kill (see Xeroxes of Ned's 1976 reaction). Again, at Rochester Museum, speaking to school children, "Rocky" was used as an example of the exploitation of hunters, etc. Ned is wondering if we can't prevent the use of the animal in furthering this ethic through a condition in the permit. I believe that this would be an infringement of a constitutional right and would be quite impossible.

At any rate, Ned is asking for a complete review of a 1977 permit to Harris and it would be swell if we could get this firmed up within the next week so as to avoid an eleventh-hour issuance.

These department memos, at least as I interpret them, prove clearly that fish and game departments, both state and federal, operate on behalf of the hunter and will, when necessary, assert their influence to protect hunters' interests and stifle any "antihunters," as they call those who speak in defense of wildlife.

At least one state wildlife management officer, Maryland's Duane Pursley, is beginning to see the light, stating, "The key to wildlife management is people management, habitat protection and restoration." The solutions are simple and obvious, but the politics involved in managing wildlife exclusively for powerful vested-interest groups gives little hope for wildlife unless and until the hunter realizes that what is best for wildlife would be in his own interests as well.

In the control of certain species in order to protect agribusiness, considerable chaos has been created at this critical interphase between man and nature. Carnivores (wolf, coyote, fox) have been eliminated by poisoning and trapping or so reduced in many areas that in addition to the problem of excessive grazing by domestic stock, a surfeit of wild rodents now faces many ranchers. Overgrazing may actually make the rangeland even *more* suitable for rodents such as the ground squirrel. Ranchers only create their own pests with poor range management. These compete with his livestock, and the real price of predator control programs is slowly being realized. Ground squirrels are now so numerous in the southwestern rangeland of the United States that they must be poisoned in order to protect the rancher's interests. The threat of bubonic plague, which is transmitted by the squirrel's fleas, has been used as a cover-up to hide the real reason for squirrel control—a rangeland mismanagement—and at the cost of still more animal lives.

State and federal agencies have spent billions of taxpayers' dollars in waging war against wildlife to protect the interests of ranchers, many of whom are grazing their stock on public lands. Coyotes, cougars, wolves, eagles, and other "pests" have been persecuted for decades—trapped, shot, and poisoned. As John Olsen describes in lurid detail (in *Slaughter the Animals, Poison the Earth*), poisons such as strychnine and cyanide, as well as warfarin, a poison which causes animals to bleed internally and drown in their own blood, have been used extensively. Until a recent presidential ban, a poison called 1080 was used extensively by state and federal agents, even though it was well known that this poison gets into the food chain* and kills many nontarget species. For example, bait containing this poison will kill a coyote, and a carrion bird or mammal eating the remains of the coyote would be poisoned, and so on. It is still used widely in Texas, law or no law regulating its use.

The coyote has been persecuted perhaps more than any other wild animal. On cattle ranches coyotes are often seen by the farmers as friends because they keep down rodents. On sheep ranches they

---

* We should also not forget the impact of crop insecticides on wildlife, DDT, for example, being responsible for the near extinction of such predatorial birds as owls and falcons. This again can create pest problems, such as a surfeit of rodents, which the predator birds normally help keep in check. The use of DDT is now banned in the United States, but it is still manufactured here. DDT sold to South America contaminates migratory birds, which in turn poison falcons and other birds of prey when they return to the United States.

can be allies, too, but since many sheep ranchers are no longer good shepherds (because they don't use sheepdogs or bring ewes into safe sheds to lamb) or cannot afford the necessary labor to tend their flocks properly, the coyote becomes a serious problem. As Hope Ryden reports in *God's Dog,* in some ranches the coyotes avoid dead sheep, which they would normally eat, because they are leery of poison bait; instead, when hungry, they will take live sheep. Again, wildlife mismanagement has created another problem, in this case conditioning coyotes to avoid sheep that have died from natural causes, sheep that they would normally eat! Humane and conservation groups were recently successful in stopping a coyote-mule deer relationship "study" in Utah, which would have entailed exterminating coyotes over a period of several years ostensibly just to see what would happen to the mule deer population. This state project, which would have received federal support, was dressed up as a bona fide scientific study but was in reality a coyote extermination program designed to please the ranching community and to eliminate any competition over mule deer for the hunters. But, as I pointed out in my affidavit, which was used in a suit against the state:

> This program may not benefit the coyote, the mule deer or the hunter on the basis of existing scientific evidence. It has been well documented that when a major prey species is eliminated, the larger ungulates, deer in this case, will ultimately perish through overpopulation and habitat destruction. A more serious aspect of the Utah coyote extermination program would be the subsequent increase in rabbits and rodents, which would lead to even greater competition between mule deer and domestic livestock for rangeland resources. Thus, the interests of both hunter and rancher would be jeopardized by such a shortsighted program, and the benefits, if any, would only be short-term and not worth the expense involved in executing the six year coyote control program.

We won this case, and Utah's "scientific study" was canned.

Trapping animals in steel traps that cause untold pain, panic, and suffering is regarded lightly by many people. Wildlife management programs condone it and often modify an ecosystem to ensure a surplus for the trapper and the fur industry—sometimes with disastrous consequences. The following discussion of trapping is adapted from testimony presented by Guy Hodge, an officer of the Humane Society of the United States, before the Subcommittee on Fisheries and Wildlife Conservation and the Environment of the House Committee on Merchant Marine and Fisheries in Washington, D.C., in November 1975, in support of a bill to discourage the use of painful devices in the trapping of animals and birds.

The likelihood of achieving general agreement as to whether or not commercial trapping is morally permissible is at best remote. We hope that a time will come when all people will view animals as more than ornaments to adorn coats and dresses. However, we are seeking to instill a new code of behavior in wildlife management, one that goes substantially beyond current game regulations, one in which it is the welfare of the animal and not the needs of the trapping industry that is the fundamental concern of trapping rules and regulations. . . . There are an estimated forty species of North American mammals in the wildlife grouping collectively termed furbearers. These species of primary importance to the fur trade include the muskrat, nutria, fox, mink, opossum, raccoon, beaver, and coyote. Only fragmentary data is [sic] available on the annual United States fur catch. A 1971 Department of the Interior survey of forty-two cooperating states reported a total of 6.5 million animals taken by commercial fur trappers. In the 1974 book, *A Voice for Wildlife,* prominent wildlife biologist Dr. Victor Scheffer placed the total annual fur catch at more than *eleven million* animals, including animals taken in connection with commercial, biological, and nuisance trapping.

The commercial fur trade is not an industry that employs a large number of persons at its base level. State game agency fur specialists estimate that there are approximately 50,000 commercial trappers in the United States. The number per state varies from less than 700 in Delaware to Maryland's 5,000 licensed trappers. It is difficult to obtain more specific data on trappers since few states require special licenses for them.

An animal's initial reaction to trapping often involves a struggle to free the affected limb, resulting in torn ligaments and flesh, broken bones, and other injuries. A Canadian Wildlife Service Report (Series 8, 1969) graphically describes such injuries:

> The stomachs of [trapped] Arctic foxes ... often contain parts of their own bodies. They may swallow fragments of their teeth broken off in biting the trap, and sometimes part of a mangled foot; almost every stomach contains some fox fur, and a considerable number contain pieces of skin, claws, or bits of bone. ...

Trappers argue that, in time, the leg of an animal caught in a steel-jaw trap will become numb from loss of circulation. But unquestionably the animal is subjected to pain and suffering when first caught and pressure from the trap jaws will, at best, provide only intermittent periods of pain relief. So intense is the animals' pain and terror that it may actually chew at its own limbs in a desperate effort to regain freedom. Escapees whose limbs are chewed off or torn free are known as "wring-offs." They are easy prey for other animals, but most of those that avoid predators face a slow death from shock, blood loss, infection, gangrene, or gradual starvation. A few, perhaps the least fortunate of all, survive their ordeal. Trapper C. A. Wambold tells the story of such an animal: "Many years ago, I caught a one-legged muskrat in a leghold trap. The poor animal had suffered loss of three legs and still lived through all that misery and agony."

Although an experienced trapper can set steel-jaw traps in such a way that they are more likely to take one particular species of animal than another, these devices are fundamentally non-selective. A five-year study conducted by the Ontario Department of Lands and Forests (Technical Bulletin, Wildlife Series #8, November 1959) showed that on two professional tended traplines, using only leghold traps, 1,350 unwanted birds and mammals were caught, while only 561 desired furbearers were taken. A more recent study in Great Britain also showed a ratio between unwanted and target species of almost 3:1.

Among the non-target species regularly taken in leghold traps are domestic dogs and cats, porcupines, flying squirrels, owls, woodpeckers, ducks, geese, and blue jays. Even rare and endangered species are not immune to the hazards of an accidental encounter with leghold traps. A series of wire service articles in 1973 revealed the deaths of bald and golden eagles in leghold traps set out in Western states to catch coyotes and bobcats. A United States game management agent determined that more than 2,500 eagles were caught in Nevada during the winter of 1972–73 and that 630 of them died from exposure.

It has been argued that trapping protects wildlife against disease, starvation, predation, and a destroyed habitat by removing surplus animals. This attempted justification for commercial trapping has been termed "patently false and absurd" by an official of the Bird and Mammal laboratories of the National Museum of Natural History. It is an established biological principle that most natural populations of vertebrates, including furbearers, are regulated by the complex interaction of environmental variables which maintain population size within specific limits. These variables include food, space, territories, predators, parasites, disease, and competition. While a species may regularly overproduce, such surpluses are required to offset high infant mortality. Certainly, if a species' population growth went unchecked it might ultimately result in the self-destruction of that animal, but it is ridiculous to claim that this would result from regulations restricting trap sets. Trapping simply substitutes for other mortality factors and has no relevance in terms of population maintenance.

The fur industry would have us believe that trapping is a fundamental part of wildlife management programs, but in truth, it is fur prices, not "stewardship," that determine the number of trappers and the number of animals that are taken. A bobcat pelt, for example, was worth $25 in 1970 but became a prize for trappers in 1976 at $250 or more per pelt. Little wonder then, with such financial impetus, that this wildcat today may be endangered in some areas. Dr. Ward Stone in the February 1974 issue of "The Conservationist" indicated that in 1960, a poor year for fur prices, New York State issued 8,140 trapping licenses while in 1973 escalating fur prices enticed over 15,000 persons to purchase licenses to trap.

A second argument that has been advanced by trappers is that trapping is needed to control epizootic diseases such as rabies. A 1973 report from the National Academy of Sciences entitled "Control of Rabies" conflicts with this claim. The report concluded that "persistent trapping and poisoning campaigns as a means of rabies control should be abolished. There is no evidence that these costly and politically attractive programs reduce either wildlife reservoirs or rabies incidence." Similar statements have also been made by the American Society of Mammalogists and the Secretary of Interior's Advisory Committee on Predator Control.

Since this testimony, however, no progress has been made to regulate trapping in the United States, and the atrocities continue unabated. There is a striking analogy between the domesticated animal and the wild furbearers that are managed (or even raised and released) in designated areas called wild "ranches." Some people feel that if it is right to utilize farm animals, it must also be right to trap "managed" wildlife. But can we justify the nonessential killing of wildlife for sport or luxury fur, especially since we already have destroyed enough natural habitat to contain our domesticated plants and animals and affected natural ecosystems with our pollutants and pesticides?

Many people still believe that wildlife management programs designed for man's benefit are ethically acceptable, citing biblical references to man's God-given authority to manage nature as his own resource. These people are deaf to the voice of the wilderness. Some still claim to hear this voice of the Great Spirit in all things. The Native American Indian trapper, for example, claims that trapping on his ancestral lands is a valid form of self-subsistence. Unfortunately the average Indian trapper today takes more animals than he needs for subsistence. Walruses are slaughtered for their ivory, and wolverines and wolves, endangered and rare species, are destroyed purely for commercial reasons. Many Indians have sacrificed their ancestral claims and philosophy of kinship with animals for modern-day commercialism.

Because he pays for a hunting license, the white "sport" hunter believes that it is his traditional right to kill wild animals. What is legally right may not be morally right, however, especially the killing of trophy animals and the horrendous sport of bow hunting. More animals are maimed by the arrow or die later from infections or loss of blood than are killed quickly. Hunters who claim they are helping the balance of nature by controlling the populations of game and nongame species are on shaky ground because the game surplus has usually been artificially created for them, and most competing wild predators have been exterminated to ensure human dominion over the wildlife "resource.'

Non-Indian trappers have many other arguments: "We kill off the 'surplus' more humanely than nature," for "nature is often cruel." "The good trapper takes as much care of the animals on his trapline as does a farmer for his stock." They try to justify their killing by employing so-called humane methods but seem incapable of considering the wild animal's right to life.

Trapping wild animals for fur should be as much an anachronism today as slavery was ten decades ago, but I suspect that we may have to wait another ten decades before the rights of animals will be understood and recognized by those who destroy and manage wildlife for recreation and profit.

Some argue that they should use the animal surplus of furbearing wild animals rather than let them go to waste (through starvation, disease, and so on), but we all know nothing is wasted in nature. I believe that no one should wear a wild animal's fur today unless it is essential for survival (few of us live in Arctic conditions). I am not so irrational as to oppose selective trapping of wild animals injurious to human interests, provided those interests are compatible with those of a given ecosystem. A humane trap is a viable alternative to an inhumane one, but it is not the only alternative for wildlife control. It is possible that if a humane trap were ever developed, it might loosen the trapper from his own conceptual trap—first by making him think more humanely and ultimately by leading him to find an alternative way of life that no longer entails nonessential killing. Fur boycotts have little impact since other countries, especially in Europe, provide a ready market, but pressure at the consumer end of the trapline may add to the growing awareness that wildlife is not ours to harvest after all.

This review of wildlife "harvesting" by trappers, hunters, dealers, whalers, and others would be incomplete if I did not mention another serious and extremely lucrative wildlife exploitation: the commercial "live" trade of wildlife. As one former international dealer and illegal smuggler of endangered species, Jean-Yves Domalain, states in his book *The Animal Connection,* this has become a multimillion-dollar business. Both private collectors and zoos will pay small fortunes for live specimens of such now rare and endangered species as cheetahs, infant chimpanzees, gorillas, and tropical birds and fish. In order to catch an infant monkey, its mother usually must be shot. In the process of capture, holding before shipment, and eventual shipment, 80 percent or more of the animals die from stress, inadequate nutrition, and secondary diseases.

Trophy hunters add to this continuing depredation of the world's fauna. Native poachers killed one of the gorillas zoologist Dian Fossey was studying in Africa for a European dealer with a client who wanted to buy a gorilla's head and hands. Not too long ago a group of American safari hunters went to Kenya for a three-week vacation and killed more than 2,000 animals, including lions, zebras, and giraffes. One of the safari guides was so appalled that he quit his job for good.

Local poachers make good money from the skins and furs of endangered species, from the ivory of elephants and rhinoceros horn—still sold in the Orient as a panacea and libidinal stimulant.

By carefully routing shipments of live animals and wildlife products through ports such as Hong Kong, where the laws protecting wildlife are not adequately enforced, and by forging the origin of some of the animals (for example, certifying that they were zoo-bred and -born), wildlife traders have a lucrative business.

Combine the above impacts on wildlife with the worldwide intensification of habitat destruction through logging, mining, agricultural expansion, population expansion, and other direct and indirect human influences, and there seems to be little hope for wildlife. And there will be no hope until it is realized that the long-term effects of such accelerating entropy—of reduction and depletion of the earth's diversity and irreparable damage to ecosystems—can only do us more harm than good.

For those who wish to keep wild animals as pets, perhaps one acceptable solution is to propagate the animals in captivity. Many ranches in the United States breed wolves, foxes, coyotes, and other wild animals for sale to the public as "pets." This trade should be stopped not only because the conditions on these ranches—like those where mink, fox, and other species are raised for their fur—are often grossly inadequate but because, as I have detailed in *Un-*

derstanding Your Pet, wild animals don't make satisfying pets. More often than not they have to be destroyed or finish up at the local zoo. Death may indeed be better than life in a small barren cage. But why breed them in the first place except for profit and short-lived pleasure and status? These are poor reasons indeed for justifying the commercial exploitation of wildlife as "pets."

A disturbing by-product of breeding exotic wildlife in captivity has been the advent of the game ranch. For a fee, hunters can bag a trophy animal from Africa or South America without having to leave the United States. Such lucrative wildlife "game" ranches are numerous in Texas, and rumor has it that some zoos actually provide the ranches with surplus stock for the trophy hunters' later pleasure. What better use for surplus stock anyway? one might argue. Once again, sheer utility and economic "necessity" (the profit motive) override any sense of ethics and sensitivity. To raise animals until they are trophy size and ready to be shot seems inconceivable in a country so advanced that it can put a man on the moon. Clearly, technological achievement and material wealth are not reliable indicators of how civilized we are. As Mahatma Gandhi once observed, one may determine how civilized a country is by the way in which the people treat their animals. We have some way to go. I see it as an ironic twist that with the increased public interest in nature and wildlife, the "back to nature" trend for many people means keeping a wild animal as a pet or wearing the furs of live-trapped or ranch-raised animals.

The problems of wildlife conservation—the protection of species and the preservation of habitats—are essentially human in origin. The fundamental issue is the ever-expanding human population which is in competition with wildlife for natural resources. We are past the point of compromise, of striking a golden mean between man and nature. While a few influential members of society are proconservation, the majority of the world population is opposed because it can be accomplished only at their expense. But appropriate technologies and methods of utilizing wildlife for food and other products will only temporarily alleviate human starvation and suffering and will accelerate the destruction of the biosphere if human population controls are not instigated. Medicine and technology, in reducing the natural population regulators of disease and starvation, are speeding up our demise by supporting population growth. It is both a biological and socioreligious necessity for many of us to reproduce as much as possible, unless a totalitarian regime forces otherwise, and even that, like Indira Gandhi's sterilization program in India, would probably fail through public (or world) opposition. It seems inevitable, then, that wildlife conservation and the preservation of our own species are clearly incompatible unless we gain dominion over ourselves. Only when human consciousness is raised so that we all realize the interdependence, intrinsic worth, and sacredness of all life will wildlife and our own species have a future. Humanity cannot continue to multiply, consume, and destroy the earth at the rate it is doing now. It is a biological necessity for us to restore harmony between mankind and nature. The more it is postponed through advances in technology, medicine, and agriculture that serve only shortsighted human interests, the less there can be of nature, and ultimately, the less there will be for and of ourselves. All human "progress" should ultimately serve the greater good of all life on earth, for we are not a species apart and must cease to think and act that way.

Ecologists have yet to define what a "natural state" is for any ecosystem since it is almost impossible to determine when and if human interference has made an area become unnatural. The energy level of an ecosystem is at its highest when there is a great diversity of species, when biological productivity and species diversity are interdependent. Thus, in terms of our own interests, species diversity should be maintained; it need not be always "managed" (by selective cropping or disease controls) but rather monitored and allowed to regulate itself. We must learn what "naturalness" is and shape our values and actions to harmonize with all existence. To allow any species or subspecies to become extinct is an act of criminal negligence since unique genetic material is the most precious resource of the world. Such a loss represents an irreversible reduction in the biopotential of earth and thus, indirectly, a loss to humanity. While the utilitarian manager with his computer and flow charts may believe that an artificial ecosystem can be regulated—be it a wildlife part or a vast field of corn or cotton—he does not have the basic knowledge to do so. Natural diversity is sacrificed for short-term gain and spurious efficiency; the costs are immeasurable, and future generations will pay for it. As Robert Smith has shown in *The Ecology of Man,* because of the complexity of natural systems, human intervention may be more catastrophic than regulatory unless human intervention per se is controlled. On the other hand, "preservation" (eliminating the human factor to which the system is coadapted) could be as disastrous as introducing human control into a pristine ecosystem.

If we are to protect the world from us, we must develop a totally closed system. We are only just beginning to recognize the real costs of open systems, which have polluted the biosphere. Swedish researchers, for example, have found high levels of the chemical PCB in Baltic seals, which may be the reason for reduced fertility and may lead to ultimate extinction. More than 130 persistent toxic chemicals have been identified in the body fat of these animals.

We are beginning to learn some of the serious chain effects of inappropriate technology in our application of chemicals in agriculture, as van den Bosch reveals in *The Pesticide Conspiracy.* Insecticides are causing even more serious pest problems than before they were first used, and they are increasing the costs of food production as well. Many contain carcinogens which get into the human body either directly or via livestock that is fed contaminated feed. (For an in-depth survey of this subject, see my forthcoming book *Farm Animal Husbandry, Ethology and Ethics.*)

Another unfortunate consequence of scientific "progress" is exemplified in the perfection of vaccines against disease. When the vaccine to prevent trypanosomiasis (sleeping sickness) is perfected, it will mean an end to much human suffering, but it will also mean the opening up of a large area of African wilderness where, because of the disease-carrying tsetse fly, wildlife resistant to the disease still have sanctuary. Conservationists are justifiably concerned that this land will soon be taken over by people and cattle and that the largest area of pristine wilderness in Africa will be gone forever. The chances of protecting even small sectors from human colonization are slim since the growing population demands food and natural resources, and we cannot deny starving people the right to life and land. Such is the ethical dilemma between the humaneness of disease prevention in man and foreseeably disastrous ecological consequences.

Extinction occurs when one or more groups, families, or species of life die out. Over the epochs of evolution there have been many such deaths on Planet Earth—the dinosaurs and the great mammoths, for example—and they are part of the normal progress of life shaped by natural forces. But now a wholly unnatural force is accelerating the death rate of species, a force created by man. The death of an individual is only a transition, but when the species becomes extinct, there will be no more individuals. A whole new cycle of creation would have to begin all over for that species to exist again, and even then, the odds of replicating such a unique expression of creation would be extremely slim.

The rate of whole species extinctions has begun to accelerate over the past 200 years as humans and their technology have spread all over the earth. Why should it be important to stop such continued extinctions? It is not only for our own good but for the good of all creation that we need a diverse, healthy biosphere.

The crises of today that engender our concern over the environment and all life may be part of an evolutionary force which will bring about an advancement in human consciousness. To comprehend the significance of the extinction of whole species, and to prevent such needless destruction, is a significant step forward for man. The wolf may become the next species to become extinct in the wild if human values and actions are not changed in time. If this does come to pass, might not the passing of the wolf be a valid sacrifice if human ignorance and selfishness were eliminated? We humans have a convenient strategy for pain and guilt—forgetfulness—but we must not forget the wolf and other kindred creatures. We must strive to keep them alive not just in books and memories, but in the few wilderness sanctuaries which we must set aside for them and preserve, irrespective of our need for land, coal, lumber, and other natural resources. If we do not, the world will be impoverished a degree more.

NATURE, CONSERVATION, AND HUMAN CONSCIOUSNESS

One question that all of us must be prepared to answer is: How much are we willing to sacrifice for nature's sake? Very little, if we are starving, as much of the world population is, and only a little more if we are affluent. Some of us would let nature go, for the rights of humans must prevail, yet our well-being is surely dependent upon a whole and healthy earth. Alistair Graham, a former Kenya game warden, in his book *The Gardeners of Eden* contends that the efforts of people to conserve wildlife "is nothing more than the outcome of repressed aggression redirected onto animals by humans paralyzed in their relations with their fellow men. The preservation of the wilderness, of the image of Mother Nature, is the cultivation of a fantasy, a desparate regression into the idealistic memory of childhood's mother-love." While I do not discount the author's own aggressive projections, his thesis deserves mention since it reflects a view relevant to the issue of self-preservation versus the preservation of nature. Graham's thesis that the attempt to preserve wilderness is a utopian fantasy may be true for some, but his view of concern for wildlife as a form of redirected aggression is misguided. Rather, it is alienation from human society that may lead many people to seek identification and kinship with nature and nonhuman animals, be they pets or "totem" wild species. The fact that conservationists are more numerous in urban areas, according to Steven Kellert, may support this latter contention. Other critics see those in the conservation and humane movements as effete and affluent idealists who, in their neurotic concern over animals, do more harm than good by neglecting the human condition: overpopulation, hunger, and loss of quality in life. While such criticism might have held true a decade ago, these movements are now much more enlightened, so that they may, for example, accept native rights to hunt if these are ecologically sound. The former bleeding-heart preservationist is now of a different cast, aware of the political and economic aspects of conservation as well as of the conflicts between human and nonhuman rights.

Our species as we know it today will someday become extinct. We are a transitional life form, evolved from our "primitive" human ancestors who lived closely with nature and who possessed instinctual wisdom, created not by the mechanistic sciences, but by the very process of evolution itself. The return to nature, to reestablish the connection with the animalness within us, is not regression to a primitive state of being, but an essential *recapitulation* of a form of life repressed by our contemporary society. Without such connectedness, our species will continue to consume and sterilize the earth, reducing the diversity of creation into a self-serving world of utilitarianism. With its domesticated plants and animals and small "sanctuaries" from token wild species to assuage our guilt and to satisfy aesthetic desires, such an impoverished world will sustain us neither physically nor spiritually. This describes the world today. The values, artifacts, and devices of our technological culture which make us feel independent of nature are as illusory as they are destructive of our humaneness and of our future. Like the overspecialized biological inventions of other species, which led to their extinction, these technological inventions may lead to our own demise since the mind of man has not evolved in parallel harmony with them. The mind is no longer an integral regulating part of the body. Such a schism between mind and body, culture and consciousness, individual and society, man and nature cannot then be healed. Extinction of one or the other or both is inevitable. This may mean not simply the death of an entire species for mankind, but rather the extinction of a mode of consciousness and related social institutions, which are as poorly adapted to the environment as is the great size of the early reptiles. A new consciousness will evolve so that future surviving members of our species will be as different mentally from us today as we are different physically from elephants and whales. On the surface, these future generations may resemble us as we today resemble physically, but not mentally, the aboriginal hunter-gatherers of Africa and Australia.

We are entering a long period of transition, and there will be even more suffering and needless destruction of life before we reach that different state of consciousness and become that new species.

In their book *Eyelids of Morning,* Alistair Graham and Peter Beard state:

> Why is it that between them [people] and the animals there is always a glass shield? . . . They are so near, yet so far. If only they were to insert a mirrored glass, they would find themselves staring at their own earnest, puzzled, *desperate* faces. The riddle would be solved. They would realize that the concern is for *their* fate, not that of the animals. It is so simple really; solve mankind's problems and the predicament of the animals will automatically vanish. But no amount of concern for the animals is going to make any difference to their destiny or to ours.

While admittedly much concern over animal welfare and conservation may be selfishly motivated, that we all are part of one great system of plantary life touches a deeper level still. Lyall Watson, in *Gifts of Unknown Things,* gives a very different view of man and nature, stating: "I believe that it is only through Earth-awareness that we can reach higher levels of consciousness. Without a deep and full appreciation and understanding of your environment, there is no possibility of extending yourself beyond it to a place with meaning and relevance." What is good for mankind should be good for all life in the long scheme of things, and while it is true that nature's problems are man-made, to focus all concern upon human problems and to ignore those of wild creatures and their habitats would be grossly negligent, for by the time we get our own house in order, there may be little left of the natural world to save.

5

Pets and Their Owners

Once each year in India there is a nationwide festival in honor of the dog. Food is put out, and countless stray pariahs eat their fill. The few people who keep dogs as pets in that country, having acquired the custom from the British, are those who can afford to feed an extra mouth, yet a visit to any small village will reveal dozens of dogs lying in the shade or waiting patiently by a baker's ɔr butcher's store. No one owns them; they are part of the village. They are an accepted and integral part of everyday life. Many are, like their human counterparts, in various states of emaciation or illness, and many females are found nursing scrawny pups, few of which are likely to survive to maturity.

Similarly in Africa and Australia we find native settlements with a scruffy assortment of dogs, and they, too, seldom belong to anyone. But they are more than just part of the scenery; they are symbiotes, not pets. They share the same space, if not the same room, with the people, and they do a good service by keeping down pests and warning of intruders—strange humans or potentially dangerous wild animals. In return, these dogs are allowed to find shelter under the eaves of huts and canopies over shop stalls. Their staple diet is garbage, human excrement, and the rare wild animal which they may kill and eat if the villagers don't get there before they can consume it. In India one or two villagers may even use some of the dogs occasionally to go hunting—or poaching—but the dogs are not trained. They are just used as beaters to flush out the quarry as the maharajas would employ the villagers themselves in the old days to bag another tiger.

Although appalled at the poverty of the people and the pathetic condition of many of the dogs in these Indian villages, I learned two important lessons. These people are generally accepting of and nonabusive to these pariah dogs because of the Hindu belief in the sacredness of all life and the Buddhist-Gandhi teachings of ahimsa—nonviolence toward life. Also, these people accept the animals because they were born and raised together. The dogs are part of the same ecosystem, both physically and psychologically. But they are not loved, and there are insufficient resources for indulging them with good food and medication when needed. The dogs, like the people, fend for themselves peaceably and usually democratically.

This kind of relationship was perhaps the first social relationship that early man had with an animal. Archaeological evidence points to the dog as being the first animal to become part of the family of man. But in India and elsewhere the dog has not crossed the threshold to become an integral member of the family. Historically the transition from outside to inside the home occurred slowly. The aristocracy began it when they selected small village pups as cuddly companions. These were the first pets, and there is some evidence that in Europe, at least, a person was not allowed to wear clothes or to possess a dog "above his station." Even if a person could afford to feed a nonworking pet or "lap" dog, there were certain social-status-related restraints which were prohibitive.

But the commoners were not without their dogs. They created many fine working breeds. The tenant farmer had his sheepdog; the lord's gamekeeper, his kennels of hounds and bird dogs. Many had their own, socially acceptable working and sporting dogs, like the terrier and whippet, and fighting dogs, like the bull terrier. These dogs were valued on the basis of performance, and the owner's esteem rose and fell accordingly. From this initial working relationship with the dog, it was a natural step for the dog to become an integral part of the family. The dog earned its right to lie by the hearth at its master's feet.

No less the cat. Imported into Europe from the Middle East, the cat earned its place in the home as a significant contributor, keeping down vermin which abounded in the towns and villages of our ancestors.

Six thousand miles away from India, in the United States we find a very different relationship between people and their companion animals, cats and dogs. I hope that in the future, the term "pet" will fall from general usage and be replaced by "companion animal," which is kept not by a "master," but by a human guardian. In some areas we may still see free-roaming cats and dogs not unlike those of the Indian villages, and we also find some people who still keep cats and dogs to perform specific tasks for them. But for the most part, people, like the aristocrats of old, keep animals simply as nonworking pets. We find veterinarians who specialize in dermatology, cardiology, ophthalmology, and so on, geneticists who counsel breeders, and nutritionists who formulate scientifically balanced diets for pets. Pets have training schools, beauty parlors, psychological counselors, and other related services. Taken altogether, pets represent an estimated $4 to $6 billion industry, according to L. E. Benning's *The Pet Profiteers.*

On the surface, such indulgence reflects the affluence of this society which many critics, such as Kathleen Szasz, dub as misguided and wasteful "petishism." While admittedly some people do overindulge their pets and have developed an almost pathological state of "petism" (which is duly exploited by pet-trade entrepreneurs), it is neither fair nor accurate to criticize all pet lovers as being misguided zoophiles. Many such critics, as we will see later, suffer from "speciesism" themselves, failing to see the real values of pets beyond their monetary worth.

Pets provide companionship for lonely people in our alienated and dehumanized society, giving a sense of family and community to countless numbers of elderly retired people. To young couples who are thinking twice about bringing children into this overcrowded world, pets are significant nonhuman companions and

child substitutes. They are always accepting and, with the unconditional love that they offer, are conducive to human emotional well-
being and mental health, as psychiatrists Boris Levinson and S. A.
Corson have shown. The greatest "value" of pets in the Western
world is to help people regain their "animal/nature connection"—
to become more fully human in a relationship that breaks down
egocentric values. More will be said of this shortly, but first, let us
explore a few basic types of owner-pet relationships.

Some pet ownership today may be termed object-oriented, as
when a family has one or more dogs or cats because: "What's a
home without a pet? We always had them as kids, and so did our
parents." For many, the Christmas or birthday kitten or puppy may
be no more or less than another play object for the children. As with
an inanimate toy, interest in the pet may wane with time as its nov-
elty fades and its appealing infantile traits are replaced by less
endearing mature behavior and temperament. Judging from euthanasia statistics at American humane shelters, animals are too often
considered disposable objects. Some adults may keep pets for purely
ornamental purposes, regarding them with as much concern and
empathy as pieces of furniture in proportion to monetary worth or
uniqueness. Like furniture and other inanimate objects, pets may
have some intrinsic worth, some sentimental value, or they may
give a feeling of identity or status.

Utilitarian exploitation involves a relationship in which an animal
is used, trained, or manipulated for the exclusive benefit of people.
This category includes the use of animals in biomedical research,
military work, and agriculture as food converters for human consumption. In the domain of pet use, the possession of an animal for
any utilitarian function—as a guard, a hunter, a guide for the blind,
or for show, obedience trials, and breeding purposes—often combines with need-dependence and object-oriented relatedness, as
with the policeman who loves his working dog as a companion or
the breeder who regards the best dog as a status object.

A pet that is kept primarily as a "learning experience" can be an
object of utilitarian exploitation if the learning is not combined with
affection or empathy. Knowledge for the sake of knowledge is un-

ethical if it does not ultimately have some ethical basis and morally sound purpose or goal.

As I explained in my book *Between Animal and Man,* the essentially utilitarian view is a destructive and dehumanizing force which seriously distorts our perceptions. To value a pet (or a person) simply on the basis of its utilitarian function is crass materialism. To rate any living creature, human or nonhuman, in relation to its usefulness is a step backward in our attempt to become "civilized." What many pet owners value is the intrinsic worth of their animal companion and the value-transcending quality of relationship that comes with unconditional love. Would that the latter were more prevalent in relationships between people, especially between parents and their children! One criticism often leveled against pet owners is that they waste too much money and concern on their pets while they ought to devote themselves to problems that concern the human race. This is ironic, for many of the problems of humans originate from those who value things only in terms of their usefulness and regard humans and other animals as things, as workers, slaves, consumers, resources, and the like.

It is pertinent at this point to mention the widespread exploitation of both pets and their owners. Because of the potentials for quick profits, unethical and inhuman practices in the pet industry are not uncommon. A few examples will suffice, beginning with the promotion of certain pet foods that are touted as being good for your pet, and if you don't feed Brand X, you don't love your pet. Some feeds, such as all-tuna-fish diets for cats, are actually unbalanced and can be very bad for pets. One company claims that dogs need "an all-meat diet," which would, in fact, be detrimental to a dog's health; ironically, this firm does not sell a 100 percent muscle meat diet, as it implies, but a variety of low-quality animal by-products, such as lungs, intestines, and cows' udders.

Some of the worst abuses of animals I have ever seen occur on the "puppy-mill" breeding farms in the Midwest, where purebred pups are raised wholesale, often under the most atrocious conditions, for sale in large retail chain outlets in the cities. Prospective buyers of purebred dogs should boycott all pet stores and find a good local breeder. But because of the many problems associated with in-breeding, I advise people seriously to consider getting a "super-mutt" from the local dog pound instead. (For more details, see my book *How to Be Your Pet's Best Friend.*)

Another exploitation is the sale of unnecessary medications for pets, some of which may be hazardous to animal health. I believe that cats and dogs should not wear flea collars constantly, except in those few southern areas where fleas are a constant problem; a comparable practice would be to take aspirin every morning just in case you might get a headache. One entrepreneur is now advertising on national television that owners should worm their pets every month. In England the British Veterinary Association would publicly oppose such unethical and potentially harmful "free enterprise" that exploits pets and their owners with profitable misinformation. The American Veterinary Medical Association has yet to take a firm stand on such matters (and, indeed, on many other matters related to animal welfare, such as dog- and cockfights and trapping).

A final area of exploitation is the capture, breeding, and sale of wild and exotic animals as pets. Many ranches in the United States breed raccoons, foxes, wolf cubs, and other animals for this purpose, but selling these animals as pets is a total misrepresentation to the public. Most of these animals either finish up their lives miserably confined to a cage or are destroyed because they are unmanageable. As many as 80 percent of all exotic birds imported from abroad and high percentages of other exotics, such as squirrel monkeys, capuchins, and margay cats, die before they ever reach the pet store. The conscientious consumer should boycott the sale of any wild indigenous animal or imported species, many of which are now threatened with extinction because of the wholesale pet industry. Local ordinances in some areas forbid anyone to own a wild animal. This is a social service since few species make suitable pets. It will also help prevent ecological disruptions, the extinction of species, and the spread of zoonoses and diseases which may infect our indigenous wild and domestic animals.

Perhaps the major reason that people have pets, especially dogs and cats, involves a need-dependency relationship, which is a common underlying emotional mode in many man-man relationships as well. The pet may fulfill many needs for adult and child alike: a companion, confidant, sibling partner in games, an unconditionally affectionate and accepting emotional support, a link with nature and with uninhibited, honest emotions and responses, or simply a refreshing break from the impersonal and often dehumanizing man-man transactions. The deeper the emotional need of the person, the more important the pet becomes in this kind of relationship. A pet can do more than "humanize" its companion through its openness and unconditional acceptance; it may, as shown by Dr. Levinson, also serve as a psychotherapeutic support, as a child or sex substitute, a guard for the paranoid, an ally for the lonely and antisocial, an inferior controllable being for the megalomaniac, or an outlet for redirected frustration and aggression. Pets are gaining wider recognition and respect as therapeutic tools, serving as an emotional bridge and social catalyst between the emotionally withdrawn patient and the therapist. Even in "normal" contexts, a pet serves a significant role as an emotional bridge in the home, facilitating interactions between family members.

As I detail in *Understanding Your Dog,* overpermissive and overindulgent raising can lead a pet to become neurotically over-attached to its owner. This is a source of many behavioral disorders in pets and is often a result of the owner's need to indulge some living creature, in essence as a child substitute. Neurotic behavior problems in pets are very much on the increase in the United States. Obesity in dogs is also an increasing problem, a physical manifestation of excessive indulgence, resulting in related complications, such as kidney and heart failure and various psychosomatic ailments. In other words, some pets are being pampered to death, much to the benefit of "pet profiteers." Nevertheless, a pet can give a person a sense of belonging, and for some people it may even be something to live for, especially for senior citizens who have little social life and emotional fulfillment outside their relationships with their pets.

Because of emotional investment and dependence, this type of relationship differs significantly from object-oriented and utilitarian relationships and is best exemplified by the way in which the individual or family responds to the pet when it is sick or after it has died or become lost. A child can come to understand the meaning of death and to cope with personal suffering at the loss of a loved one. Knowing that a pet will not live as long as the child will and experiencing the death of a pet can force a child to face the ultimate reality. Knowing that all living things will die can give a refreshing clarity to relatedness, from which a reverence for life may arise. Seeing a pet suffer in sickness can help foster empathy and compassion and may also help some children become more caring when they mature.

There is another dimension to the social value of pets, which is seen in what I call the transpersonal relationship between pet and owner. Here the pet is appreciated for what it is, instead of what it supplies in emotional gratification as it satisfies the owner's needs, expectations, and dependencies. A person's perception of the pet shifts from one of dependency to an ego-free relationship. This change in perception has been recognized and analyzed in human relationships by the humanistic psychologist Abraham Maslow, but it is no less applicable to the human-animal bond. In this type of relationship, each individual is free to be himself without the binds of conformity, expectation, dependency, and conditional affection.

As with a child, however, the adult in relating to an animal in this dimension has a degree of responsibility which must not be surrendered in a permissive ideal of natural laissez-faire (a misguided naturalistic ethic). With increasing maturity of the child and, to some degree, of the pet, responsibility ideally shifts from the parent/owner to the child/pet. In human relationships, when this normal transference does not occur, there is considerable conflict between parent and child, for whom love and responsibility are confused. The parent does now allow the child to assume responsibility for its own life, and the relationship is governed by need-dependencies primarily on the part of the parent.

One cannot expect a pet to mature to this degree of responsibility in relation to others (though basic obedience training helps to a degree). Yet some owners hold that a pet should be allowed to live as natural a life as possible—to reproduce freely and to roam and hunt as it pleases. Living easily with a pack of dogs in the hills may be a nice Thoreau-like pastoral idyll, but such animals may be shot by hunters, fall into traps, eat poisoned bait, compete unfairly with natural predators for prey and carrion, kill domestic livestock, contribute to automobile accidents, and even attack people. Just as with a child, the pet must be protected. The natural relationship must be combined with responsible pet ownership. While some pet owners may need to be educated toward greater empathy with their pets, others need to be educated toward greater responsibility.

When there is a relationship of responsible care, empathetic understanding, and appreciation of the animal for itself, a person may for the first time experience a oneness or communion with another living being. Many people find it easier to establish such a relationship with an animal than with another human, whose ego defenses are an additional barrier to the individual's own barriers. These are absent or at least minimal in a pet. The unconditional openness and receptivity in the pet can lead to a need-dependency relationship, satisfying such needs as that of mothering and indulging or dominating and controlling.

Interestingly a longtime trainer of German shepherds recently told me that he had started to "ease off" (relinquishing some of his need to control others, including his dogs) and was amazed at what he was beginning to learn about his dogs. In essence they were becoming his teachers, and the one-way man-animal communication had shifted into a more reciprocal transpersonal relationship with obvious benefits to both. J. A. Boone in *Kinship with All Life* lucidly describes this change in man-animal relatedness which occurs when one ceases to impose one's wants and will upon another being and, instead, begins to empathize, to feel-see and appreciate the animal for itself.

A person who has experienced a transpersonal relationship with an animal, especially in late childhood, may recognize its significance and pattern later and bring it into mature relationships with people. Accepting others for what they are, with respect, humility, and understanding, is analogous to the unconditional acceptance of a pet. People who are good with animals are usually good with children, combining transpersonal relatedness with compassionate care and responsible control.

Stewardship is a new relationship emerging today. It is one of great responsibility. Unlike "management," which even under the best guise is nothing more than utilitarian exploitation, stewardship entails constant monitoring of every human interaction in any biological system including man-made systems—from the soil of our farmlands, the genetics and metabolism of high-yield dairy cattle to the gait and temperament of a German shepherd. The latter is a good example of unnatural selection, in which animals are bred to conform to man-made criteria, some of which may be detrimental to pet animals. Breed clubs of purebred varieties of cats and dogs are now beginning to identify, monitor, and correct some of the destabilizing consequences of domestication, excessive inbreeding, and unnatural selection. The physical and psychological degeneration and emotional problems of our pets, especially purebred or "pedigree" ones, necessitate our most concerted stewardship. Also, since some of the behavioral problems that pets develop are linked to emotional troubles within the human family or stem directly from the owner, therapy involving pets and humans is now becoming a reality.

Pet keeping, especially when irresponsible owners are involved, is not without its problems. There is an ever-growing awareness of the impact that urban pet and stray dogs have on the public's health and general well-being. In addition to the publicity, ecological changes in the urban dog populations have strained the relationship between man and dog, as I. Nowell describes in *The Dog Crisis*. All these changes were caused by man.

The number of dogs registered with the American Kennel Club has nearly doubled since 1963, with more than 1.1 million dogs registered by 1972. It is estimated today that there is 1 dog for every 5.9 persons. Any increase in the dog population must lead to increased contact between people and dogs. It is not surprising, as Alan Beck has demonstrated in his book on free-roaming urban dogs, that diseases and bite injuries involving animal contact are occurring more frequently within the general population.

Overpopulation also means an increase of stray dogs and a greater annual destruction rate. For example, in Baltimore, more than 15 percent of the estimated dog population is destroyed by the pound annually, and automobile traffic kills nearly 10 percent yearly. High mortality in a growing population means a lowering of the age distribution. Again, to take Baltimore as an example, according to Dr. Beck, the mean age of impounded dogs was only 2.3 years, with more than 60 percent of the population under two years of age. A young population is composed mostly of new, nonimmune individuals, more susceptible to disease and worm infestation. Young animals are also more likely to bite and to expose humans to a greater risk of aberrant parasitism.

Another major change is in the average size of the dog. The dog population is becoming composed of larger dogs. Smaller breeds—poodles, beagles, and so on—continue to be registered by the AKC at approximately the same rate, but the registration of the larger breeds shows marked increases. There are almost twice as many German shepherds and significantly more Doberman pinschers, Saint Bernards, great Danes, Siberian huskies, and malamutes. This trend may be motivated by the public's awareness of urban crime. Larger dogs seem better equipped to warn and protect their owners. But increased biomass of the population also means increased waste output, an enormous urban problem. Fecal output varies, but averages 340 grams (0.75 pounds) per day for a large dog. This means that the streets and sewer systems of a large city will receive more than 187 tons of feces daily. In New York, a state law went into effect in 1978, requiring dog owners in cities with populations over 400,000—in this case Buffalo and New York City—to clean up after their pets. In New York City the law has been remarkably effective as most owners have complied. Many welcomed it; after all, dog owners probably benefit most since they are in the streets more frequently than non–dog owners. There's no question that clean streets are healthier for people as well as for their dogs. But there was one consequence that shocked humanitarians. When the "pooper-scooper" law came into effect, the local pounds all of a sudden were full of abandoned dogs. Hundreds of pet owners, it seems, would rather get rid of their dogs than clean up after them.

Larger dogs also inflict more serious bites, and this may be related to an increase in the number of reported bites. In the United States the bite rate is now about 500 bites per 100,000 people, but it is estimated that far less than one-half of the bites are reported. Interestingly, recent statistics show that contrary to popular belief, the unsupervised dog, not the stray, is the source of the biggest bite problem.

Through a rigorous program of owner education and animal control, successful animal shelter operations can reduce animal bite injuries and the dangers from several zoonoses. Continuous dissemination of information, including news releases, interviews, and stories through the news media and pamphlets, keep the public alert and protect them from animal-related diseases. But more is needed. It is time for the social and legislative forces of society to respond humanely, but strictly, by exercising greater control over the size of the dog population, the dogs' freedom to roam, and their promiscuous defecation. The New York State law proves that such laws can be effective. Several additional insights and possible solutions are detailed in Robert Allen and William Westbrook's *Handbook of Animal Welfare.* The dog should not be considered a pest to expel from society. In fact, the controls necessary to safeguard the public would also benefit the canine population. Dogs that are under direct supervision or control are healthier, live longer, and appear to be better adjusted, perhaps because a pet's real social group includes the family of man rather than free-roaming dogs.

Other contemporary problems threaten to change long-existing relationships between man and pet. Many high-rise apartments and condominium units outlaw any kind of pet. Surgical modifications—declawing, neutering, and debarking—are often indicated today in order to preserve the pet-owner relationship and to appease or otherwise satisfy social pressures. The ethics of such practices are questionable, but a noisy and untrainable dog that has been devocalized might, in the final analysis, be better off devocalized than dead. But how far should we go in making our pets adapt to our needs and life-styles?

No pet (working farm cats excepted) should be allowed to roam freely today, not only for its own safety but for the social and ecological reasons already described. How many pets can adapt to a more confined life is debatable. Selective breeding, surgical procedures, and proper training early in life—all to facilitate adaptation—are serious contemporary concerns. Some would hold that the cat is the pet of the future since it is more adaptable to apartment life than most dogs. It is true that dogs are no longer allowed to run freely in city parks and are not allowed in some parks at all, even on a leash, making them difficult city pets.

The changing life-style of the family is another pressure on the dog as pet. Few dogs adapt well to being left alone in an empty house or apartment when both husband and wife work. Some dogs become house wreckers, bark excessively, or become unhousebroken. Professional dog walkers and sitters have appeared and dog care centers have been established for a valid service, and they can make the difference between an adjusted and a neurotic dog. A more questionable service is performed in the cities by attack-training schools. Legislation should require that all these schools be inspected and licensed since many employ extremely inhumane training procedures. Also, owners of attack dogs should at least be certified as competent dog handlers, and some should probably have a psychological evaluation. It has been shown that a burglar alarm system is safer and certainly more reliable than an attack dog.

No one needs, or should be forced, to justify choosing to live with an animal, loving it unconditionally, and accepting it as an integral member of the family. Only a "speciesist" excludes domestic animals not only from the family of man, but from the scope of moral concern. Animals do have rights intrinsically, by virtue of their very existence, and once born, a relatively helpless pet has a right to a good home. This *is* a burden of responsibility on us humans since to a great extent we created pets. Many breeds of dogs and varieties of cats are extremely dependent. Selective breeding for specific traits has resulted in some cases in physical and/or psychological changes which make the animals unable to fend for themselves in the wild. Being so created, do they not have a right to the most understanding, compassionate, and responsible care?

Such "rights" of a pet are often confused with the "right" to own a pet. The antipet faction attacks only the latter, and this puts its adherents in an untenable position when the owners uphold their right because they are *responsible* owners and because the animal has a right to be with such people.

More extreme antipet people are crazed by paranoia over the possibility of contracting some disease from an animal. (If they wish to avoid getting sick, they should avoid people, instead, since they are the main vectors of infectious and contagious diseases!) Others extend this paranoia to the point that *no* animal should be in the house or be touched by their children. Another extreme view argues that since pets today rarely perform any specific function, they should be done away with to preserve our limited resources and to give priority to more urgent human problems. One lady wrote chastising me for wasting research funds in my studies of dog behavior and brain development "when people are sick and starving and children need help and research on their problems." This I see as a confused utilitarian with good intentions. Like those who fail to see the many values of having a pet, others see no value in research with animals. While admittedly there is much needless research, often entailing unnecessary suffering, animal studies can and do give valuable insights into both animal and human problems. My own research in cat and dog behavior, for example, has done much to help people and children relate better to their pets by understanding them better—the key to communication and communion. Many people in their letters to me have revealed a narrow world view that sees only human beings and their concerns as significant. To demean all pet ownership is to reveal an immature and limited, if not ignorant and insensitive, mind. While admittedly some pet owners are irresponsible and need to mature, nonconstructive criticism and antipet talk will not help them or the pet problems that they create.

Ironically, many pet owners still value their animals for selfish reasons. The pet's intrinsic worth is not appreciated; the animal is valued only to the extent that it satisfies its owner's needs. They often have illusory and unreal *expectations* about pets, knowing and caring little about the animals' basic needs and natural behavioral tendencies. Dogs like to bark and roam; they don't like to be left alone in an apartment for extended periods. Cats like to claw furniture, sometimes to spray the house, and to go out acourtin' and acaterwaulin'. By understanding and appreciating a pet and learning to relate better to animals, we will be capable of relating more effectively to our own kind since selfish demands and unrealistic expectations are a barrier to any form of meaningful relationship.

Pets play a positive role in other ways. As S. A. Corson describes in *Pet Animals and Society,* the unconditional love of a pet is now being used as a therapeutic "tool" for bringing emotionally disturbed children and schizophrenic adults out of their shells. These pets are therapists, not "emotional slaves" for people who need animals to dominate and control or overindulge. Nor do these therapeutic animals serve simply to alleviate their owners' senses of inferiority or insecurity as might a show dog or attack-trained dog.

Many owners are criticized for attributing human qualities to their pets. There is not much wrong in being anthropomorphic to a degree since there is now good scientific evidence to prove that cats and dogs have emotions and sensations comparable to our own—fear, pain, anxiety, jealousy, guilt, joy, depression, anger. The brain centers mediating such states are virtually identical in man and other animals. This knowledge brings us closer to being morally obliged to consider the rights of animals. The right to "own" a pet may be questioned, but the intrinsic rights of animals cannot.

This "rights" issue has been neglected for too long. The recognition of animals' rights and the liberation of animals may elevate us all to a higher level already discussed—humane stewardship. And it is through pets—as companions, as co-therapists, and, indeed, as teachers—that many people will learn. These animals can make us more human, compassionate, patient, understanding, and responsible humane stewards. The mistakes that we have made with our pets—the abuses, excesses, neglects, exploitation, genetic deformities, and emotional problems—all are lessons at their expense, but we are learning to avoid them. And without pets in our lives, especially in the critical years of childhood, we would surely be impoverished. We need them, for the many reasons alluded to in this chapter, as they have come to need us.

I have already discussed the exploitation of wild animals as pets and, in the previous chapter, as victims of wildlife management, but there is another way in which wild animals come under man's

dominion—in zoos. Zoo animals fall into an odd category, being neither pets—although some can be petted—nor truly wild animals,
especially after having been bred for several generations in captivity. Some species are now even extinct in the wild and exist only in
zoos.

Zoos have been with us for a long time. The Romans brought
many varieties of wild animals back from military expeditions and
kept them on display until they were slaughtered in public arenas as
entertainment. Thousands of African mammals were killed until one
Christian, Telemachus, threw himself into the arena as a protest
against such inhumanity, an act which purportedly put an end to
these atrocious public spectacles. Since the Middle Ages, public
zoos have been popular urban centers for entertainment. But
today's zoos and wildlife safari parks are radically different from the
early zoos of iron and concrete. They no longer merely present passive displays of living animals simply to entertain the public but are
concerned with education, research, and conservation. The animals
profit from this new awareness as exhibits are improved to simulate
native habitats and to stimulate the inhabitants. The psychological
well-being of captive animals is improved, and their behavior is
more natural. Zoo visitors profit by gaining a greater insight into the
true nature of a wild species. But enlightenment is not without a
price. It takes money to run a modern zoo, and zoo directors realize
that they must compete with a wide variety of leisure-time activities. Concession stands, miniature railroads, and other carnival
amusements, as well as dubious circuslike shows with performing
chimps or big cats, lure many visitors to some of our large zoos and
wildlife parks. And some of these visitors show little respect for the
animals they've come to see. They flaunt the rules by feeding animals, and in some cases they inflict deliberate injury. The Frankfurt
Zoo has an exhibit of items confiscated from visitors, or found, on
postmortem, inside the animals, that were used deliberately to
cause the animals to suffer and even to die. Contrasting with such
"zoopaths," in misguided efforts to establish a closer rapport with
the animals, some zoophilic visitors have been injured and even
killed by reaching into a cage to feed or pet an animal. There are, of
course, serious and concerned visitors and bona fide students, along

with devotees who visit the zoo so regularly that they come to be recognized by some of the animals.

Zoo visitors and their responses to the animals would make an interesting study. My own observations have led me to the conclusion that, unconsciously, man reflects upon himself when he visits a zoo since in one way or another something of every living creature is embodied in his own essence. Anthropomorphism is a natural product of human thinking and perceiving in relation to animals. Although on the surface it may be based on misconceptions, it is more deeply rooted in the psyche of our being as a vague awareness that man and animal are one. Only man's heightened ego has created the illusion of man and animal as separate entities. Beneath this illusion is a collective unconscious that recognizes man's union with animal—and empathizes.

6

"Factory Farming":
The Hidden Cost of Suffering

T he sheer magnitude of the livestock industry is difficult to conceive. Each year this country produces 3.3 billion broiler chickens, 85 million pigs, 112 million beef cattle, and 9 million sheep, and our milk and eggs come from a total of 11 million dairy cows and 280 million battery hens.

The level of cruelty, unnecessary suffering, and privation of animals, described by Ruth Harrison in *Animal Machines,* is even more difficult to conceive and to accept. Much of what goes on in this industry is behind closed doors—literally—often in partial or total darkness. What the consumer doesn't see, he doesn't grieve. Styrofoam cartons of impeccable eggs, neatly trimmed meat in plastic wrappers, or a delicate slice of veal cordon bleu served on a silver platter do not tell the story.

Beneath this illusion of clean and wholesome food is the agribusiness reality of mass production of meat, eggs, and milk from farm animals whose daily existence is often far from clean and wholesome. Economically justified suffering and cruelty, protested in *Animal Liberation* by Dr. Peter Singer, are part of the business. Gone is the small family farm with its free-ranging chickens, mud-wallowing hogs, and dairy and beef cattle grazing contentedly in green pastures. Most chicken and eggs and increasing quantities of pork and veal come from creatures that never see the light of day.

Beef and dairy cattle are also being swept into this trend of total confinement.

The popular term for such livestock production systems is "factory farming," which has one primary characteristic—confinement. Animals are kept indoors, some for part of their lives and others for the duration of their existence. The confined animal is wholly dependent on the stockman not only for food and water but also for the cleanliness and temperature, humidity, and light control of its environment. Depending on the system, the animal may also be subjected to varying degrees of crowding, social deprivation, and the subsequent thwarting of various basic instincts and needs.

This space age form of farming is claimed to have one major advantage to the producer and consumer alike: More can be produced for less. But there are many hidden costs, especially in terms of animal welfare, which should be recognized and accounted for. Today we pay proportionately less for most farm animal products than we did fifty years ago, but often at the expense of animal suffering. It is frequently said in support of factory farming that no farmer mistreats his animals since his economic livelihood is dependent on their well-being. But this is simply not true; the major, if not sole, criterion of the animals' well-being is *productivity*, which is not a scientifically valid indicator of psychological well-being or necessarily even physical health. (One "efficiency index" for broiler production, for example, is the number of pounds of meat per square foot for floor space.) Also, large factory farms may be run to maximize profit margins with cost-saving efficiencies (such as overcrowding) that actually reduce productivity. And when there is market monopoly, lack of competition can reduce the need for optimizing productivity, and the animals' welfare may be neglected.

Some producers claim that animals have a better life totally confined indoors in "controlled environments" than they would have outdoors exposed to the elements, predators, and other variables. On a few farms this may be true, but by and large this is an outright fallacy. For example, some argue that tethered sows don't suffer from fight injuries as they would if kept in yards. But if the yards or fields aren't overcrowded, fighting is not a problem. It is often a symptom of bad husbandry when it occurs, and keeping sows tied down or penned alone all their lives is not a humane solution. Like many aspects of factory farming, it is a rationalization, a substitute for good husbandry and humane stewardship. It may reduce labor and increase productivity but at the expense of the animals' well-being; arthritis, obesity, and infertility often result. Generally, confinement systems are designed to reduce labor costs and for the convenience of the operators. But now from the bitter lessons of chronic infertility in sows, mastitis and foot problems in cattle, and chronic respiratory ailments in pigs and poultry, farmers have learned that the environment must be designed first for the animals; otherwise, confinement systems will continue to fail. One of the greatest costs to the modern livestock farmer is in drugs and vac-cines for the diseases which are often a direct result of the factory system.

Some claim that factory farming is justified to "feed a hungry world." But it is grain, not animal products, that the United States supplies to the hungry world. It is also grain that we feed to our live-stock, 90 percent of the annual harvest being fed to them. Chickens are the most efficient converters of feed, and beef cattle can digest many feed by-products that humans cannot. But pigs and veal calves are less efficient food converters. Most of what they eat we could utilize ourselves. Acres of cropland could be more efficiently used to grow cereal and vegetable products for human consumption than to be processed through an animal for conversion into costly animal protein.

Most readers have probably never visited a factory farm and will benefit from a closer look at the system and how it works. As I've already stated, crowding and confinement are the major features, but there are other environmental stresses as well as some, such as accelerated production, which are directly caused by man.

Crowding is especially severe in the raising of hogs and broiler chickens. Broilers may have one square foot or less of floor space per bird and no perch space, and hogs barely sufficient room in the pen to turn around in without stepping on another animal. Battery hens have even less—four or five birds are often kept in cages no larger than 12' × 16' × 14' high. Overcrowding is stressful physically and psychologically and can lead to feather pulling and tail biting vices, fighting, cannibalism, and losses as a result of secondary infections. The common solutions are to debeak (remove part of the upper bill) in poultry, to dock the tails of pigs, and to control crowding, stress-related diseases with vaccines, antibiotics, and other drugs. Symptoms alone, not the basic causes, are treated. The animals are still stressed, but they live long enough to produce a sufficient profit margin to make such farming practices worthwhile. The risk/benefits, in terms of human health, and the cost/benefits, in terms of animal suffering, have not been fully accounted for. The risks and costs are, in my accounting, greater than the benefits. Less crowding would be more humane and could also be more profitable, but tradition is hard to change.

The physical environment in which factory farm animals are confined is a cruel one. Even the animal's last contact with reality, the ground, may be stressful. Slatted floors, with spaces often too wide for calves and pigs, may cause lameness. Straw bedding is rarely provided, and the hard concrete combined with the weight of a full-grown sow also causes lameness. Beneath the slatted floor of many pig houses is a tank of liquid manure, which creates a dank, ammoniated environment, chilling in the winter and excessively humid in the summer since the ventilation system is often inadequate.

Battery hens and growing poults are kept in wire-floored cages, which have a steep slope for the egg layers for easy collection of eggs. Such a surface causes foot problems and constant discomfort; the birds have nowhere to perch. Tests have shown that if given a choice, they will avoid these thin wire floors. Dust can be a serious problem in deep-litter broiler chicken houses, which, together with the ammonia from the animals' excrement, can lead to chronic respiratory problems.

Outside, cattle in feedlots wallow in ice-cold mud and excrement after winter rains. Dust in the summer is churned up by the cattle and can aggravate respiratory problems. Feedlot animals are rarely provided with shade or shelter from the sun or from cold winds. Concentrated diets can make them more susceptible to extremes in temperature. In the summer of 1977 several hundred dairy cattle in

California died from heat stress, while dairy herds that were provided with shade sheds had no losses. In the winters of 1973 and 1978, thousands of beef feedlot cattle died from exposure. These losses could have been minimized by providing them with windbreaks and raised areas above the freezing mud and manure of the feedlot pens.

Confinement in barren stalls, pens, or cages is extremely monotonous. Being deprived of varied stimulation leads to chronic boredom and understimulation stress, which may increase susceptibility to certain diseases and lead to "boredom vices," such as excessive mouthing on pen bars, pecking, grooming, nervous tics, and repetitive motions.

When the barren environment, with or without crowding stress, is combined with severe physical restriction, animals are unable to perform many natural actions or to satisfy basic needs. Crowded in small pens or battery cages, or tethered in separate stalls (as are sows and veal calves), they find it difficult, if not impossible, to groom, preen, stretch, turn around, and lie down comfortably. Social and emotional needs may also be frustrated, especially in veal calves, breeding bulls, and boars.

One solution is an especially cruel one—darkness. In darkness, animals move less, so they don't waste food or energy. They eat only when the lights are switched on. Twenty to twenty-two hours' darkness is usual for veal confinement systems. Lack of light may also reduce crowding stress and is often employed on some intensive pig and poultry farms. This ultimate extreme of confinement—isolating creatures alone in pens or crates in total darkness—is surely one of the most disturbing products of human ingenuity motivated by profit. Not surprisingly, new evidence indicates that calves will do better if they are not raised this way. While an animal in a field will consume more food (and money) just walking around or playing during the daylight hours, it may, in the final cost analysis, do better since it will be healthier and require fewer drugs to keep it healthy.

In fact, sickness and death are standard fare on a factory farm. Care is motivated more by economics than by ethics. Good animal husbandry has been replaced by administering drugs in the feed and water to prevent illnesses that are to a large extent created by bad husbandry. Essential vaccines are costly to the farmer and actually increase the animals' susceptibility to many diseases. Also, with too many animals to look after, sick ones are rarely noticed, and if they are, it may be too late or too costly and time-consuming to treat them.

Another major flaw in the factory farming system is that when things go wrong, they go wrong in a big way, and the animals can't do anything to help themselves. They are helpless against contaminated food or water, a virulent bacterium or virus, a failure in the heating, ventilation, automatic watering or feeding or cooler-sprinkler systems. The animals are wholly dependent on men and machines, and they have no escape, nor can they rectify things for themselves, as they might under more natural conditions. For example, cattle on the range or in pastures naturally seek shade or shelter when necessary, but in feedlots this is rarely possible.

Farm animals are equally helpless against the effects of dietary imbalance or deficiency. Problems began with overstocking of pastureland. Overcrowded, the animals were forced to graze where the pasture was contaminated with feces. They became infested with parasites. More problems came later when weeds were destroyed and replaced by high-yield grasses and other plants. With a narrowed choice of food, the animals became subject to metabolic and nutritional deficiency disorders, such as milk fever, grass staggers, and bloat, especially in more susceptible high-yield cattle. (Under ideal farming conditions, with a diversity of plants in the pasture and of nutrient components in the feed, they select and regulate their diets, largely preventing disease and deficiency. Animals possess a "natural wisdom.") With lack of diversity, they could not regulate and correct themselves for certain dietary needs. Further, highly palatable seeded plants, such as clover, occurring in an artificially imbalanced overabundance, led to other problems, such as photosensitivity, laminitis, and scours. The animals were not equipped with the "wisdom" to regulate themselves when faced with an unnatural abundance. The introduction of certain plants which increased productivity disrupted the animals' inborn nutritional wisdom.

On a confinement farm, where the animal cannot graze, it is

wholly dependent on man for its nutritional needs. Most diets, often barely adequate, are formulated on a "least cost" basis. Feeds are compounded from various natural and unnatural (by-product) sources and are fed to the animals. They cannot regulate themselves without free choice of food.

The science of nutrition, with analyses of parts per million of each essential nutrient, is far from being a reliable tool for optimal, scientific formulation and regulation of the confined animals' feed. There are still many unknowns. Claims that any given formula is perfectly balanced and contains all essential nutrients would not be true. For example, the "standard" nutritional requirement for phosphorus in poultry is too low, making the birds extremely susceptible to heat stress.

It would be particularly advantageous for nutritional research to include animal behavior indices in their studies of various dietary formulations. Free-choice situations, designed to facilitate critical evaluation of the animals' nutritional wisdom, could lead to the animal's telling the researcher what it needs in its diet. In addition, social variables, such as crowding, and environmental changes, such as high ambient temperature, should be incorporated into the research analysis of dietary requirements.

Being force-fed extremely rich food can lower the animals' abilities to withstand other stressors, such as disease and extremes in temperature. Lack of roughage (hay and grass) can cause rumen ulcerations and liver abscesses in cattle. Pigs are fed highly concentrated rations that are rarely fed as pellets (because of costs). Instead, they are given a dry feed that has the consistency and effects of sand and gravel, causing gastric ulcers. Recent studies have shown that if fed a little hay, cattle and calves will grow better and won't develop ulcers. The same is true for pigs if they are fed a pelletized feed. Veal calves are denied roughage (which they crave) and are fed a totally liquid diet deficient in iron for sixteen weeks so that they will have pale meat. Given some roughage and iron, they are much healthier, but the meat would be red and not fetch a good price when graded. Yet when cooked, it looks and tastes the same as "white" veal and would be more nutritious. In the final analysis, therefore, humane concerns may complement profit motives: Animals that are fed more natural rations will be healthier, and good health means more profit. Increasingly the farmer is realizing that there are limits to cutting corners and that giving some consideration to the natural needs of his livestock is not a false economy, but a sound investment. In a word, a return to *husbandry* and a rejection of the agribusiness trend of maximizing output at the expense of the animals' well-being would be indicated.

An often-overlooked cause of suffering, stress, and ultimately disease in factory farming animals is the way in which they are pushed to their limits to produce milk, meat, and eggs. Meat animals are fed arsenic and other appetite stimulants as well as growth-promoting hormones. Highly concentrated feeds that are low in natural roughage are used to produce more milk and to "finish" or fatten off beef, cattle, and hogs. This approach causes many problems. For one thing, it lowers the animals' stress resistance to disease and temperature extremes.

Broilers that are pushed to their limits may put on so much weight that they collapse because their bones are too weak and immature to support the abnormal weight, or they die suddenly from what appears to be a heart attack, a seizure which is called a blowout or keelover. They are often raised under continuous artificial light to stimulate appetite and accelerate growth. Battery hens are accelerated to produce more by being given a longer day under artificial light. At the end of one laying cycle, they are either destroyed (and put into soups or pet foods) or deprived of water and starved for up to ten days to force them to molt. Then they begin to lay again. Many die under this acute stress. Others burn out from sheer production exhaustion. Still others collapse with soft bones depleted of minerals used to make the eggs and shells.

On top of all these intolerable stresses, farm animals are subjected to unnecessary physical pain and suffering. Branding of cattle, castration of pigs, lambs, and young bulls, and dehorning are usually done without the use of an anesthetic. Recent studies have shown that castration of hogs and cattle and debeaking of chickens are unnecessary practices, as M. Kiley-Worthington shows in his book on farm animal behavior, and should be abandoned. The marketing of entire—noncastrated—boars and bulls would have a major health advantage to the consumer, for bull and boar meat contains less saturated fatty acids, which are implicated in coronary heart disease. Many established animal mutilations—docking the tails of lambs and pigs, debeaking poultry, and dehorning calves—could be eliminated by improvements in husbandry. Further physical abuses, injuries, and deaths occur when the animals must be caught and penned for shipment to slaughter. Transportation itself is one of the most acute physical and psychological stressors. Abuses by handlers during loading and unloading (especially with electric prods) contribute significantly to the millions of dollars that are lost from transit trauma.

The conditions under which farm animals are transported for slaughter must be improved. They are often severely overcrowded and may be shipped long distances (often more than 1,000 miles by road or rail) without adequate rest, exercise, sanitation, ventilation, food, or water. Existing regulations are inadequate and poorly enforced. A decentralization of slaughter and packing facilities would help greatly in reducing the toll of animal suffering and economic losses from deaths, injuries, and acute diseases associated with transportation stress. An estimated $1 billion is lost annually as a result of injury, sickness, and death associated with livestock transportation. More than $5 million was lost to the beef industry alone in 1976 from cattle being killed or injured in transit, and another estimated $70 million from treating shipping-fever. Other losses affect the "finisher" of pigs, cattle, veal calves, and poultry since many of the animals he receives to fatten will die from stress-related diseases during the first few days following shipment.

Slaughter techniques need further evaluation and refinement. Electrocution, for example, may cause paralysis but not unconsciousness in some animals. Kosher slaughter especially needs to be greatly improved, eliminating the cruel (and actually very unkosher) method of shackling and hanging an animal by one hind leg before its throat is cut. A 1,000-pound steer, hanging by one leg, will twist and struggle, tearing tendons and fracturing the bones in the leg that is shackled. A more humane cradle restrainer has been developed but has yet to be adopted by kosher slaughterhouses.

John Macfarlane, a long-experienced livestock consultant, recently gave me the following staggering illustration: If all the live-stock that die in transit, plus the parts discarded because of bruising and crippling, were loaded into railroad cars (at 38,000 pounds per car), a stock train forty miles long would be filled . . . every twelve months. He observes that "in the United States there has never been a federal law written that was intended to bring about kindness to animals for kindness' sake. Laws have been passed that made life a bit more tolerable for livestock, but they have been closely tied up with profit and loss ledgers." Macfarlane also notes that there has never been systematic research done on *any* of the electrical shock-ing equipment used in slaughter to prove or disprove the conten-tions of the humane groups. Nor has any been done on the ventilation systems of livestock trucks. Prior to passage of the Hu-mane Slaughter Act, many slaughterhouses opposed the use of stun-ning guns because of the extra cost (a few cents per animal), even though these are most humane when properly used. Macfarlane contends that the carbon dioxide tunnel pit used especially to kill hogs is far from humane because animals struggle to escape for up to forty seconds. A humane death should be instantaneous and with minimal prior trauma or anxiety.

Macfarlane concludes that "there is no such thing as a completely humane method of preslaughter stunning because no method is any more humane than its human counterpart will permit it to be."

How does the factory farm affect the human consumer of its products? For one thing, the widespread use of antibiotics in animal feeds could lead to drug resistance in bacteria pathogenic to humans and animals alike. For example, one out of every ten hogs tested by the Food and Drug Administration for antibiotic residues in the meat in 1976 had illegally high residues. Hormone implants which are used to stimulate growth in beef cattle may be linked with cer-vical cancer in humans. Pesticides, nitrate fertilizers, herbicides, and molds contaminate grains and other crops used in the animals' feed. Some of these substances may be stored in the animals' fat, muscles, and internal organs or be concentrated and excreted in milk and then be ingested by humans. Although most of these sub-stances are carcinogenic, their use is often justified on the grounds that they help reduce production costs. Although we cannot buy health, we should at least be able to buy healthy food and to trust that what we eat is good for us. To these hazards we should include the additional element of nitrites. These are added to preserve and color-stabilize most processed meats. When cooked, nitrites form carcinogenic nitrosamines. Reforms and alternatives are difficult to instigate when there is economic dependence on the use of such substances.

The question of the quality of the product to the consumer remains unanswered. The lack of flavor and slimy or watery texture (which may be stress-related) of pork and chicken meat and the runny, tasteless battery egg are well recognized. Could the "wisdom" of our taste buds be telling us that these are not good foods? With corner-cutting in feeding and synthetic formulation of dietary ingredients, who knows what essential trace elements—vitamins and other substances essential for our health (and not yet known to science)—are missing in the animals' feed and in the animals' meat, eggs, or milk that we consume? This is the price of progress which future advances in the science of nutrition may help correct, but in the interim, animals may suffer, and the consumer may be short-changed.

How does factory farming offset the environment? Overgrazing and predator and "pest" control on public lands have an ecological and wildlife impact. Sheep ranchers especially practice predator control by indiscriminate poisoning and trapping. The contribution to the diet of the nation (per capita annual consumption of lamb is less than two pounds) is insignificant compared to its impact on the land and on our native wild fauna. Sheep may become the next farm species to be raised in confinement; crowded feedlot "finishing" stations for sheep are already well established in the West.

An important political issue discussed by Wendell Berry and John Hightower is the growing agribusiness control of production, distribution, and prices and its takeover of the small family farm. Land-grant colleges receive government grants from our taxes, but the fruits of much of their research benefit agribusiness development and profits rather than the consumer or local farming community directly.

On the international scene, multinational corporations have invested in foreign countries (cheap land and labor) to produce cash crops and meat for United States consumption. Much of the meat in the fast-food chains comes from beef raised abroad at the expense of human rights and health. In countries such as Costa Rica and Haiti, peasants have lost their land and suffered malnutrition and starvation. Wildlife habitat has also been lost.

There are many solutions and resolutions that can be made to improve the lot of factory-farmed animals. Know what animal you eat. Be a vegetarian or "conscientious omnivore." Be willing to pay more for animals from farm cooperatives that are concerned with the welfare of their animals. Many are, since healthy and happy animals are easier to manage and are better producers, especially for the smaller operator, than sick and sad ones. More research funds are needed to design facilities which meet the animals' behavioral needs, to study and compare animals under different systems, and to breed more adaptable strains. More veterinarians and animal scientists must be encouraged to study the behavior of farm animals, and funds provided to study all aspects of farm animal welfare.

Farmers and consumers must come to understand that farm animals are not mindless and emotionless cogs in the complex machinery of factory farming. This understanding, empathy, and compassion, as Wendell Berry eloquently details, were once part of farming. Farmers "husbanded" their land, crops, and livestock. An ethical attitude may be slow to return without the spur of humane legislation because of the many distracting problems and priorities which intensive farming has created. And the problems themselves have created new specialist fields and supportive industries and jobs. Unfortunately, most attempt to solve only the symptoms, not the underlying cause, which is bad husbandry, with its by-products of cruelty and suffering.

Professor G. M. Teutsch of Hanover University has provided an excellent analysis of the ethical aspects of farm management. He cites the Eight-Point Statement of the Socioethical Institute of the University of Zurich, which reads as follows:

(1) Man, animal and plant participate in this one world and this one environment. This means that they live in relation and interdepen-

dence. (2) Unlike animals or plants man is able to break through the ecological balance system and by doing so is able to exert power upon the world of living beings. From this fact fatal consequences have resulted for nature. (3) This power of man constitutes his responsibility for his environment and therefore for the animals living with him. (4) Compared with the powerful position of man, animal has no similar chance. It is subjected to human superiority. Therefore human power must be limited by man accepting a fellowship of creatures which finds its expression in an attitude of respect for animals. (5) Man is not permitted to continue in his reducing the variety of living nature. On the contrary his activities should aim at regulations by which nature will be able to keep its right balance. (6) To the extent of his dominating power man is responsible for those conditions of life which comply with the natural needs of those animals under his control. In particular animals ought to be considered to be more than mere objects of human action. (7) In principle man may be entitled to make an economic use of animals. But when he makes such use he must provide for conditions of life which are in accordance with the animal's natural needs and which guarantee their physical and psychical health. (8) The influence exercised upon the genotype of a species may not impair the ability for living at any time and in any environment.

This is one of the most succinct statements to guide human thoughts and actions toward humane stewardship of all life on earth and is particularly germane to our economic use of farm animals for food and other by-products.

In the final analysis, what is humane and in the best interests of the animal may be to the best interests of the consumer and to some extent to the livestock producer as well. The "golden mean" between animal exploitation and humane treatment must be established, and consumers who care should be prepared to pay a little more for better-kept animals. Those in the livestock industry should also be willing to explore and implement improvements and reforms in their practices of livestock production, transportation, and slaughter.

There are still some good "husbandrymen" of our land and animals in America, and they must be supported and encouraged because the advances in technology should be applied to enhance productivity only by those who really care for their animals and the land. Otherwise, the misapplication could mean an intensification of animal abuse and environmental destruction.

Writing this chapter has been a task of self-restraint since it is difficult for me to describe in objective and nonjudgmental terms the many abuses in the factory farming of animals. Dairy cows near collapse under a broiling sun, veal calves isolated in darkness, kosher slaughter, broiler chickens being scalded alive, hogs crippled on concrete slats, overcrowded poultry cannibalizing each other are just a few of the many surface symptoms of a deeper problem. The problem is not with the animals, but with people. It is one of attitudes and values, and it is these that should be changed. To interpret these symptoms as deliberate cruelty is a gross oversimplification and an unfair judgment. Exploitation, reverence for "efficiency," the profit motive, alienation (from nature and animals), and the blind spots of unthinking habit and tradition underlie these surface symptoms, which can be generalized to other fields of human activity from environmental destruction to corporate consumer irresponsibility. What is needed is not simply more legislation, law enforcement, and bureaucracy, but a change of heart and mind, an ethical transformation to a more humane, enlightened, and compassionate regard for all life.

This is not, therefore, a judgment of those involved in the factory farming of animals, but rather an appeal to reason, and a plea for humane stewardship, and a challenge to explore and implement reforms where needed. And more research is needed to define what is stressful for farm animals and what conditions are best for their welfare. The mirror has been held up, and while some may deny the reality of what they see, others may justify the abuses and privation of basic freedom as cost-saving benefits of progress or as unavoidable aspects of the system. But few can be blind to the truth that the hidden cost of factory farming is animal suffering.

After having read this chapter, many readers may be left feeling helpless against the inertia of giant agribusiness and government. Groups working toward humane reforms in this field as well as in other areas of animal exploitation are listed in the appendix. These are nonprofit, tax-exempt organizations which you may wish to join and support to further the implementation of humane reforms. Regular publications by some of these organizations will also keep you informed and involved.

The plight of farm animals is of the greatest magnitude compared to all other fields of animal exploitation. The complexities of factory farming are indeed enormous, and I have presented only a few of the major welfare problems. There are many more, and there is much documented evidence in support of my overview which I have compiled in an in-depth study, soon to be published, entitled *The Animal Factories: Do You Know Who You Eat?*, and in a technical book, *Farm Animal Husbandry, Ethology and Ethics*. Veterinarians and animal scientists have shown that many of the practices of factory farming are not conducive to the animals' welfare and that there are humane alternatives. But these have yet to be adopted. In Europe there is far greater public concern over the welfare of farm animals, and codes of practice are now being adopted by many member countries of the European Economic Community.

What kind of agriculture would be in the best interests of farmers and the nation as a whole? What long-term investments should be made to protect all interested parties since short-range goals too easily lose sight of the fact that we have finite resources? The American continent has been under the plow for a mere 200 years, a fraction of what the European and Asian continents have been subjected to.

This land of plenty may soon become exhausted. Soil erosion (estimated by some experts as being as high as 5 billion tons lost per annum) is one major concern. Another is the fact that American agriculture is dependent on fossil fuels not only for running farm equipment and for transporting grain and livetock but for the manufacture of chemical fertilizers, pesticides, and herbicides. Some five to ten calories of fossil fuel are now used to produce one calorie of food, and ironically, 90 percent of feed grains produced are fed to livestock. Critics often remark that American agriculture is geared primarily to feed animals, not people. Such a practice is not just inflationary. With the development of vast monocultures, the very ecology of American agriculture is unsound.

In addition to the above economic and ecological concerns (which have certainly given short-term gains but which in the long run are counterproductive), there are two other major trends in U.S. farming which must be addressed. These are sociocultural and humane concerns, detailed in reports by Wendell Berry and myself. As will be shown, the "welfare" of the farmer, the land, and the quality of life in rural communities and of the animals on factory farms are closely interrelated.

Briefly, as a consequence of capital-intensive corporate monopolies, the free enterprise system and cooperative ambience of rural farming—the cultural bedrock of the American family farming culture—are being rapidly destroyed, as Wendell Berry describes in his book. In its place, labor- and community-destroying, fossil-fuel-dependent, and energy/capital-intensive factory farming of land and livestock is taking over. Under the not always egalitarian and benevolent system of vertical integration, the farmer either becomes a piecework worker for the corporation or is forced to sell out because he doesn't have the capital to compete or access to essential materials (feed, fertilizer) or market outlets for his produce.

When the land and livestock don't really "belong" to the farmer anymore (because he is now vertically integrated or is a manager for a company the investors of which he may never see) a very subtle and counterproductive element is introduced.* Essentially this element works against the traditional sense of *pride* (in one's work, land, animals, produce, and so on), *personal investment* (one tends the land with care, for one's sons will inherit it), and *empathy*.

Empathy is diluted and eventually eliminated when the stockman does not own the animals himself, is a hired hand or manager, or has thousands of confined animals to tend to. Automation and elimination of farm labor also reduce the amount of direct human

---

* This is, in terms of quality of husbandry and degree of productivity, best exemplified in the USSR, where the per acre yield was three- to fivefold greater on the peasants' own allotments than on state-run cooperative farms. American corporate socialism may be creating an analogous problem.

contact animals receive. Yet research has proved conclusively that *good husbandry,* under which the animals receive plenty of human contact, increases productivity and decreases disease problems in chickens, pigs, cows, and calves. In essence, empathy pays.

The lack of empathy and frequent human contact is a major reason why, on the large, impersonal (and "deanimalized") intensive factory farms, overall productivity is lower and disease problems are more prevalent than on a well-run medium-size family-owned farm. Such hidden costs are of concern to the animal welfarist, economist, and consumer alike. Buffered by feeding high levels of antibiotics and other drugs, and by mass production and market monopolies, the intensive farm animal factories can still turn a profit. But as has been shown in the United Kingdom by authors D. K. Britton and Berkeley Hill, bigness is ultimately counterproductive.

Both family farmers and their animals are caught today in an ever-tightening cost-price squeeze. With escalating land costs, more and more livestock are being raised in confinement. With high setup costs for total confinement, building space is a costly item. Consequently the animals are often overcrowded and unduly stressed and deprived of their basic behavioral needs under highly intensive factory animal farming.

A second Industrial Revolution has taken place during the past four decades. Since the end of World War II this revolution toward intensified factory-style agriculture has been subjected to increasing corporate control and monopoly. This revolution has had serious negative impacts socially, culturally, ecologically, and economically.

At this time in history we have reached a critical point at which we can see that further application and intensification of existing systems would have predictably disastrous consequences. Research surveys by agronomists, ecologists, and veterinarians indicate that there has been an *overapplication of technology,* including the use of chemicals and drugs, and an *overintensification of production,* from vast plant monocultures to overstocked concentrations of confined, intensively raised farm animals. As Marvin Harris in *Cannibals and Kings* observes:

... when certain kinds of state-level systems of production undergo intensification, despotic forms of government may arise which can neutralize human will and intelligence for thousands of years. This implies further that the effective moment for conscious choice may exist only during the transition from one mode of production to another. After a society has made its commitment to a particular technological and ecological strategy for solving the problem of declining efficiency, it may not be possible to do anything about the consequences of an unintelligent choice for a long time to come.

He concludes:

Since evolutionary changes are not completely predictable, it is obvious that there is room in the world for what we call free will. Each individual decision to accept, resist, or change the current order alters the probability that a particular evolutionary outcome will occur. While the course of cultural evolution is never free of systemic influence, some moments are probably more "open" than others. The most open moments, it appears to me, are those at which a mode of production reaches its limits of growth and a new mode of production must soon be adopted. We are rapidly moving toward such an opening. When we have passed through it, only then, looking backwards, shall we know why human beings chose one option rather than another. In the meantime, people with deep personal commitments to a particular vision of the future are perfectly justified in struggling toward their goal, even if the outcome now seems remote and improbable. In life, as in any game whose outcome depends on both luck and skill, the rational response to bad odds is to try harder.

Today we have such an opening, a moment of grace in which to debate the future of American agriculture. Tomorrow it may be too late. A critical assessment of all the interdependent variables and vectors in U.S. agriculture is needed, from the interests of producer and consumer to the immediate and long-term welfare of farm livestock and land respectively. A government which has the sense and sensitivity to undertake such a task could, for the first time in the history of mankind, take a positive step toward maximizing human interests and at the same time ensuring that the "costs" to the environment will be minimized. As the Secretary of Agriculture, the

Honorable Bob Bergland, said in his address to the National Farmers Union in Kansas City, Missouri, on March 12, 1979, we do not yet "have a workable policy on the structure of agriculture. . . ." He says, "Surely, it is time to develop a national farm structures policy," and, he adds, to "design policies to save the family farm."

It is the general consensus among animal scientists, veterinarians, and others involved in the livestock industry that since animal welfare and productivity are closely correlated, industry's concern over maximizing productivity will guarantee a high standard of animal welfare. However, on the large, intensive farm, overall mass production, based not upon individual performance but upon output per unit of building space, is the modus operandi.

Individual animal performance/productivity is often suboptimal on large factory farms but is still profitable because of the economies of scale. Optimal productivity on an individual basis is of secondary importance to overall productivity with low-cost inputs to maximize returns. In other words, if a particular production system or scale of production promises to produce more for less, then that system will be adopted. Therefore the claim that, in the interests of profit, farm animal welfare is satisfactory on intensive factory farms (otherwise individual productivity and performance would be adversely affected) is true only in theory.

It may be true on the small farm or on exceptionally well managed factory farms. But on large farms, with millions of laying hens or broiler chickens, or with thousands of hogs or cattle, it is simply not true, because of the economies of scale and the criteria used to determine productivity that are based upon individual performance.

7

Laboratory Animals

Millions of animals—dogs, cats, monkeys, rats, mice, guinea pigs, rabbits, gerbils, and countless other lesser-known species—are used each year in laboratories. An accurate count is not available, for no records are kept of the numbers of rats and mice used, even though these are the most common laboratory species. A conservative estimate, on the basis of a 1971 Rutgers University survey, would be in the region of 100 to 120 million. By far the greatest number of animals is used for commercial purposes, particularly in the search and screening of profitable, though often superfluous, new drugs and in the safety testing of nonessential products, such as cosmetics, household and other chemicals, and of synthetic food additives.

Large companies have their own laboratory animal facilities, where generally the standard of animal care is in compliance with existing laws and guidelines. The Institute for Laboratory Animal Resources (a division of the National Academy of Sciences) and the American Association for Laboratory Animal Care (AALAC) have done much to improve these standards, and all large research facilities now have a resident veterinarian. There are, however, many private testing laboratories which conduct animal experiments on a contract basis for commercial companies and government agencies. Some of these private laboratories not only have substandard animal facilities but also have conducted substandard tests, even falsifying research data. The Good Laboratory Practices Act, with the aim of enforcing standards in this area of the commercial use of animals, is now in operation under the administration of the Bureau of Veterinary Medicine.

Far fewer animals are used today in universities and colleges for research and for teaching purposes than a decade ago, mainly because of cutbacks in federal funding. Large universities have followed the guidelines of the AALAC and have become accredited with this national organization after improving their laboratory animal facilities and hiring specialist veterinarians to oversee things. However, animal care facilities in small colleges are still relatively in the Dark Ages. Most do not require students working with animals to complete a basic course in laboratory animal care (including postoperative care), nor is veterinary treatment for sick animals always provided.

Only the larger research establishments breed their own animals. Many are supplied by commercial breeders and animal dealers, all of whom must now be licensed with the Department of Agriculture (USDA). The Animal and Plant Health Inspection Service, which is a division of the USDA, is responsible for inspecting these and university facilities. It also enforces regulations for adequate care and transportation of animals to research laboratories. Compared to farm animals, laboratory animals have far better protection under existing laws, primarily because the researcher needs whole and healthy animals to work with. Animals of unknown genetic origin or unhealthy animals are of little use to most researchers. It is via the Animal Welfare Act, administered by APHIS, that laboratory animals now have some protection under the law. But there are still serious omissions. Rodents (rats, mice, and so on)—in other words, the majority of animals used for research and teaching purposes—are not covered by this act, nor are farm animals. Also, no provision is made to give cage-confined dogs any exercise, and worse still, an investigator is not obliged to give an animal an analgesic or other treatment to reduce pain and suffering if such treatment might interfere with the experiment.

A major abuse in research has been the overuse of primates in experiments. Thousands of primates are used each year in the United States for military research (such as the testing of new weapons, neutrino radiation, and so on) and for the commercial testing of drugs and vaccines. The kidneys of green monkeys, for example, are used to grow polio virus, and live rhesus monkeys are used to test the safety and effectiveness of new batches of vaccine. Primates are used because it is generally believed that they are the closest animals to man and therefore the best test models. This is not necessarily true. For example, rhesus monkeys are used for long-term safety tests of human birth control pills, yet according to Dr. Andrew Rowan, their steroid metabolism is quite different from that of the human female.

Under mandatory regulations only primates (or primate tissues) can be used for certain tests and commercial vaccine production. Such regulations, drawn up by committees that are not always composed of the most knowledgeable experts, need to be changed in the light of new advances in cell and tissue culture replacement techniques. Cultures of human diploid cells, for example, could be used in the production of polio vaccines.

The search for research alternatives has been hampered not only by the inertia created by regulations but by the plentiful supply of primates and lack of funds and incentives to develop effective alternatives. Instead, more primate breeding facilities—government and privately owned—are being set up here and in their countries of origin. Recently considerable public concern has arisen over the status of primates in the wild. Most of them are now on the endangered species list. However, the United States supply of rhesus monkeys from India was stopped only when Prime Minister Morarji Desai learned that the animals were being used in military research, an apparent violation of earlier terms of supply. Conservationists intervened when they learned that the United States was planning to import pygmy chimpanzees for military research, a plan which could have resulted in extinction of the wild population. Wild chimpanzees are now threatened with extinction partly because they are needed by drug companies to develop a new hepatitis vaccine. If alternatives to the use of primates are not found soon, and if wild habitats are not protected from human encroachment, most species will exist only in zoos, laboratories, and breeding centers in the near future.

There is an additional note of irony which places these creatures in greater jeopardy. The same persons concerned with the importation and supply of primates for research sit on the importation-regulating endangered species committee, which ostensibly serves to protect threatened and endangered species from human extinction. Because of the alleged necessity for using such animals for the benefit of humanity, there are strong pressures to lift the ban on importation. This clearly violates the Endangered Species Act and illustrates the ineffectiveness of animal protection laws in the face of human need and corporate pressures to further their commercial interests.

How valid is research involving the use of animals? There is an extremely disturbing trend in the care and raising of animals for research. The standards which have been set and are enforced by the USDA address only the physical health concerns of laboratory animals. The behavioral, social, emotional, and environmental needs of the animals are not adequately considered. It is not generally realized, much to the detriment of good research, that to deny or frustrate an animal's basic behavioral and social needs can be stressful and influence the validity of any studies done on it. A clean cage, water, and a balanced diet are not sufficient to produce a normal, healthy animal. Yet it is believed that the more sterile and automated the system is (for feeding, watering, cleaning, and so on), the better for animal and researcher. A genetically standardized animal in a perfectly controlled environment is seen as the ideal. But when social contact, including human contact for some species, is drastically reduced, it may be to the detriment of many laboratory animal species that need some form of social contact with their own kind or with man but are being denied both under present standards. As I have shown in *Laboratory Animal Science, Ethology and Ethics,* this is especially important since most laboratory animals have to be handled at some time for experimental purposes, and if they are not used to human contact, they may react badly to handling. Standardized and regular handling of laboratory animals should be part of routine care, but with labor costs and increased automation, this important element in their lives is gradually being eliminated. Increasingly, too, animals in research are isolated from their own kind, for health reasons, for the sake of the experiment, or for sheer convenience. Even rats will develop behavioral and physiological stress reactions when socially isolated. Their susceptibility to diseases, drugs, and other treatments is greatly increased by social deprivation.

Present standards for the care or breeding of laboratory animals, though still inadequate, have greatly improved since the Animal Welfare Act was passed more than a decade ago. The values and priorities underlying present federal regulations are concerned primarily with the animal's physical well-being. It should be free of disease and physically "normal." Such concern neeα be motivated not by humane considerations, but by purely utilitarian and commercial reasons since health is essential if the animals are to be reliable "research tools."

The behavioral needs of the animals are also important to good research. Highly inbred laboratory rodents or highly sociable wild-caught rhesus monkeys kept in isolation in small (but clean) cages cannot be regarded as normal.* Under present standards and practices of laboratory animal care, we may be unwittingly creating genetically and environmentally repressed, uniformly abnormal, and sometimes even psychotic creatures. Research findings derived from them cannot be safely extrapolated to man or other animals without extensive field trials.

For example, long-term isolation of a beagle or a rhesus monkey can cause serious behavioral, emotional, and physiological changes, including stereotyped pacing, depression, anorexia (refusal to eat food), or excessive eating, drinking, and grooming (which may lead to self-mutilation). I have seen cancer research and pollution studies in large laboratories where such beagles and rhesus monkeys were used. The behavioral changes and stresses were not considered by

* Curiously, the recommended cage sizes for dogs, cats, primates, and other laboratory animals are almost twice the size in the United Kingdom, compared to the U.S. guidelines.

the investigators, yet they do influence the results by increasing the animal's susceptibility to spontaneous or induced diseases, chemical toxicity tests, and cancer tumors.

The animal researcher must first define the value and relevance of his research. But he must also look again more critically at the kinds of animals he is using in his research. The "healthy" (disease-free) animal in a spotlessly sterile cage may have a scientifically formulated and approved diet and a controlled indoor environment (light, heat, humidity, and so on), but unless it is a wholly preadapted laboratory "race," it may, like millions of cats, dogs, and primates, suffer physically and psychologically. Such suffering is not only inhumane but an uncontrolled variable which may totally invalidate the conclusions drawn from many studies. The suffering and sometimes death of animals as well as the research money will have been wasted. (Many of these studies are funded by the taxpayer—$2 to $3 billion per year—in the United States.) And then, if it is a genetically and environmentally preadapted ("laboratory-phied") species or race, any conclusions derived from experimentation upon it may be of very limited value unless it is a known model of some specific human disorder. Clearly a radical change is needed in this entire field of laboratory animal care and use not only from the humane viewpoint but from the scientific value per se of using animals for research that are raised and housed under present standards.

With increasing concern over occupational safety hazards and industrial pollution, the need for more and more laboratory tests to evaluate the toxicity and minimal safety levels of chemical compounds is intensifying. This means that an increasing number of animals will have to be used to help ensure human safety and protection from known, potentially harmful chemicals. It may soon be written into law that for all new compounds and all existing chemicals in common use (an estimated 60,000 to 70,000), animal toxicity tests must be conducted. To the vast list off industrial chemicals and their by-products, we must append the 4,000 or more medical drugs (plus 2,000 or more stabilizers, diluents, and so on); 5,500 or more chemical additives used in the processing, flavoring, and preserving of food; 30,000 or so chemicals as well as live vaccines that are used in agriculture (pesticides, herbicides, antibiotic and other animal feed additives). The Environmental Protection Agency, given the responsibility of safety-testing pesticides, is reportedly ten years behind its scheduled program. Its "success" record is poor, few dangerous chemicals, such as Kepone, having been removed from the market (but by no means from the environment). The safety-testing of Kepone and other pesticides was recently exposed as a fraud, and the tests conducted by certain private contracting laboratories were found to be totally inadequate and to favor the interests of the manufacturers. (Hence Congress passed the Good Laboratory Practices Act, mentioned earlier.) Present attempts by the federal Food and Drug Administration to regulate the addition of antibiotics to animal feeds are being opposed by private industry and agribusiness. It has been shown that the accumulation of antibiotic residues and the appearance of drug-resistant bacteria follow the use of antibiotics in animal feeds. And these are passed along to the consumer, giving good theoretical/biological grounds for concern. Even so, the drug and agribusiness industries do not seem to feel that this warrants any concern. Actual proof of human sickness seems to be the sole criterion for any type of reform. What, then, is the point of using animals for safety-testing in the first place? Anyone with vested interests, such as manufacturers or users of potentially hazardous chemicals, will oppose and discount animal test data as being irrelevant. "Rats aren't people" is the familiar cry. Ironically, it is the very nature of their products that necessitates the safety tests in the first place. It is also ironic that test animals are used in the research and development phases of industry as well as in the safety-testing of potential environmental and occupational hazards, which are a product of industry. This is a kind of double jeopardy from the animals' point of reference.

Caught between the government bureaucracy and private industry are the millions of laboratory animals that are used for testing purposes. Some individuals today are coming to regard these animals as "political-industrial prisoners." From an ethical viewpoint, should animals be used as extensively as they are, primarily for the screening of potentially profitable new products? The environment and consumer alike may well be better off without many of these products in the first place. This is the root of the issue.

To attempt to regulate industry and impose more animal safety tests in order to protect the workers, consumers, and the environment is inadequate, if not impossible. No government bureau could ever effectively regulate the proliferating chemical/drug industry in this country today. When test results are contrary to the manufacturers' vested interests, they will be vehemently opposed by the manufacturers. More animal tests are not going to help. Even if a substance is "safe" under laboratory conditions, its possible synergy with other substances or cumulative effects in the environment, human body, or both can never be adequately evaluated. Partial or total replacement of animals by microorganisms, tissue cultures, or other test models, as discussed by A. N. Rowan, will help alleviate potential and actual animal suffering and may also reduce costs, but in the long run it may help neither mankind nor the environment if industrial proliferation continues. Like the proliferation of nuclear weapons, production of chemicals by private industry necessitates restraint. Pressure on industry from Congress, consumers, and especially the scientific community for restraint will do far more than animal tests to ensure our safety.

In studies involving drugs two independent agencies found that "three out of every four drugs approved for marketing by the United States government between late 1975 and 1978 were of little or no therapeutic gain over existing medicines" and that "less than 1%" (of investigational drugs approved for human testing) "offered important therapeutic gain" (C. Joyce, *New Scientist,* April 6, 1978). Evidence to date suggests that the drug industry is concerned more with proliferating a diversity of drugs to support investments and further shareholders' profits than with human health and animal life and suffering.

A tragic irony for laboratory animals in the safety-testing of new drugs and chemicals is that each country has its own criteria and regulations, and individual countries may not accept results from other countries. This leads to an enormous waste of animals through needless repetition of identical tests. Also, several independent companies may be developing and testing the same or similar drug, each trying to satisfy extremely costly FDA regulations and get onto the market first. Again, this is nothing more than a waste of human resources and animal lives.

CARCINOGENS AND OTHER MAN-MADE HAZARDS

Recent studies indicate that 80 to 90 percent of all human cancers are related to chemical contaminants in the environment. It follows that cutting down on the development of new chemicals will keep more of them out of the environment. There are already countless potential carcinogens in our environment, including the rays of the sun. Natural carcinogens were present in our food long before we ever invented fire. Now that we roast and fry some foods and add chemicals in the preserving and processing of others, our dietary intake of carcinogenic substances has increased considerably. It is, therefore, impractical and impossible to eliminate all potentially harmful natural and man-made elements from our environment, but this does not mean that we should not endeavor to reduce them.

The saccharin controversy opened a Pandora's box; social, economic, and medical issues make this a multifaceted problem. It is not simply that since saccharin has been shown to cause cancer in rats it should be taken off the market. Informed consumers and their physicians can weigh the odds and make their own decisions.

And in the case of smoking, countless numbers of animals—beagles, monkeys, and rats—have suffered in studies to show that it is dangerous. But informed people still smoke and will continue to do so until physiologically and aesthetically safe alternatives are available. Many smokers live a full life and never get cancer or emphysema. The practical sociopolitical issue is: Should the government attempt to protect the public by taking all potential and known carcinogens off the market, or should the consumers be informed and be given the freedom to make their own choice?

The Tris fire-retardant problem is another recent controversy. Dr. B. N. Ames, using his bacterial (salmonella/microsome) test, found that Tris is mutagenic. Subsequent experiments showed that it can cause kidney cancer in rats and mice and that it can be absorbed through the skin of rabbits. Since there was no proof that Tris causes cancer in man, the applicability of animal tests to human safety was strongly contested by the manufacturers. Both rats and mice of cancer-prone strains were used, and rats were found to develop kidney cancer at much lower doses than in mice. Is the susceptibility of humans modeled by the rat or the mouse, or by neither species?

As these examples may indicate, we should first question what animal testing entails—in other words, what species and strains are used and what tests are conducted. Considering the complexities of drug actions and of age, sex, and species differences in response, one would anticipate a wide range of species models and test procedures. This is not the case, however; one discovers a disarmingly simple routine procedure of giving male rats massive doses of the test substance over a short period of time. This is not valid research, and even though it may be cost-saving, it may not be lifesaving. To make any inferences about the carcinogenic potential of any substance in man from such simplistic tests would not be scientifically valid. There must be verification, either by another test species or bioassay, or, as often is the case, clinical data from human subjects. This sophomoric oversimplification of biological systems gains credence only through the consensus of a minority of biomedical technologists. But it is nothing less than institutionalized and bureaucratized bad practice.

A one-species test study using only one dose-rate parameter has been claimed to be the most economically realistic and expedient way of identifying potential carcinogens. Former FDA Commissioner Dr. Jack Kennedy justified the dosing of test animals with amounts of a suspected carcinogen far larger than humans are ever likely to receive by stating:

> . . . no one could breed, raise, sacrifice and examine test animals fast enough to find one case of cancer out of 20,000 animals—there aren't enough breeders, examiners, time or money. Instead we use fewer animals. And to compensate for that, we use high doses. And over the years we have established that the system works. Animal

tests identical in principle to those used for saccharin have demonstrated cancer in animals for virtually all the chemicals known to cause cancer in people.

The commissioner's last remark is particularly disturbing. It clearly reveals much of what is sometimes done *post hoc* with animals in the name of research. Known human carcinogens are given to animals, and "virtually all" of them cause cancer in animals. This is hardly surprising. And if it is known that certain chemicals are carcinogenic to humans, why test them further on animals? This procedure is called animal modeling, but in order to know that one has the right *animal model* for some human disorder, one must know a great deal about the human disorder. Admittedly fine-grain tests and experimental treatments may be evaluated on the animal model, yet this is often not the case. Continuing research on animal models can lead to an ever-narrowing and increasingly irrelevant focus—i.e., *reductio ad absurdum.* This is not only a waste of time, talent, and finances, but also a needless waste of animal lives.

The most serious limitations to all tests for carcinogens and other potential biohazards are those variables which are encountered under "real" field conditions. Individual human variability—resistance or susceptibility—may be affected by genetic, sex, age, and demographic variables. Life-styles and associated stresses and crises, personalities or temperaments, nutritional and other variables (intercurrent metabolic and endocrine disorders; addictive habits such as alcoholism, smoking; exposure to air, food, and water pollutants; pregnancy; and so on) must also be considered. The question of cancer, which may now affect one in every four people in this country, is not a simple biomedical problem that can be solved by oversimplified laboratory animal tests that do not embrace some of the real-world variables. Cancer is as much of (if not more than) a cultural, social, and economically related problem as it is a biomedical phenomenon.

Animal tests are becoming mandatory for an increasing range of consumer products and occupation-related hazards. To question their validity in relation to human health is to expose the primary motives behind the development of many new nonessential compounds. The primary motive is often profit, and to oppose a rigorous reappraisal of all animal test procedures today is to set financial interests above ethical concerns for human health and humane concerns over the needless waste and untold suffering of animals used in such tests.

Some antivivisectionists would have no research done on animals. This is a limited and unrealistic view since in many cases it is the only way to test a new vaccine or drug which could save many lives—human and animal. Often the drugs being tested will treat or alleviate disease in both animal and man.

But it can be argued that if disease were prevented, drugs would be less necessary. Western medicine and biomedical research in general must begin to focus more on rigorous study of health and preventive medicine, rather than on after-the-fact therapy and pathogenesis and on treating symptoms instead of addressing the underlying causes. In Eastern philosophy and medicine, prevention is a key to the science of health. One visits the physician to maintain a balanced state of ease (or health, as distinct from dis-ease). In Western biomedical research this approach is just beginning to be explored in spite of the traditional and entrenched modes of scientific thought and methodology (see page 148). The antivivisectionist must be patient and work with optimism to guide scientific inquiry along these more humane paths. Opposing all biomedical research with animals will not facilitate the evolution of science. Demanding a critical and objective appraisal of animal usage in terms of values, ultimate goals, and possible alternative modes of investigation will have more effect. Complete opposition will merely slow down the infusion of ethical values and humane standards since a researcher who has to defend experimentation in general may not be free to reflect objectively upon what he is doing in the name of scientific inquiry and progress. Through open dialogue with nonjudgmental critics, the credibility and relevance of an investigator's project should be explored. For example, a research project may be very good science—well designed, sophisticated technique, animals well cared for, and so on—but really of no relevance; drug addiction studies in animals are a good case in point. Research projects are usually funded after review by a panel of scientists. Such peer review is questionable if the proposal is judged only on its scientific merit, not on its relevance, as is too often the case.

A noted orthopedic surgeon, who had conducted considerable experimentation on cats and dogs, shocked a close friend by stating that "animals don't feel pain—at least not like people do." Obviously even some of the most prestigious and skilled members of the biomedical field have to be educated toward a more factual and empathic understanding of animals. This could help revolutionize many areas of science, which have become, like archaic religions, rarely relevant to social and environmental priorities and lack any firm moral or ethical philosophy.

Without the pressure of constructive criticism and the hard facts demonstrating animal pain and suffering, inhumane animal experimentation will continue. Animals are often treated with as much empathy and understanding as inanimate objects not only by many unenlightened biomedical technologists but also by many hunters, sportsmen, fur trappers, and factory farmers. We all are guilty in varying degrees of being ignorant, and although we must habitually kill in order to live, life would be infinitely better if we killed knowingly and sparingly.

Federally enforced standards of care and treatment and protective laws are no substitute for empathy and understanding, but they are a start. Richard Ryder, in his controversial book *Victims of Science,* states:

> . . . in the matter of alternatives to laboratory animals we are at the beginning but the potential is surely there—all that is needed is the political, commercial, legal or moral incentive. If scientists cannot mend their morals then laws may have to provide the final impetus to *oblige* experimenters to develop humane methods—necessity has, after all, so often found itself pregnant with invention.

Reverence for all life is a state of mind, not a law that has to be legally enforced. It must be demonstrated through science and be expressed in thought and action in all of man's relationships; biomedical research is one important relationship with animals in which such progress is urgently needed today.

Catherine Roberts, in her book *The Scientific Conscience,* expresses deep concern over the motives and goals of scientific research and particularly on how objective detachment can lead to inhumane treatment of animals. She observes:

> Eight years ago Michael Polanyi (in his book, *Personal Knowledge*) did so, thus pointing the way. With elegant logic and eloquent persuasion he attacked the modern delusion of detached scientific objectivity. Maintaining that scientific knowledge is a union of the objective and the personal, he regarded the continued neglect of the personal element of scientific motivation as both dangerous and immoral. The attainment of scientific knowledge is not, according to Polanyi, detached and impersonal achievement, but rests ultimately upon belief, and failure to recognize this fact only widens the gulf between science and humanism.

There is a general consensus in the humane movement that if the treatment or use of an animal involves unnecessary pain or undue suffering (fear, anxiety, or depression—e.g., after separation from mate, companions, or parent), it is being treated inhumanely. This thinking can take us in two directions which are not always constructive. We must distinguish between necessary and unnecessary pain or suffering. At the same time we may be led into the trap of having to demonstrate "how much" pain or suffering the animal experiences, often with the outsider's view that animals surely don't or can't feel pain the way human beings do. The point is not how much or how necessary the pain or suffering is but rather that there is any pain or suffering which must be justified by researchers.

There can be no question that nonhuman animals do experience pain and other forms of suffering. All life forms avoid noxious (harmful) stimuli which even at a relatively low level of evolved consciousness (beyond simple tropism or reflexive reaction) must be experienced subjectively as pain. If this were not so, no organism could exist. At a higher level of neural complexity and consciousness, at which pain responses can be conditioned, *expectations* of pain (fear, anxiety) must also be considered. In more socially dependent gregarious species and infant animals dependent upon parental care, separation and severance of social bonds must also be reckoned with in determining the nature and extent of an animal's suffering instigated by man.

Demonstrating the consequences of thoughtless or inhumane treatment of animals is difficult. Changes in overt behavior may be ambiguous or not evident at all. Physiological changes may also be ambiguous and even analogous, as with a wild animal that is simply afraid but reacts to this psychological stress as it might to a direct physical stress.

With a human being, we only have the other person's word and our own experiences and empathy to know that he or she is suffering or experiencing pain. But can we ever be *really* sure, unless we are in his or her shoes? Hysterics, hypochondriacs, hyperaesthetic schizophrenics, or paranoid psychotics may overmagnify their reactions to certain physically or psychologically noxious stimuli. Do not some of us conclude that the suffering is all in their minds or imaginations? But their fears and sufferings are real, even though the same stimuli to a "normal" man would be nonthreatening and innocuous.

A paranoid schizophrenic is not unlike a terrified wild animal. Both have great flight reactions when approached. So, too, perhaps is the analogy between a catatonic schizophrenic and an animal "frozen" (cataleptic) with fear. There is also a similarity between a hyperaroused autistic child who feels no pain (or at least does not react to painful stimuli, such as a red-hot stove ring) and a hyperaroused animal that shows no overt reaction to noxious stimulation.*

How then, given the fact that the emotional, cognitive, and perceptual states of man may vary so greatly, can we hope to determine to what degree any person or animal may suffer under a given set of circumstances? The reaction will vary according to prior experience, expectations, and the individual's shifting state of consciousness. We can no more generalize about the subjective element of suffering from one person to the next than we can about suffering in animals compared to man or the varying degrees of suffering in individual animals of different species, ages, sexes, and so on.

* For further details see Michael W. Fox, *Integrative Development of Brain and Behavior in the Dog* (Chicago: University of Chicago Press, 1971).

We must logically conclude that objective evaluation of the phenomenon of suffering in animal or man can be done only on an individual basis and under a carefully defined set of conditions and that *no* generalizations for all individuals of the same species under the same conditions can be safely inferred from such observations. At best we can say that where there is sentience, there is the capacity to suffer, and we must logically assume that the laboratory animal may well suffer.

Is such suffering justified? Here the focus is on the responsible scientist. The justification of his or her actions must be cast in a strict ethical framework—namely, of man's right to take nonhuman life or to cause suffering in other sentient beings in relation to the nonhuman's right to life and to humane treatment under man's jurisdiction. The nature of these rights is discussed in detail later. In brief, it may be concluded that an animal's rights are violated if its death or suffering is not essential for human survival, health (including that of nonhuman animals), or the integrity of the biospheric ecosystem. To kill or cause animal suffering for nonsurvival purposes (as in the product-testing of any nonessential consumables) or to satisfy scientific curiosity (or "knowledge for knowledge's sake") is ethically untenable.

Drs. W. M. S. Russell and R. L. Burch make a particularly cogent point concerning the question of distress in nonhuman animals and their abilities to cope with it:

> But insofar as we are employing our intelligence, we can control from moment to moment the direction and focus of our attention. The sequence of moods in a lower animal, however, is rigidly controlled by internal and external changes according to a code of rules, largely preset for a given species.
>
> In this respect, animals are functionally similar to neurotic humans, and, since we are all neurotic to some extent, most of us can recall a state of mind (anxiety, depression, etc.) in which one or a few preoccupations absorbed our attention exclusively, and an unpleasant narrowing of our sensory, intellectual and emotional horizons was impossible to combat for seconds, minutes or, in severe cases, hours. The lower animal is therefore specially vulnerable to unpleasant conditions. When it is in a distressful mood, this

is very distressing indeed. There is good reason to suppose that distress is associated with paucity of information, and an animal in distress can only attend to its own misery. Extreme pain, as well as neurosis, can produce this effect in man. . . . In general, the lower animal is the slave of its own moods. Its behavior is very largely automatic, and we know that we ourselves are most vulnerable when our behavior is most automatic. Nor can a lower animal obtain the precious relief of verbalizing its distress. Far from deficiencies, we should logically treat them with special consideration. These points are stressed because similarities between man and lower animals are so often unduly emphasized, in a laudable endeavour to promote humanity. The differences are much more cogent. No sane person regards a baby as insentient, because he cannot talk.

Is it possible that animals (most warm-blooded animals at least) are *more* rather than *less* sentient than we and, therefore, more likely to suffer especially when experimented upon?

ARE ANIMALS MORE SENTIENT?

One who is regarded as being highly emotional—hypersensitive and often overreacting to sensations and sensory and social stimuli— would presumably suffer more than a person with a more mature, inhibited, or stoical personality.

Since animals—cats, dogs, primates—belong to the former category and most of us adult human beings to the latter, is it not logical to suggest that animals may suffer existentially (in the here and now) more than we? Humans, who may internalize more, may suffer less in the existential time frame and more in the dimension of worrying about the future: anxiety. Animals, too, as Pavlov and other animal psychologists have shown, can show anxiety reactions. They are not totally existential. While we can rationalize, reason, and otherwise cope with certain anxieties, animals cannot. Thus, they are likely to suffer more than we in this dimension as well as in the immediate here-and-now existential dimension. So it may be hypothesized that animals (at least mammals) are *more* sentient than we, rather than less, even though they may be *less* objectively aware of their sentience. Objective awareness can also reduce one's immediate fear, pain, or future-focused anxiety. Animals, to the best of our knowledge, lack such objectivity, a third reason why they are likely to suffer more than people. Let no one today argue that animals have different nervous systems mediating pain. The basic system is identical in all mammals, including humans, and all share the same natural opiate receptors (or enkephalins) to dampen intense pain.

In *Victims of Science*, Richard Ryder summarizes his detailed appraisal of research involving the use of animals. He found no good reason for assuming that other animals do not suffer in a way similar to humans. Yet in recent decades there has been a steady increase in the use of living animals for research. Many experiments entail considerable suffering for the animals involved. Even ordinary laboratory life causes suffering. It is probable that more than 100 million animals die each year in laboratories throughout the world. Many die in the experimental testing of weapons. Many primates—man's closest evolutionary relatives—are being used for experiments. About 250,000 apes and monkeys die annually in the laboratories of the world, threatening several species with extinction. It is known that more than 5 million vertebrates annually are experimented upon while alive in British laboratories. About 85 percent of the experiments are without anesthetic, although many of these entail pain even if not severe. It seems likely that an increasingly large proportion of painful experiments upon animals, all over the world, are of a "nonmedical sort," so cannot be justified on the grounds of medical necessity. Such experiments include the poisons-testing of toiletries, cosmetics, nonnutritive food additives, weed killers, insecticides, and other commercial products, such as detergents and oven cleaners. Research on animal pschology is another area of nonmedical experimentation. Much animal research—medical and nonmedical—is scientifically invalid; nowhere is this more evident than in the vast field of poisons-testing of commercial products. But commercial profit is the main motive for the enormous use of animals in research. A secondary motive is career ambition. Apace with commercial experimentation there is a growing "laboratory-animal industry," the vested interest of which is in maintaining the increase in the use of animals for research.

Ryder also found that nowhere in the world is there legislation which provides adequate protection for laboratory animals. The British law is obsolete and ineffective and still allows the infliction of severe pain. Reforms should include prohibition of all cruel non-medical experiments. And government backing must be given for the development of alternatives to animals in research. Promising alternatives to the use of animals for research already exist and could be further developed; in some cases such alternatives are considerably cheaper than animals. Many great reformers of human society have also shown an interest in animal welfare; in recent years there has been a reawakening of concern among politicians, scientists, and laymen.

The interests of other species must not be ignored. Selfish "speciesist" prejudices are even unlikely, in the long run, to promote the worthwhile survival of man himself.

Dr. Ryder's findings were based on studies made in England, but there can be no doubt that they summarize the state of laboratory animals throughout the world.

In the United States the Animal Welfare Act gives the veterinarian in charge of laboratory animal care some jurisdiction over how animals will be treated before, during, and afer experimentation. But one of the major flaws in enforcing the animal welfare regulations is that there are not sufficient veterinarians or inspectors to go around. Not all Ph.D's or M.D.'s or high school teachers are able to recognize where and when a given animal experiment is inhumane or unethical—in other words, (a) when an experiment is a needless repetition of research already well documented (a common flaw of high school and college science projects), (b) when the degree of physical or psychological suffering of the animal overrides any possible value derived from such a study, either as a learning experience (for the student) or as a contribution to scientific knowledge, (c) when a more humane alternative is available, or when an organism of lower sentience (or tissue or egg embryo preparation) may be used as a replacement, (d) when the experiment is poorly designed with inadequate hypotheses, controls, and statistical validation, (e) when the researcher is performing "basic" research which cannot be justified for the betterment of society or of the animals themselves, and (f) when the experiment is conducted purely for profit motives, not for the ultimate benefit of society, as in the development and testing of new, nonessential commercial products.

Clarification of these categories will suffice to illustrate the main thesis of this chapter: *The rights of animals in research are being violated to such a degree that they virtually have no rights.*

NEEDLESS REPETITION. High school science fair projects: injecting rats with weed killer, hamsters with Valium or with common household chemicals just to see what happens; inducing acute myocarditis in guinea pigs by injecting a muscle-destroying chemical into their hearts. College projects: blinding rats and giving drugs (such as amphetamines) to see how their performance in a maze is affected; effects of electroshock, starvation, and other variables on learning ability or aggression in rodents; conditioned aversion studies, "learned helplessness," maternal deprivation in primates and prolonged social deprivation. "Learned helplessness" studies are particularly in vogue with psychologists in the Untied States because they are ostensibly a good model for depression in man. Rats are shocked or half drowned, and dogs restrained and given repeated electrical shocks until they literally give up all struggling because there is no possible escape. Such research has been condemned by the British Research Defense Society (a proresearch organization). This kind of research and other emotionally stressful studies are being conducted in psychology departments at many universities in the United States. The research has no clinical applicability to depression in man and is an example of creating a model for generating data— psychology as a pseudoscience at best. If, as some psychologists claim, animals subjected to such trauma are "high-fidelity models" of analogous suffering in man, how can they justify such torture? Concern for the welfare of these animals is often put down as sentimental anthropomorphism, but the scientists themselves are surely guilty of being unscientifically anthropomorphic. A terrified dog that is totally incapacitated from repeated abuse is hardly comparable to a depressed patient.

In veterinary and medical schools, dogs are still being poisoned with strychnine and other drugs as classroom demonstrations, and rodents injected with virulent diseases. Various surgical operations, including breaking and pinning a bone, are performed on the *same* dog at weekly intervals. Such animal abuse in the name of education is ethically untenable. Many schools agree and have stopped such inhumane practices. Animals should not be made sick or physically injured for students to learn. The answers are in textbooks and in real-life clinical cases. Breaking a dog's leg under anesthesia and then repairing the fracture is a meaningless exercise since the injury is nothing like a real fracture. Alternatives, including the use of "bionic" models and computer simulation, are now being used in the more forward-thinking schools.

UNJUSTIFIABLE SUFFERING. One class of studies will suffice here—the prolonged restraint of primates and other animals in holding chairs or devices for weeks, sometimes months, for a wide range of studies. The ethics of using such animals for evaluating the effects of addictive drugs, such as cocaine, and other self-induced poisons, such as tobacco and alcohol, are also questionable. For further details see Dallas Pratt's *Painful Experiments on Animals* and J. Diner's *Physical and Mental Suffering of Experimental Animals.*

NEGLECTED ALTERNATIVES. Nobel Laureate D. C. Gajdusek reportedly used more than 120 chimpanzees, a threatened species, in his research. The researcher himself admitted almost ten years ago that the more plentiful squirrel and rhesus monkeys could have been used instead.

The Ames bacteria test method for preliminary screening for carcinogens is one particularly effective partial replacement for higher life forms. Other replacement alternatives are needed in biomedical research and testing not only for humane reasons but for economics as well.

INADEQUATE EXPERIMENTAL DESIGN. Among the flaws of many college honors and higher degree theses are inadequacies in design. Weaknesses in design often lead to excessive numbers of animal subjects being used and to groups being discarded when results don't turn out or when, through improper procedure, experiments must be repeated. It should be emphasized that in many, if not most, colleges, the students take care of their own animals. Students may be inexperienced, untrained, and indifferent and are generally unaware of the Animal Welfare Act. At one college a large rat colony was virtually wiped out twice by student caretakers not providing them with water during the summer.

NONRELEVANT "BASIC" RESEARCH. "Knowledge for knowledge's sake" is a politically sensitive area. Some scientists still "sacrifice" animals or subject them to physical or mental suffering simply to satisfy their intellectual curiosity. The academic pressures to publish (or perish) are real, too, and result in a number of needlessly repetitive experiments or "variations on a theme." Making irrelevant additions to the body of scientific knowledge is not only a confusion of priorities but a gross misuse of public funds. This should be interpreted not as an indictment of all basic research, but rather as a plea for a more purposeful and integrative approach to basic research to avoid waste of animals and resources. Many basic studies could be terminated by the investigator asking himself, "Do I really need to know what I think I want to know?" as, for example, the investigator who wants to know how the coatimundi moves its nose. A chance "breakthrough" discovery, a new line of investigation, could come from such work, but surely this is a blind way of "fishing," an unscientific hit-and-miss game of chance.

COMMERCIAL TESTING. This area, above all others, warrants rigorous review. Reforms in established procedures and a total reevaluation of standardized methods are urgently needed. Such gross tests as loading dogs' stomachs with new floor or boot polishes to establish the so-called L.D. (lethal dose) 50 (which is a wholly unscientific measure agreed upon by a general consensus) are used instead of sound sequential testing using more sensitive physiological indices other than sickness and death. The Draize eye test is another atrocity, perfumes, deodorants, and other nonessential commercial products being placed into rabbits' eyes until the concentration known to cause severe eye inflammation (often leading to extremely painful injury and blindness) can be quantified. Analgesics are rarely used because, it is argued, such drugs may interfere with the test. Interference is a common argument of biomedical scientists and psychologists, and the Animal Welfare Act as it now stands permits them to perform painful experiments if pain-relieving drugs were to interfere with the experiment. Many of these tests are not only inhumane but poorly designed and needlessly repetitive, especially when companies do not share or make public their test data. They are motivated less by the desire to ensure consumer safety than simply to satisfy federal guidelines and ensure good profits, a fact revealed by Senator Edward Kennedy's Subcommittee on Biomedical Research and Testing which examined the atrocious experiment designs and record keeping of several commercial testing laboratories. Other tests, no less inhumane, include the instigation of acute pain reactions by a variety of bizarre methods in developing new analgesics.

One area which Richard Ryder did not cover in *Victims of Science* is the high school science fair, which does not exist in England. I have briefly mentioned high school science education above, but it deserves greater attention.

In a time when the scientific community itself is questioning the ethics and scientific value of the use of animals in biomedical research, American educators must also question the use and abuse of laboratory animals by schoolchildren. Inappropriate and inhumane animal projects are commonly conducted within the school's realm of jurisdiction. It is still considered necessary for a student on the elementary or high school level to conduct an experiment which causes pain, suffering, or discomfort if it can be justified as a "learning experience."

At the high school science fair, animals are often used in experiments that are unnecessary repetitions of work already well documented in great detail in scientific literature. The student may gain manipulative and basic experimental skills, but these can be learned in more humane ways without causing the suffering and death of the animals involved. It is far more important for a young scientist to develop ethical and humane values as well as the powers of observation and quantitative and qualitative analyses of data. The latter can be derived from more humane experimentation. For example, there is a wealth of fascinating experiments that the student can design in the field of animal behavior which would provide an excellent learning experience and familiarize him with scientific methodologies without entailing the destruction or suffering of animals.

Students participating in the high school science fair must submit a protocol in which their projects are outlined in advance of experimentation and completion. The protocol is an essential part of the evaluation process to determine whether a project is of superior quality, under specific standards and guidelines, such as those established by the Humane Society of the United States in the case of animal experimentation. It is important that all aspects of the project be within the comprehension and capabilities of the student undertaking the study. If by chance an exceptional student submits a protocol for an exceptional project calling for the use of animals, then his or her experimental procedure should be accomplished in a full-time laboratory facility under the direct and continuous supervision of a qualified biomedical scientist, trained in correct animal care and experimental procedures. But animal experimentation should be the exception not the rule.

The following examples from the 27th International Science and Engineering Fair, held in Denver, May 10–15, 1976, reveal the paucity of regulated criteria governing the use of animals in student experiments:

> EFFECTS OF CAFFEINE ON ALBINO RATS. This study involved injecting caffeine in high doses, which, of course, caused considerable physical distress in rats. It was needlessly repetitive and nothing more than an exercise in applied skills for the benefit of the student.

> STUDY OF THE HEART IN GUINEA PIGS. In this case the project was "supervised" at home by the student's father, a physician. The student injected sodium tetradecyl into the heart muscle of the guinea pigs to simulate a coronary attack. This chemical causes acute and undoubtedly extremely painful damage.

THE INFLUENCE OF PHOTOTOXIC RAYS ON THE SKIN. Mice were exposed to ultraviolet and infrared rays after areas of their skin had been denuded. The suffering of these radiated animals cannot be justified since their suffering was needlessly repetitive, demonstrated nothing new, and contributed nothing to the future mitigation of suffering in man or animal.

PREVENTION OF THE BENDS BY BREATHING OXYGENATED LIQUID. This experiment, approved by a professor of psychology and a professor of surgery and anesthesiology, reached the national finals but was dismantled and not shown to the public. All animals used in it died. This was testimony to inadequacy of design, basic knowledge, and, above all, humane concern.

NITRITE: A COMPARISON OF NITRITE CONTENT IN CURED MEAT AND ITS EFFECTS ON MICE. The student (who used rats instead of mice) described findings already well documented in scientific journals. Effects were not obtained until 100 times the FDA limitation level of nitrite was given. It took twenty days for one rat to die.

The Denver fair is by no means unique. A recent science fair in Kansas included such school and home experiments as injecting rats with insecticides, dosing hamsters with Valium, and inducing lead poisoning in infant rats.

There is a marked difference between gaining biomedical knowledge in a laboratory and the pursuit of a learning project at school or at home. There is absolutely no way that the two can be equated. The school science project is not going to produce new findings that would justify injuring an animal. Therefore, sharp limitations should be placed on the way animals can and should be used if the student is not working in an established laboratory under qualified supervision. If animals are caged, they should be a laboratory species already adapted to such conditions. The use of wild animals or those species, such as dogs, cats, and monkeys, the instinctual and socioemotional needs of which cannot be satisfied under confinement should be prohibited. There is no ethical or scientific justification whatever for conducting any classroom or home experiments which cause pain or suffering to any type of animal.

The following range of experiments should not be performed or accepted by a science fair unless they have been conducted in a well-recognized laboratory facility, and only then as an integral and contributing part of an ongoing biomedical and professional research project: any form of surgery; the injection of or exposure to microorganisms which can cause disease in man or animal; exposure to ionizing or other radiation; treatment with cancer-producing agents; injection or other treatment with any chemical agent; exposure to extremes of temperatures; electric or other shock; excessive noise, noxious fumes, exercise to exhaustion, overcrowding, or other distressing stimuli; deprivation of food, water, or other factors essential for survival (including deficient diets).

It is fair to say that the child who is conditioned by either parent or teacher to indifference and apathy toward the pain and suffering of any sentient creature is being desensitized and taught to repress his or her emotions, affection, and compassion, reactions which have been implicated in the development of psychopathic personality disorders. Cruel science fair projects tend to discredit true science; further, they inhibit the aim of education which, in its fullest sense, entails the development of the whole person and human nature, involving ethics and sentiments as well as the intellect. On the other hand, experiments in which animals are observed in a natural state (or seminatural—in zoos or farms) for normal behavioral purposes and are not exposed to any injury, pain, fear, or anxiety should be encouraged and praised. Such projects foster greater understanding and respect for life.

There is a great need for improvement in values and attitudes after a rigorous scrutiny and objective evaluation of the goals, purposes, whys and hows of biomedical research. At the high school level this is indeed critical since the unthinking acquisition of values, skills, and methods of experimentation with animals may be detrimental to the student, limiting his or her vision. The student may not be able to conceive of alternative methods and subjects (cells instead of rats, for example) or to explore untrodden areas if his or her early training is narrow in terms of values and attitudes.

Today students can tell *how* they performed their experiments, but few can clearly articulate *why*. Expertise and sophistication of technique are valid accomplishments but are only means to an end. Too often they become an end in themselves, and the animals used are then mere tools. For many students, this has become a major factor in their disillusionment with biomedical research. For others, the use of animals to answer human problems is a ludicrous and often inhumane game, when "animal models" are created to satisfy purely intellectual curiosity and to produce ego gratification. The answers to human problems are usually best answered by the study of man himself. This is not to say that all research on vertebrates should be abolished; this is only to say it should be carefully scrutinized for its validity. Unfortunately great pressure to experiment with animals is being constantly exerted on students and scientists. There should be concern for the perpetuation of such unthinking immemorial usage. With enhanced scientific and humane education and more rigorous regulations, this circle may be broken. Young students may then be freed from the narrow confines of current biomedical research, and their creativity may add to our understanding of man and nature. The words of the National Society for Medical Research have a ring of irony—*"Study life to protect life,"* an edict which may lead to the justification of animal suffering under an all-encompassing umbrella of protective relevance to man. To protect life from death is perhaps of questionable value, but to protect all life from unnecessary suffering (and to protect nature from man) is to begin to understand man in and through all life. Herein is fulfillment for the emergent biomedical scientist, through a life of service, purpose, dedication, and ultimate personal significance.

The science fair can help foster such awareness of future years as an annual focal point for young people interested in the many areas of science and medicine, as it has in the past—but more so once the intrinsic values, motives, attitudes, and goals underlying biomedical and scientific research are recognized, understood fully ... and changed when necessary. A rational, objective, ethical, and humane appraisal is needed each year, for each exhibit and for each and every person, field of science, and area of human interaction with the natural world. Let no scientist or educator claim that high school students must experiment upon animals in order to become biomedical researchers. England and Sweden, for example, produce some of the best biomedical scientists in the world, and in both countries high school experimentation on living animals is not permitted.

Against this rather cursory overview of animal use and abuse in research, testing, and education we may well ask if laboratory animals do have any rights at all. That such animals are abused at all must surely be one of the most urgent ethical issues facing those who use them for research and teaching purposes. Further federal regulations may help bring about a wider recognition of animal rights, although such an externally imposed set of rules is a weak and fragile substitute for an internalized set of humane ethics and responsible compassion toward all life. The latter can come only through educational reforms which may amount to a radical change in societal values and attitudes toward nonhuman life. Federal regulation, at best, requires constant supervisory monitoring and more and more bureaucratic regulations.

HUMANE ALTERNATIVES

An excellent book entitled *The Principles of Humane Experimental Technique,* by W. M. S. Russell and R. L. Burch, thoroughly explores contemporary research problems and suggests what alternative techniques are available. The authors emphasize that inhumane treatment of animals may fall into two categories—namely, direct—during actual experimentation—and contingent—in the total picture of laboratory animal husbandry. The general care of laboratory animals is partially covered by the Animal Welfare Act of 1970, but the treatment during experimentation is neglected. These authors urge that inhumanity can be reduced by following the three Rs of animal research—*replacement, refinement,* and *reduction.* Briefly this means: using life forms of lower sentience—invertebrates, microorganisms, tissues cultures, and so on (the fallacy of having to use animals close to man as ideal models is clearly exposed); improving experimental design with known genetic stock;

and better controls of environmentally induced variability so that fewer animals are needed to secure consistent and significant results. Needless repetition is then avoided; improved testing procedures and statistical designs and analysis of data also facilitate a more judicious use of animal subjects.

Richard Ryder states:

> It cannot be denied that out of all the millions of experiments performed upon animals, some useful knowledge has been gained. But equally it must not be forgotten that this knowledge often could have been acquired by other means and that many of the greatest discoveries of all have owed nothing to the use of laboratory animals and indeed might never have been made if animals had been used. To impose suffering, allegedly in order to reduce it, and to take life, allegedly in order to save it, are self-contradicting claims. They are made even more dubious when one bears in mind that at the time of the experiment any benefits that might be accrued from it are merely hypothetical and uncertain.

Some basic research scientists rationalize their social responsibilities away, saying that their only role is to seek knowledge and it is for others to apply it—for better or for worse. Scientists—indeed, all people, nonscientists, corporations, and governments alike—must become more socially responsible, and their work more socially relevant. It is for the scientist to judge the relevance of his work especially if his research entails public funds and animal lives or suffering. Since science has become the new religion of our culture, its priesthood must be radically reformed and the members become, if not good leaders, exemplary upholders of the highest standards of ethical conduct and compassionate concern. If the scientist is genuinely concerned to improve the well-being of mankind and to alleviate suffering, he may be better employed in the "real" world and help directly, rather than create more suffering in the laboratory. Laboratory research is not often of direct value to real-world problems. At best, the benefits, without reality-focused field research, are indirect. The researcher must be encouraged to reevaluate his own personal priorities in relation to the urgent priorities that face humanity today and to be free to change, to get off the treadmill of continued research, without loss of prestige, tenure, and so on. He may be overly defensive or simply disoriented when put through the "reality test" by being asked *why* he is doing such-and-such a study involving animals' lives or suffering which he believes to be justifiable. Richard Ryder observes:

> Those genuinely human motives are most likely to prolong life or alleviate suffering by bringing existing medical knowledge to bear in those parts of the world where men and women are suffering and dying because they cannot afford any treatment. Yet many scientists prefer to spend their lives in laboratories causing untold suffering to animals in questionable medical research with a strong commercial motive; these researchers are not convincing when they plead that humanity is their overriding concern.

Ryder also asks, "How much will the attitudes of callousness, the blunting of sensitivity, and the disregard for the sufferings of animals . . . affect the whole outlook upon life of future generations?" We should ask how it affects us today. The person on the street may not see any connection between his life and relationships and the abuses of animals in biomedical research, but there *is* a connection between the "hardening of the heart" of science and the hardening of the hearts of people in other walks of life. The growing sense of alienation and competitive individualism, the lack of responsible compassion and cooperative support are apparent in this culture today.

If science is to serve society, it must become *humanized* and more ethically responsible and relevant. Surely this is what the concern about the uses and abuses of animals in research is really about, and if we can improve their lot, it will be a small, but significant, positive step for humanity as well. Indifference toward our animal kin—"deanimalizing" them as tools or test subjects—is analogous to the indifference toward our own kin. Most would agree that there is an increasing trend of impersonal indifference—of "dehumanizing" others in society today. While few would define the virtues of doing this to our own kin, the analogous process of "deanimalizing" our animal kin is self-evident, and there are more offenders than defenders. How we regard and treat animals in research is of growing concern today. Such concern is a symptom of greater awareness of our ethical responsibilities and moral obligations toward all life: to our fellow creatures, both human and nonhuman alike.

8
Science over Nature

O ne of the most lucid analyses of man's dominion over nature
via science and its application as technology has been given
by William Leiss in *The Domination of Nature.* His thesis is
that science has become knowledge for power for the sake of domination instead of for the enrichment of our lives in other ways. He
observes that the real significance of the natural sciences is not:

> ... an increasing "power" over external nature; rather, their real
> significance with reference to the mastery of nature lies in the po-
> tential effect which they may have on human behavior within a
> peaceful social order embracing the human race as a whole. Under
> such conditions the rationality that is embodied in science may in-
> deed serve as an instrument of man's self-mastery: to understand
> the world means in part to be at home in the world, to experience
> the harmony and order of its elements, to transcend that propen-
> sity, arising out of insecurity and fear, to project alien and hostile
> forces onto natural events. Science shares this task of pacifying
> man's nature with religion, philosophy, and the arts, indeed with
> human culture in general.

Science through its technology has been used to dominate and
exploit nature, including even inner human nature. It was once
thought that science and technology would remedy the social ills of

humanity by mastering nature. Instead, they have only compounded and increased those ills. What is needed is mastery over the relationship between nature and humanity. In describing the drastic change in our approach to nature, Leiss quotes Werner Heisenberg: "... the human attitude toward nature changed from a contemplative one to the pragmatic one. One was not so much interested in nature as it is; one rather asked what one could do with it. Therefore, natural science turned into technical science; every advancement of knowledge was connected with the question as to what practical use could be derived from it."

Leiss goes on to observe:

> The idea of the mastery of nature must be reinterpreted in such a way that its principal focus is *ethical or moral development* rather than scientific and technological innovation. In this perspective, progress in the mastery of nature will be at the same time progress in the liberation of nature. The latter, like the former, is a rational idea, a concept, an achievement of human thought; therefore the reversal or transformation which is intended in the transition from mastery to liberation concerns the gradual self-understanding and self-disciplining of *human* nature. As a rational idea "liberation" can apply only to the work of consciousness, to humane consciousness as an aspect of human desires. Success in this endeavor would be the liberation of nature: a human species free to enjoy in peace the fruits of its productive intelligence.
>
> Science and technology will be no less important for us when they are deprived of their rank as the principal forces in the mastery of nature. In fact, I think that their great accomplishments would be far more secure as a result. As we have seen, according to the prevailing conception the conquest of nature is regarded as the enlargement of human power over nature, with science and technology serving as the instruments of this drive, for the purpose of satisfying material wants. Pursued in this manner, mastery over nature inevitably turns into mastery over men and the intensification of social conflict. A vicious circle results, imprisoning science and technology in a fateful dialectic of increasing mastery and increasing conflict. The attractive promises of mastery over nature—social peace and material abundance for all—remain unfulfilled. The real danger that the resulting frustration may be turned against the instruments of mastery themselves (science and technology) must not

be underestimated. As integral factors in the ascending spiral of domination over internal and external nature, they are bound to an irrational dynamic which may destroy the fruits of their own civilizing rationality.

The liberation of science and technology from the thrall of this dynamic is a task that primarily involves the reconstruction of social institutions. Theoretical reflection plays a part in this process by suggesting changes in the categories through which individuals and groups interpret the significance of their activity. To dethrone science and technology as the guiding forces in the mastery of nature is a necessary step not only for them, but for the idea as well. Freed from a historical association that has become anachronistic, the idea of the mastery of nature would be open to new meanings. Considered as moral progress, it would indicate more forcefully the most demanding challenge that confronts us: not to conquer external nature, the moon, and outer space, but to develop the ability— widely dispersed among all individuals in society—to use responsibly the technical means presently available for the enhancement of life, together with an institutional framework which will nourish and preserve that ability.

A detailed and scholarly investigation led Leiss to make these logical, but revolutionary, conclusions. He is not alone in his views, however, and notes that they are shared by philosophers Max Horkheimer and Herbert Marcuse. According to Leiss, Horkheimer says:

> ... despite all improvements and despite fantastic riches, there rules at the same time the brutal struggle for existence, oppression, and fear. That is the hidden basis of the decay of civilization, namely that men cannot utilize their power over nature for the rational organization of the earth but rather must yield themselves to blind individual and national egoism under the compulsion of circumstances and of inescapable manipulation.

And Marcuse:

> ... there is no possibility of a reversal of scientific progress, no possibility of a return to the golden age of "qualitative" science. . . . The transformation of science is imaginable only in a transformed environment; a new science would require a new climate wherein

new experiments and projects would be suggested to the intellect by new social needs. . . . Instead of the further conquest of nature, the restoration of nature; instead of the moon, the earth; instead of the occupation of outer space, the creation of inner space.

In coming to know a little of the intrinsic complexities of nature through the scientific method, we have come to believe that since scientifically verifiable facts are infallible, we, too, are infallible when we apply such knowledge to shape nature for our own ends. Unfortunately science has become the new religion, and its adherents believe that the scientific method and its application are the only way to think and live (especially when there are economic justifications). Worse, it has bred arrogance and blind faith in the infallability of objective knowledge. With less "know-how" our ancestors were more cautious in their interventions with nature. Even today the forest people of New Guinea will say a prayer for the spirits of those trees they must cut down and an Amerindian potter will thank the spirit of the earth before digging up enough clay for his needs. Simple ignorance may underlie certain fears, superstitions, and cultural traditions, but these traditions can temper rash and potentially destructive actions. Today we need less know-how and more "know-why." We are replete with facts but short of wisdom. In the recent past we have arrogantly thrown caution to the wind, and today we are beginning to pay the costs. The application of scientific knowledge without ethical and ecological considerations is worse than doing nothing because of superstition or cultural taboo. In fact, it may well be our undoing. If we are to survive, we must develop a very different orientation toward the world. The naturalist Aldo Leopold wrote: "A thing is right when it tends to preserve the integrity, stability and beauty of the biotic community."

No contemporary political and socioeconomic system has accomplished this. From democratic to totalitarian, all systems exploit nature with a technology that is discordant with the natural order and with people to varying degrees. There is nothing wrong with technology, but there is something wrong with the values that underlie its application.

While Leiss's analysis of the impact of science and technology on nature may move one to seek allegiance with antitechnology neo-Luddites (or castigate his views as neo-Marxist), it is the shortsightedness and lack of conscience/consciousness of utopian technocrats and our dependence upon and support of biocidal socioeconomic systems that should be addressed. There are no intrinsic evils in science or technology; there is only the misapplication of the latter and the unethical means and ends which contaminate the former. As the late E. F. Schumacher has shown, we need not abandon technology if it is appropriate. In *Small Is Beautiful*, he presents an economic argument based upon Buddhist ethics that is a strong directive, but no panacea, to change mankind's domination of nature into one of a more harmonizing stewardship. Victor Ferkiss, in *The Future of Technological Civilization*, presents a detailed and convincing argument for such ecological humanism. He states:

> ... the two greatest challenges facing humanity today are the relationship between man and nature and between man and the machines he has created, it is vital that economic arrangements in society be so ordered as to curb those economic forces which destroy the balance between man and nature and to counter the economic forces which make it difficult to control the development and use of technology.
>
> The primary task of human society in the decades ahead will be to create a balance between a growing population and its claims on economic goods on the one hand, and the limits on such claims imposed by our finite resources of energy and space on the other. Future ties will have to create this balance within cultures which allow human beings to coexist with nature and to maintain sufficient continuity with their cultural past so as to retain their identity. To accomplish this will require control by society as a whole—through its political institutions—of the total pattern of economic life.

He contends that the economic goals of ecological humanism must break the following four vicious circles:

> Present-day society is locked into four positive feedback loops which need to be broken: economic growth which feeds on itself, population growth which feeds on itself, technological change

which feeds on itself, and a pattern of income inequality which seems to be self-sustaining and which tends to spur growth in the other three areas. Ecological humanism must create an economy in which economic and population growth is halted, technology is controlled, and gross inequalities of income are done away with.

Some of the major conclusions of Ferkiss's political philosophy for technological man are as follows:

The world and humanity are one entity, one system in equilibrium. Earth is humanity's only home; humanity is one people in relationship to the earth. We are all passengers on the same spaceship. The capacity of the earth to sustain human life is finite and the relationship between human numbers, human technology and the earth's resources is the most basic factor in maintaining the total system of the world and humanity in equilibrium.

Human societies and humanity as a whole exist within a natural system. The world, including mankind's physical habitat and other living species, serves human needs, but the natural world has rights of its own. It is not a servant but a brother and a collaborator.

Human beings have a discernible common nature which is the source of human values. The human body and the human mind are aspects of the same reality, and both have needs the fulfillment of which constitutes the content of human values. Each individual and each human group has [*sic*] a unique destiny, but a destiny which can only be fulfilled within the balance of the system of society and nature as a whole.

Because of the shared nature of humanity, there is a social common good which consists of the subsistence, order, and purpose of particular societies and of human society as a whole. All individual human goods are necessarily subordinate to the achievement of these common goods, since individuals can only survive and develop if the social system as a whole survives and develops. A common world requires a common order to seek the common good; a planetary political order is needed to deal with matters of planetary concern.

While this last statement may sound ominously socialistic, it is surely obvious that for the well-being of all humanity, an egalitarian form of socialism is needed with the ethical underpinnings and global political-economic structure of ecological humanism. Man's domination of nature must give way to a more enlightened relationship with all creation. The environmental crises, the exploitation and abuses of animals and nature alike, detailed in this book, not only are symptoms of our state of consciousness but should also be seen as critical reflections of our state of being-in-the-world. For humanity to progress, we must begin to address these ecological and humane issues and become ethical and responsible beings. Progress can no longer be seen in terms of advances in a science and technology that serve the good of mankind exclusively or certain more materially affluent or influential segments of society.* Progress is in service to the greater good of all life, and this is the difference between domination and stewardship.

We may aspire to more than a liberal, democratic, and egalitarian society and give it up if we feel dissatisfied, but we will never be fully satisfied, be perfectly content all the time. Liberal civilization is as fragile as nature. The alternative totalitarianism will destroy man and nature, and noble tribal communism is impossible because of the numbers of people and their continuing dependence upon existing labor systems. A few can homestead, live in communes, farm, and so on, but the majority are inextricably dependent upon what is. They cannot financially or psychologically break free. They and the systems must be supported and helped—humanized. World-negating gurus and dropouts who go back to nature have no place in the real world, for in turning their backs upon less fortunate fellowmen, they turn their backs on what they supposedly love most—nature, life, and so forth. Who will be left to protect nature if the "enlightened" ones give up civilization and live in the hills? Many have indeed given up, by surrendering to selfishness and despair. As John Passmore clearly articulates in *Man's Responsibility for Nature*, our ecological problems aren't simply and exclusively scientific problems; they are social problems. To solve them, we must face a subset of problems—scientific, technological, economic, moral, political, and administrative. Scientific ignorance and arro-

* See also R. Allen, *How to Save the World: Strategy for World Conservation* (London, 1980).

gance coupled with technological incapacity are serious limitations. Alternatives must address costs and benefits. Some of our greatest obstacles to social change are our social habits and life-styles; government agencies and corporations are not wholly responsible. The sad truth is that most people don't want to make any sacrifices. Many "experts" have argued that pollution, for example, is a justified price to pay for a high material standard of living, and in intensive factory farming, the "price" (in terms of animal suffering) is justified because we can have cheaper animal produce for food. Factory farming, like pollution, is a social problem. A utopian, as John Passmore emphasizes, justifies any cost (to others) to eliminate a problem, while a conservative does not see there is a problem and may rationalize it away as a necessary or unavoidable cost. To conservatives, utopians are insane idealists, and to utopians, conservatives are blind and insensitive egomaniacs. A moderate, who sees both sides, is judged by the utopians as a conservative compromiser who "sells out" to the establishment and is judged by conservatives as radical. Middle-ground rationalists are on lonely turf, lacking the zeal and fervent support of utopian extremists and the strength of consensus and status quo of the conservative establishment.

But the middle-ground rationalists will have their day because all actions have environmental effects, and we must protect Eden by assessing direct and indirect costs, benefits, and consequences.

Apocalyptic prophecies must not be substituted for the need for responsible concern, commitment, and thoughtful action. By "thoughtful," I mean we must be wise, humble, cautious, and aware of our values and goals. Passmore states vehemently: "Mystical contemplation will not clean our streams or feed our peoples; no invisible guiding hand, whether Providence or History, guarantees our salvation. In the biosphere—man has no tenure; his own folly may, at any time, lose him his precarious occupancy." He goes on to state that his sole concern "is that we should do nothing which will reduce their [other people's] freedom of thought and action, whether by destroying the natural world which makes that freedom possible or the social traditions which permit and encourage it." Otherwise, repressive totalitarianism may result, and with it the bureaucratized inability to think freely and act to save both mankind and nature.

Inflation, loss of jobs, and a general lowering of the standard of living are annually cited to counter conservationists and animal welfarists, yet often their reforms have had the opposite effect, being cost-saving and generally improving the overall quality of life. One must agree with Passmore that "it is cruel foolishness to expect people to turn their lathes into pitchforks," yet changing economic conditions may give them no other options but to do just so.

Few countries have reached the point of "ecological transition" that we have in the United States. But we all must be prepared to make some sacrifice, be it financial or in our life-styles. Passmore's insight here is that "in order to solve that set of problems which Galbraith has collectively designated as 'public squalor,' the West, to a striking degree, would have to embark on precisely the courses of action which are essential for the solution of its ecological problems (the opposite situation holds in the developing countries; there lies the tragedy)." Clearly the West must change its economic habits. Predictably, though, it is more likely to be forced upon us by changing circumstance than by deliberate foresight.

Human conscience and consciousness *must* transcend greed, ignorance, shortsightedness, and selfishness and such concepts as individualism, competitiveness, and materialism. The growth and monopoly of the scientific-technological-industrial complex must be regulated since the gross national product (GNP) is an illusory measure of the quality of life.

THE ECOLOGY OF CHEMICAL BIOHAZARDS

Few gave a second thought when organic chemists and chemical engineers began to synthesize new compounds. We have already seen how the development of certain new chemicals has affected the lives of millions of laboratory animals used in testing their safety, but many also have had an enormous and unforeseen impact on the environment. Those not biodegradable or recyclable, and those produced for nonessential purposes at the expense of the fossil fuels, have come to concern environmentalists and economists alike. More important, however, are our initial ignorance and earlier unconcern about the nature of such synthetic compounds. Because they cannot self-replicate and multiply like bacteria or viruses, there seemed to be no grounds for concern. But like any alien organism or new creation, they will find a niche which could be anywhere in the environment; it could affect the survival of certain species (like the mercury and DDT effect on the eggs of birds of prey) and by its magnified effect have an even greater repercussion on the entire ecosystem. If the pattern of incorporation is not in harmony with the existing living elements, disease follows. Unlike most natural pathogens, these new man-made nonliving "pathogens," following their incorporation into the body, affect or change the structures of the cell, causing mutations, developmental (birth) defects, cancer, and lowered resistance to diseases and other environmental pollutants. The human genetic repair system may already be overloaded with other pollutants, leading to a greater susceptibility to agents which, in a healthy body, might not cause chromosomal and other cellular disruptions.

Like mutation, the structure of the new chemical compound may be changed through the action of body enzymes or other natural agents—changes which we may never be able to predict—and become either inert or even more dangerous in its effects upon the very molecular organization of life.

New drugs, insecticides, herbicides, synthetic ingredients in paints, rubber, and plastics, food preservatives, red dye, Kepone, PCBs, and so on are not inert, as we are now learning. They may not be alive and self-replicating, as viruses or bacteria are, but they are as much a part of life as the mineral molecules and amino-acid chains, chemical enzyme systems, and carbon, sulfur, and phosphorus cycles in water, soil, and all life forms. The fundamental life units are chemical, just as the nonliving synthetics are. We have long ignored this molecular connection between the living and the nonliving and have not understood that changing the structure of the latter will affect the former. We now know that new synthetic nonliving materials may have profound consequences upon the structure and organization of the living, from the microcosm to the macrocosm—the cell to the biosphere. In crossing the bridge between living and nonliving, we have unknowingly contaminated, perhaps irreparably, both shores of creation. Our next and most important priority is surely to restore the natural order of life and to harmonize humanity with nature, not to create further disharmony with new chemical compounds. The earth is our flesh, and we cannot avoid contaminating ourselves when we contaminate the air, soil, and water.

To a degree, life forms can adapt to change, especially when they can rapidly mutate and develop resistant forms. Unfortunately man cannot mutate at the same rate as insects, which can quickly evolve to withstand insecticides and, like bacteria, produce enzymes to destroy such alien compounds. Or they may use them "against" us, as when new gonorrhea bacteria thrive on penicillin or when insects, with insecticides stored harmlessly in their exoskeletons, are lethal to birds, our biological allies. What new biochemical processes are our own bodies developing to combat the alien chemicals we have created? Generations may suffer and die before resistant human strains evolve through the rigors of such unnatural selection pressures. Only time will reveal the extent of the damage to date. But more important, now that we know that fundamentally there is no separation at the molecular level between the living and nonliving, will we begin to treat both with greater respect? We can "mutate" in one respect much faster than insects, bacteria, or other life forms; we can change ourselves for the better by changing the way we think and act to protect ourselves and all life on earth. Our "genes" are the right values and perceptions which we all could acquire instantly. Therein is our hope because we are the one animal with the capacity for rapid mental evolution.

Many rational scientists and citizens alike fear that the worldwide plethora of new chemical compounds could have disastrous consequences—as yet unforeseeable and wholly unpredictable. This is not overcautious conservatism. The potential harm of such substances may greatly outweigh the immediate short-term advantages they offer. Rather than face these hazards, some adopt a wait-and-see attitude, like the corporation executive who told the news media that he thought that the FDA ban on saccharin "was premature." Must we wait for the evidence from animal tests to be verified by humans? And when animal tests are inconclusive, do we wait until another cancer epidemic occurs in people and then isolate the new carcinogen with more animal tests? Hindsight may be all very well for the next generation, but not for those who are incapacitated or have died in the process. It is now apparent that most forms of cancer are man-made.* And it is time to address the causes, not the symptoms. To study and then to correct only the symptoms of chemically induced carcinogenesis is bad medicine, and no amount of animal tests can make it good medicine. The real issue is a human one, not one of chemical carcinogenesis alone. Improvements in animal test procedures without our addressing these sociopolitical, ecological, and economic issues will be fruitless and, worse, lead to a false sense of security. A beginning would be to maintain enforcement of the most stringent regulations controlling the production and dissemination of all known categories of carcinogens (and related teratogens and mutagens) and to inform consumers about such potential hazards. (Beverages in the United States, for example, have no list of ingredients on the can or bottle.) A moratorium on the development of any new compound belonging to any category or family of related carcinogens should also be enforced. This would not only help protect consumers and the environment, but also obviate the difficulties of having to withdraw a substance from the market that, as in the case of saccharin, would cause financial and other hardships to those who have become dependent upon its production or consumption. Restrictions should also be applied to the exportation of all American products that are biohazards. International regulations are essential. After all, we live on a small planet, and we cannot escape the indiscretions of one company or of one or more foreign nations. Until more effective international regulations are drawn up, a minority will continue to profit at the expense of animal and human health and suffering.

HOLISTIC MEDICINE

Holism is a philosophy which takes the "whole" as being fundamental to reality. Holistic medicine treats the "whole" patient, not

---

* See S. S. Epstein, *The Politics of Cancer* (New York: Anchor, 1979).

just his specific symptoms—headache, stomachache, and so on. An essential aim of holistic medicine is to teach the humane ethic of a reverence for all life and to explain mankind's role as one of humane stewardship, rather than dominionistic, competitive, parasitic, and biocidal.

Humaneness implies respecting the lives of others, including all nonhuman creatures, and the environment and habitats which we share and affect by our presence and various activities. Self-respect is also an important corollary. *Health* implies not merely the absence of disease but harmony in all relationships, as in mind and body, within and between individuals and society, between different species in their habitats and also between humans and the biosphere, the whole environment that constitutes earth. Inhumane attitudes and actions can be contrary to the rights and health (physical, psychological, social, and environmental) of others.

The interconnections between mind and body and thoughts and actions are well recognized. Similarly understood are the interconnections and interdependencies of species, habitats, and ecosystems which make up the "mind-body" of the biosphere, from which humankind is inseparable and wholly dependent. "Sickness," whether it is caused by natural diseases or destructive human actions, is rarely confined to one segment or species. Cause and effect sequences reverberate between interdependent/interrelated parts in the "seamless web" of the biosphere.

Wendell Berry aptly summarizes the holistic view of health (in *The Unsettling of America, Agriculture and Culture*) as follows: "That absolute good, I think, is health—not in the merely hygienic sense of personal health, but the health, the wholeness, finally the holiness of Creation, of which our personal health is only a share."

The health of the biosphere is a reflection of the physical health of mankind (health embracing the harmony not only within the body and between individuals in the family and in society but also between nations). But what of mental/spiritual health? There is no obvious analogue here in nature, or is there?

A desecrated segment of wilderness that has been destroyed by logging or strip mining and a lake that has been polluted by untreated industrial waste are just two examples of man-induced physical sickness and death, reflecting certain mental attitudes and values which are pathogenic—unhealthy. They can be seen and felt and do have a measurable effect on the unfortunate people who have to live, permanently or temporarily, in or near such pits of human entropy. Contrast this psychic impact of a sick environment with the transcendant, spiritually renewing effect of unspoiled wilderness on the human mind (and body).

Therefore, it is for something more than mere human survival that we should be humane stewards and conserve wolves, forests, lakes, eagles, whales, and oceans. It is essential for human health and for the well-being of future generations. Humane stewardship in maintaining health and harmony within the biosphere and between all living things is as important as medicine in ensuring the physical and mental health of our species. Our well-being is inseparable from that of all other life forms, and to believe otherwise is both suicidal and biocidal. One step in the right direction has been the environmental impact statement which must be completed before any major ecological intervention is sanctioned. Until the holistic approach to medicine and health care in general becomes more widespread, however, we cannot be too optimistic, and the humane/conservation movement will not attain its full (and vitally needed) effectiveness. Medicine has been almost exclusively humanocentric, with often disastrous, ecologically biocidal consequences. As a misguided form of human altruism, by treating the symptoms of human suffering and sickness and not addressing the political, religious, economic, and ecological causes and consequences, medicine has added more to the burden of suffering on earth than it has to its alleviation.

This misguided approach is gradually changing as we learn from our mistakes and from the man-made global crises which face us today: pollution, depletion of resources, overpopulation, unequal distribution of power and resources, famine, and disease. Medicine alone cannot be blamed for all these crises, but it has certainly failed to heal humanity.

Further deficits are evident, notably the increasing incidence of physician- and treatment-induced (iatrogenic) problems, as Ivan Illich has shown in *Medical Nemesis*. Medical practice and research have splintered into many specialist fields—cardiology, nephrology, hematology, neurology, and so on. Yet all these specialist fields are, in the organic reality of the body, intimately interrelated and inter-dependent. Needless to say, a certain amount of specialization, a knowledge of the units and subsystems of any organic complex, such as the human body, is essential. But no less essential are a synthesis of these subsystems and a holistic, *integrative* approach to modern medicine. Two examples will suffice to illustrate the need for this approach. Of the $800 million and more spent each year on cancer research, the National Cancer Research Institute 1977 Report re-veals little progress. Over the last ten years, no cancer cures have been found, and the average life expectancy of a cancer patient has been increased by only four to five years. This is principally because research has focused on symptoms and carcinogenic processes, not on the environmental, demographic, and nutritional variables. Too much laboratory research, especially with animal models, accounts for much of this insignificant progress and attests to the severe limi-tations of the specialist/reductionist approach to medical problems.

A more holistic orientation would enhance biomedical research by fostering an awareness of the psychological or emotional and *ex-trinsic* (environmental and social) complexities of health and dis-ease. We have made great progress with the mechanistic and *intrinsic* (within-body) complexities, but without more understand-ing of the context and psychological influences, more knowledge of the body is of little value. And worse, the therapy prescribed may then have been inappropriate, iatrogenic, or ineffective against the underlying extrinsic and mental causes.

Another serious flaw in biomedical research and the practice of medicine is their regard for the patient as a "body machine." Such a mechanistic view, reflected in the design of many biomedical ex-periments involving live animal and human subjects, is supported by a reverence for scientific "objectivity." In terms of empathy and compassion—important factors in healing and in the responsible use of animals in research—such objectivity leads to clinical detach-ment and apparent indifference toward the patient-as-a-fellow-being.

The mechanistic view tends to oversimplify the problems of

health and disease by its narrow focus upon systems/processes/ mechanics within the body, not on the dynamics and relationships between body and mind. Added to this mind-body dichotomy is the isolation of the body from emotional influences. For many in psychiatry, mind-body separation is just as prevalent as it is in other fields of medicine that specialize in various systems of the body.

Humane education can promote health in its broadest sense: to respect all life and to treat others (both human and nonhuman) as you would have them treat you; to respect and cherish the earth and any part thereof as one would one's own body; to uphold a nondiscriminating reverence for all life and to live by a code which constrains selfish actions and values in relation to the rights of other living creatures; to seek always the greater good for others through harmony in body, mind, and spirit.

Health, humaneness, harmony, and peace are interdependent and inseparable parts of right living. Empathy, compassion, unconditional love, humility, and understanding are the keys to conscious and conscientious living and to a happy life constrained within the moral and ethical dimensions of a world-conscience. Health then becomes synonymous with human fulfillment, and for all educators, researchers, and healers, this is surely the greatest challenge of the times and a primary goal for our species.

9

The Question of Animal Rights

I am often asked why many people prefer animals to people. I myself often find it easier to empathize with animals (and children, too). Is it a difference in me or in others that affects my reactions? Some people state that people can't be "trusted" or are impossible to reach and to love, compared to animals—and children, too. Adults tend to conceal their emotions and often "put on a face" (friendly or otherwise). They seem to lack the genuine openness characteristic of a trusting animal or young child. Adults also tend to get lost in the roles and games they play, such as living up to an ego ideal of how one ought to appear to others—efficient, knowledgeable, courteous, worldly, sophisticated, or even superior and always in control (top dog). Sometimes they lose themselves so completely in their role that their whole identity is lost in what they do. They become what Theodore Roszak, Kenneth Keniston, and others describe as robots or mannequinlike automatons, lacking in feeling and empathy except when related to the all-important role. At its mildest, this is seen in impersonal professionalism; at its worst, it is an obsessive-compulsive neurosis of seemingly alienated people, who lack fellow feeling or empathy for others. Perhaps this is why some people prefer animals. Animals are "more real and alive" or "natural."

Most people automatically respond to a person who is open, natural, and at ease with himself. Yet many people are surrounded by an invisible cage the bars and walls of which are the ego's defenses. These defenses are built up as a protection against certain fears, insecurities, and dependencies which may remain unresolved throughout life. Prejudices, negative expectations, and inflexible attitudes are also part of the mental defense that can make a person live in a self-made prison of illusion and delusion. The ego's insecurities have to be worked through, as such humanistic psychologists and therapists as Alexander Lowen, Erich Fromm, Carl Rogers, and the Polsters have shown, before anyone can trust himself (and others) to be free and open and to accept and love others unconditionally. Most of us have some form of ego armor which prevents us from being at one with the world as a whole. An animal that is timid and withdrawn is cut off from contact by a wall of fear, which only love, empathy, and patience can penetrate. The ego defenses make a comparable wall for man, and it is important for people to recognize and understand this before they blame others for their faults. People need to be liberated from their fears and insecurities, as much as a wild animal in a cage needs freedom in order to be fully itself.

It may be easier for some to empathize with and even love animals than people. Animals expect little. They are not usually contentious or manipulative; they are nonthreatening in the sense of being accepting and unjudgmental; they are open and direct in expressing their needs and feelings. Because they are existentially in the here and now, they are attentive to a person in that eternal moment of relatedness. It is easier for an animal than it is for some people to accept someone's love and attention. People may feel threatened or manipulated by love, especially if it is conditionally given.

The need to care for someone or something is often satisfied by a pet. Likewise, a pet may give its owner a sense of security and belonging that is sometimes denied because of one's attitudes or because of the attitudes of society (especially toward senior citizens). Pets alleviate loneliness and alienation from other people.

A major barrier to empathic understanding is the tendency to judge and identify the wrongdoer with the wrong that is done.

Rather than deplore the destructive and selfish values and actions of people, we deplore and reject the people. It is essential to understand, as one might in an animal or child, that untoward behavior in adults stems from such underlying factors as ignorance, immaturity, fear, insecurity, and greed. Otherwise, conflicts of values and interests will never be resolved. As we would educate a child or patiently train and socialize an animal, rather than judge and condemn them, so might we educate others to be more humane, empathic, and ethical in their relationships with both people and animals. Also, we tend to dislike others when we see in them qualities or habits that we don't like in ourselves. The better our self-awareness and acceptance of our own limitations and weaknesses, the easier it will be to understand, accept, and love others.

Ideally, man should prefer neither animals nor people. Preferring animals over humans may be an escape from reality and unresolved conflicts of attitude and aspiration. To prefer people to the exclusion of all else of creation is to deny the fulfillment and meaning that life offers.

Liking and not liking imply that there is conflict between reality and fantasy. Instead of seeing what is there, we see what we want to on the basis of expectation, judgment, and prior experience. For example, you have seen one cow and you've seen them all; all Chinamen are the same. The mind classifies, categorizes, and rubricizes or stereotypes so that we do not see and cannot appreciate the uniqueness of each living thing. And worse, reality is often judged and classified in relation to one's feelings, attitudes, needs, and values: useful/useless; beautiful/ugly; good/bad; and so on. Likes and dislikes are, therefore, simply attitudes of mind-conditioned reactions, habits, expectations, and prejudices which limit the way we perceive and respond to everything in our world. These attitudes are self-limiting. Like the ego's defenses, they are based upon fear, selfish needs, and ignorance and deny us the freedom to be and to see things—animals and people—as they are.

One who prefers neither animals nor people, but who understands their strengths and weaknesses and through them can enjoy and share in that one reality which is life, is truly alive and fully human. But in times of crisis is human life to be saved or sacrificed over animals' lives? When the chips are really down, can any sane and humane person consider an animal's life above that of any human being?

Noah was a good steward and conservationist. He took a pair of every living species into the Ark, making no distinctions and valuing all equally. This tale contains an important message for today in times of population crises and ecological chaos. In times of crisis, we should value all life equally and not seek to save only our own kind or sacrifice other creatures so that our own needs and priorities may be satisfied. But practically speaking, could animals still have rights when people are faced with such crises as famine and overpopulation?

A recent visit to India gave me a firsthand opportunity to explore this question. There the attitude toward animal suffering in the midst of so much human privation and misery presents a test case. The problem of the free-roaming dog overpopulation in India is of serious public health and humane concern. In 1975 Kushwant Singh, editor of the *Illustrated Weekly of India*, presented a critical statement of India's position: "We gave the world the concept of *ahimsa* or non-violence. Yet we inflict some of the most brutal cruelties on our animals. . . . Callous indifference is as criminal as active cruelty." Indifference may be through ignorance of empathic understanding or through acceptance of suffering as another's fate or Karma, or it may be a defense mechanism against the everyday horrors of the reality of animal (and human) suffering in India. Bachi J. Karkaria, staff writer on the same magazine, concluded:

> Why should we give to a charity for animals when millions of our people are starving? How can you expect a *tongawalla* to feed his horse if he cannot feed himself? How can he afford to retire his animal when he cannot retire himself? How can you convince a poor bullock-cart driver to reduce the load and make two trips instead of one? Isn't the sympathy of the SPCA people absurd and misplaced?

But to answer his own questions, he argues that there are at least four justifications for the humane/animal protection movement.

One, the child who today kicks a dog in the stomach is more likely tomorrow to do the same thing to a man. Cruelty is cruelty. Its definition does not change with the object against which it is directed. There is no difference—of degree or kind—between hurting a human and hurting a beast.

This is a valid dictum, which is often dismissed by such beliefs that animals don't feel pain as we do, but it must also be qualified. Namely, the motive is not to teach people not to be cruel to animals so that they will be kind to each other but rather to help people understand that any act of unnecessary cruelty is inhumane, be it directed to a fly or a man. The ethic of ahimsa and reverence for all life does not and cannot make any distinction between animal and man.

Karkaria continues:

Two, by exploiting the animal, we are exploiting ourselves. Cruelty has been the major factor in driving 1,115 species to extinction in the last four hundred years. Man is not going to be the last animal to be left on earth. People who make their living from an animal should be convinced that it will serve them better if it is healthier.

Seeing what I have seen in India, I would temper the word "cruelty," which implies some element of intent or judgment, with "ignorance," which leads to the exploitation and mistreatment of animals and people alike.

His final points are:

. . . poor, ill and handicapped people certainly need our help. But they can at least speak out their own problems, make their plight known themselves. The dumb animal cannot. If underprivileged humans have only a small voice, the animal has no voice at all. How many of those who clamour that the rights of man come before the rights of the animal have done anything to better the lot of man? Not supporting the SPCA is often part of the larger irresponsibility of not supporting anyone at all.

It might be argued that human resources are finite and human needs must take precedence over animal welfare and conservation.

To make the terrible distinction between whether animals or people should be given aid and allowed to live forces one into a position of placing relative values on lives of animals and man rather than having a reverence for all life. Each living thing is valid in its own right by virtue of its existence per se. Animals and people should have equal rights to exist. We should try not to judge, in terms of human needs and priorities, whether certain groups, classes, or races of people, and species, communities, and ecosystems of animals, are more valuable than others. All decisions and actions derived from such a line of thinking would be tainted with racist and ethnocentric judgments biased by one's own prejudices and selfish, utilitarian values. Instead, realizing that resources are finite, we must learn to live more economically; good economy is good ecology.

The humane movement, in India or in America, is one positive step toward a more compassionate and responsible way of life. Man's acceptance of his responsible role on earth as a humane being is yet to come. The state of the world and our treatment of animals reflect the state of human consciousness: Ecological chaos parallels social disorganization; inhumane treatment and abuse of animals parallels exploitation and manipulation of people.

THE HISTORY OF ANIMAL RIGHTS

Although most past moral philosophers knew little about animals, they still had a lot to say about them, much of which reflected their indifference, ignorance, and anthropocentrism. For example, Aristotle (circa 320 B.C.), Kant (circa 1800), and St. Thomas Aquinas (circa 1250) all had a totally anthropocentric regard for animals. Believing that animals had no rights per se, they were concerned with animal suffering and cruelty under man solely from the viewpoint of man. It was concluded that a person should not be cruel to animals not because there was anything *directly* wrong with causing an animal to suffer, but because of the negative effects such actions and attitudes might have in man's treatment of his own species. C. W. Hume points out:

> If, in the Holy Scripture there are injunctions forbidding the in-
> fliction of some cruelty towards brute animals . . . this is either . . .
> lest anyone, from exercising cruelty upon the brute, should go on
> hence to human beings . . . or because the injury inflicted on ani-
> mals turn to a temporal loss for some man. . . . God's purpose in
> recommending kind treatment of the brute creation is to dispose
> men to pity and tenderness to each other.

Some segments of the humane movement today support this utilitarian view. They stress that it is morally wrong to treat any creature cruelly, and if a child is taught to be kind to animals, it will
automatically be kind to its fellow humans.* While this view may at
least aid in alleviating some of the suffering of animals, it is still
human-focused, and concern for animals is not the primary concern.
The possibility that animals may have certain intrinsic rights takes
second place to the first concern of man's conduct toward man. This
is probably the reason why so little attention has been given in the
past to the question of rights of nonhuman animals.

Kant and other philosophers argued that rights belong only to rational beings who are defined as those beings with language, a
"soul," or God-given dominion. Beings without such qualities do not
fall within the framework of our moral concern. As Andrew Linzey
has shown in his book *Animal Rights,* this humanocentric and illogical assumption still contaminates our culture today. Why, in fact,
should nonhuman beings not fall within the framework of our moral
concern? Why should they not have souls? We know now that many
animals have language.

If we are rational and responsible beings, by the same token it can
be argued that we do have moral obligations to all creation. I call
this the humane imperative. Only rational beings can act immor-
ally; hence the need for moral constraints for such beings. Kant's
flaw in not realizing that there is a humane imperative prevented
him from seeing the real significance of man's moral obligations toward all life. The uniqueness of mankind was conveniently misinterpreted as something separate from the rest of creation. But it is

---

* Cases of animal cruelty often correlate with earlier abuse of the person by
parents.

surely because of this uniqueness that we are obligated to fulfill the humane imperative of responsible stewardship and reverence for all life.

Other philosophers, such as Descartes (circa 1600) and his followers, regarded animals as instinctive machines which had no rights again because they lacked reason and were nonrational. Behavior research in the late twentieth century has shattered this view but has not convinced many well-known thinkers, who argue, for example, that animals are not rational and that since they cannot reciprocate our respect for their rights, they have no place in our moral community. Newborn infants and brain-damaged patients cannot respect the rights of others, so they, too, following this argument, can have no rights either—which is absurd.

Charles Darwin observed that "the difference in mind between man and the higher animals, great as it is, certainly is one of degree and not of kind." Recent research in behavior, ecology, psychology, anatomy, and biochemistry is affirming our inseparable kinship with all life, not only with our closest relatives, the primates, but, through the connectedness of evolution, also with carnivores, reptiles, and even slime molds and plants, as I have described in detail in *Between Animal and Man* and in *One Earth, One Mind.*

One reason for man's demeaning attitude toward other animals is his projection of his own faults onto them. There is no evil in nature, only in the minds of men. Animals have been scapegoats in this regard for centuries. This is reflected in our language, rich with derogatory animal metaphors (beast, bitch, ape, pig, swine, ass, wildcat, sloth, snake in the grass, and so on. We say we are bullish, bearish, kittenish, hungry as a lion, fat as a pig, and so on). We also make animals into inanimate objects—"it" rather than "he" or "she." Often only pets are referred to by gender and given a familiar, rather than impersonal, name. This is closely tied to the eating of animals. We may eat roast duckling because we enjoy "it," but we could never eat "Dorothy," for "she" was an Easter duckling and one of the family. Linguistically we establish proximity, and we cannot eat those whom we regard and speak of as close, unless we become cannibals! We get to know an animal as an individual with a personality rather than a genderless object like an apple or potato, and we can no longer kill and eat it. Familiarity may thus breed attachment, not contempt or indifference. No doubt aware of these considerations, Plutarch (circa A.D. 100), a staunch opponent of Aristotle and his humanocentered world view, states for the animal, "Kill me for thy feeding but do not take me off for thy better feeding." Interesting, too, that so many of our food words are different from the animal. We say steak, hamburger, veal, poultry, venison rather than cow, chicken, deer and so on. We disassociate what we eat from what lives.

As Claude Lévi-Strauss has urged, one must study the unconscious infrastructure of cultural phenomena rather than the surface manifestations. Animal names not only have behavioral or archetypal similes (for example, "sssnake") and reflected reference to admired or scorned human qualities but also mirror social ideals and negative qualities of the times, especially in fairy tales. Animal symbolism tends to change in accordance with changing social values. Both myths and animal stories for children can give insight into the relationship between man and nature at a given time in history. A sleepy, fat woodchuck, for example, may at one time be regarded as an archetype of contentment, at peace with its world, and later as a lazy layabout, being given as an example of a "bad" archetype, in contrast with an "industrious" beaver that embodies the social archetype of the work ethic better. Similarly, competitive individualism and survival of the fittest may be revered values in society, and appropriate animal archetypes are created in fairy tales to instill such values with positive regard for young readers. Thus, we are guilty not only of demeaning our animal kin but also of misrepresenting them for the service of society. The human traits projected upon them help create an anthropomorphic and unreal understanding of animals in children. Once grown, such children lack an objective understanding of animals, and the issue of rights may seem ludicrous, if not impossible to understand or accept.

Scientific studies of animal behavior are now gradually dispersing the clouds of confusion over the nature of animals, thus indirectly laying the groundwork for a rational appraisal of the question of animal rights. The more we come to know about animals, the more we are impelled to care. We can no longer claim ignorance as an excuse for indifference and inhumane treatment of animals. The irrefutable light of scientific proof reveals that man is not the only animal that is rational, ethical, moral, has emotions, dependencies, feelings, anxieties, and sensations. There are more similarities than differences between man and animal, the will to live being the prime aspect of all life. Animals are even more human than we may wish or care to accept, and the boundary between man and other animals is becoming less and less clear-cut as research progresses. That man alone, and no other sentient being, should continue to have rights is obviously illogical and unethical. We should, as Peter Singer urges in *Animal Liberation*, give all creatures equal consideration of their interests and correlated rights.

A few past philosophers were exceptions to the general view of man's dominion over nature and of the mechanistic preconscious world of animals. Schopenhauer, opposing Kant, stated: "The morality of Christianity has no consideration for animals, a defect that is better admitted than perpetuated. . . . And so we must remind the western Judaized despiser of animals and idolator of the faculty of reason that, just as he was suckled by his mother, so too was the dog by his." Jeremy Bentham (circa 1798), a radical who fought against slavery, said: "The day *may come* when the rest of animal creation may acquire those rights which never could have been withheld from them but by the hand of tyranny . . . the question is not Can they *reason*? nor, Can they *talk*? but, Can they suffer?"

The philosopher John Locke emphasized that man and animal share the same natural rights for life, liberty, and prosperity and the right not to suffer at the hands of others. The quality of "human rights" is basic to one's existence as a nondiscriminating element of society, and the same holds for animals, both wild and tame. Animal and human rights must not be degraded or exploited, although it is obvious that in certain situations some rights of the individual must be forsaken for the general welfare of others. For example, obeying leash laws and not allowing one's dog (or cat) to roam free and live "naturally," neutering to help reduce the pet overpopulation problem and make the animal more adaptable and less frustrated sexually may seem inhumane and a violation of their rights, but we must impose such restraints in certain contexts just as people must abide by certain rules and social constraints.

And in contemporary times Albert Schweitzer observed: "A man is really ethical only when he obeys the constraint laid on him to help all life which he is able to succor, and when he goes out of his way to avoid injuring anything living. He does not ask how far this or that life deserves sympathy as valuable in itself nor how far it is capable of feeling. To him, life as such is sacred." This state of consciousness embraces a reverence for all life with an ethically responsible and rational world view. It is the kind of mind that thinks twice before felling a tree or even turning a stone. To know that there is life everywhere that one may inadvertently destroy and to seek alternatives to killing whenever possible are to act with conscience. We have been guilty of acting unconsciously and without conscience for too long.

Aesthetic and emotional motives also underlie efforts to protect wildlife and wilderness. The humane and conservation movements place considerable emphasis on these subjective human valuations. My daughter at the age of seven said to a friend about to step on an ant, "How would you like it if someone stepped on you?" In other words, "Do unto animals as you would have them do unto you." This is a positive moral injunction, but of limited value because it places the animal in a context contaminated by human values and morality. The animal is not seen separately in its own right. Any rights for animals or nature at the aesthetic and emotional level are extensions of the rights of people for aesthetic and emotional enjoyment of things of nature, which still do not have intrinsic rights themselves. What is needed is an objective, rational, and ethical view of animals independent of self-serving human valuation. Each sentient being should be valued in and for itself; a wolf is a wolf is a wolf. This transpersonal level of thinking and relating contrasts the basically selfish motives behind man's relationships with nature and other animals.

Human survival needs can and will take precedence over all other considerations, and this reality must be reckoned with. I might, for example, take the life of the last tiger on earth if the survival of my children depended on it. But if I had not explored other alternatives first to avoid such an action, I would be guilty of unethical conduct and of denying the animal's rights. Rights are always relative even when they are respected and upheld. Yet often there *is* an alternative to extermination (or other actions such as declawing a cat). Unfortunately, rarely do we search since it is easier to destroy than to seek or create new alternatives. We are also guilty of confusing our basic survival need with selfish, materialistic needs, as when economic survival is mistakenly equated with basic survival.

In summary, therefore, any life form should have, by virtue of its existence, the right to life. This right provides it with due consideration over all human rights except the human right to basic survival; if an animal's right is to be overruled, all alternatives must have been first explored to avoid unnecessary destruction of life.

Man's role as steward of ecosystems today brings up the delicate issue of having to destroy some animals in order to regulate the balance of nature. This is a human prerogative which is not infrequently abused because of some vested interest (for example, of hunters versus the wolves of Alaska), which is often concealed under the guise of "conservation management." If wild animals are ours in trust, they constitute common property, like a national monument. Then the people, as their trustees, have the right to prosecute those who violate such common trust by killing or otherwise exploiting for profit. States' rights to animals as "resources" are clearly unethical and undemocratic in this regard. Common property has value, however, which may be weighed against some other value such as land development. But the best defense of animals is on the basis of their own intrinsic right to life, rather than on their being common property in trust. The Endangered Species Act, protecting all listed animals, was challenged recently, when the survival of an entire species of the snail darter fish was threatened by a hydroelectric dam development. The argument was that the species was insignificant relative to the importance of the dam.

Another argument—any life is better than no life at all—rationalizes the mistreatment and unnatural privation of livestock bred for human use and consumption. But man does not have the right to treat as he chooses the life that he has created. Such would be animal slavery. In fact, he has a greater responsibility to see that they do not suffer under his care.

Some will argue against the rights of wild animals the relationships of which in nature constantly violate such rights. An example that might be given is that of a wolf killing a deer. It may seem that the wolf is violating the deer's intrinsic right to life. But the relationship is more complex. First, the wolf kills only for survival and not, like man, for sport or financial gain, which are certainly violations of the deer's rights. Also, the deer fulfills its right to escape or defend itself and indeed sometimes does so successfully. Third, and most important, the deer is adapted from the point of view of population to such predation. It "expects" to be killed, or it lives to be eaten. This evolved relationship is in the best interests of both species. The wolves are fed, and the deer population is regulated. There is an impressive analogy here with man and his domesticated farm livestock. Domestication is a special form of evolved relationship, but the benefit is not as mutual as between the wolf and deer, unless it is argued, wrongly, that having given them life, man has free license to do as he chooses to such domestic animals. Objectively the relationship between man and pig, sheep, cow, or horse is more one-sided. The animals are exploited solely for man's benefit. The relationship becomes less one-sided only when such creatures are treated humanely and allowed some degree of fulfillment under social and environmental conditions as natural as possible. Economic considerations here should take second place over our ethical obligations. It must also be remembered that unlike the wolf, man can choose not to kill such creatures (or to consume less of them) and avoid the ethical dilemma of humane concerns versus economic exploitation by seeking alternative food sources.*

---

* Vegetarianism is becoming less of a health fad and more of an ethical response to factory farming animal abuse (a recent Roper poll indicates that there are some 7 million ethical vegetarians in the United States). It is also an economically and ecologically sound practice since it is estimated that in order to produce one pound of meat, anywhere from eight to twenty pounds of vegetable protein is wasted, and the latter is no less nutritious for man than flesh per se.

The rights of animals cannot be adequately comprehended or defended simply on the most basic grounds of survival and utilitarian needs or on the grounds of aesthetic and emotional valuation. It is at the highest transpersonal level of awareness and relatedness that sentient beings can be seen to have rights. Acceptance of the fact that our animal kin possess equally the intrinsic right to life will not only be to their benefit but also to the ultimate well-being of humankind. The growing concern for animal rights today reflects a positive trend in the evolution of human consciousness.

Animal rights are based not only upon the existence of the animal per se but also upon its capacity to suffer, to feel pain, to experience fear and anxiety. While it may be argued that since a "dumb" pig doesn't know it's being fattened for slaughter, it cannot suffer anxiety, this evades the issue. An animal, not knowing what is going to happen to it, may suffer more and not less than a man who "knows." Any vet experienced in treating animals, especially wild species, is aware of this and the fact that some may die of fear/anxiety. Even pigs, on the way to slaughter, develop stomach ulcers under the emotional and physical stress of transportation.

To rate the degree of pain sensitivity and capacity to suffer in terms of an animal's evolved proximity to man is a racist extension if rights are based upon such logic. The forebrain is not involved with pain perception anyway; that is the role of the thalamus, which is well developed in all mammals, including man. To avoid pain actively is a survival mechanism in all creatures, and their right to freedom from unnecessary pain, and associated fear and anxiety, is intrinsic to their existence.

Suffering is particularly pertinent in discussing our moral obligations toward animals. Some factory farming methods, various biomedical experiments, housing of wild animals in captivity, and keeping pets confined may produce considerable physical and psychological suffering. We must first determine objectively whether the animals are suffering, and if no alternatives are available to eliminate such proved or possible suffering, that suffering must be justified in terms of the ultimate benefit to others (both man and animal alike). The basic right of an animal to life implies also the right to live without suffering. For some species this may also entail keeping it in as natural an environment as possible in order to allay undue privation or suffering from confinement and social deprivation. If feasible, the conditions that will allow some degree of self-fulfillment through its relations with man, conspecies, and a natural or seminatural environment should be provided.

We must examine the right of all creatures to freedom and to an environment which allows them space and social contacts to express many of their natural instincts. Undue privation is physically and psychologically frustrating and stressful, and is ethically inhumane. Singer lucidly states: "Why, for instance, is the hunter who shoots wild ducks for his supper subject to more criticism than the person why buys chicken at the supermarket? Over-all, it is probably the intensively reared bird that has suffered more."

Would it then be ethically acceptable to eat the flesh of genetic strains of domestic animals that are content simply to eat and sleep and, through selective breeding, have no instincts left to experience frustration or deprivation? With no instincts, they would have to be artificially bred, raised, and perhaps force-fed. Economically, for the agribusiness conglomerates, this must surely be an attractive goal—to convert domestic animals into "fleshy vegetables."* Why not then today eat vegetables instead and avoid the predictable suffering of billions of animals over the ensuing years before humane reforms are instigated or until such time as they are sufficiently mutated to become placid protein-converting machines—if such mutations are indeed possible? Even the most domestic of farm species today, if given the opportunity, can quickly become feral or revert to the wild; although repressed, natural instincts may be easily reactivated under optimal (natural) conditions.

The question remains open: How far can we go, ethically, to create unnatural animals genetically, surgically, and by drug or hormone treatment? Becoming a vegetarian is one way of avoiding this obvious deanimalizing process, but is not the sole reason for choosing to mitigate animal suffering by boycotting the meat market.

---

* Ironically, with the emphasis on high productivity and great muscle mass, hogs, cattle, and poultry are becoming *more* rather than less sensitive to stress.

Once the species barrier is broken, and our humanocentric world view changed to responsible and empathetic stewardship, to continue to eat the meat of fellow mammals, especially of those that have been treated inhumanely, is ethically reprehensible for many people.

Man must learn to be as responsible for nature as he is for himself and his family. We must learn to love all our neighbors, not just people, but trees, lakes, buzzards, and all, for each creation has its own intrinsic worth and "rights" quite distinct from our own human-centered needs and "rights." While it can be argued that animals and other creations can't have rights because they are not members of the human community, such an argument negates the fact that we are a part of the community of earth, and being so, we have obligations to all nonhuman life, which in turn has rights, as we also have. Their rights need not be identical in kind, nor do the nonhuman possessors of rights have obligations to us (neither do human infants), since we are the supreme or dominant controlling species and therefore the givers and protectors of these rights. In his stimulating and provocative book *Man's Responsibility for Nature*, John Passmore, in arguing against animal and nature rights, states that "bacteria and men do not recognize mutual obligations nor do they have common interests." He misses the point here that reciprocal respect for rights and common interest are not adequate criteria for deciding that animals (or human infants) can't be given rights.

In humaneness and respect for the intrinsic worth, and, therefore, the rights of all things, is the preservation of civilization and the world. As animals and nature gain "rights," so people lose certain rights in their power over animals. In man's losing the right to pollute a river, it may be argued that the river isn't given the right not to be polluted. But we have duties toward animals because they have interests (needs) and, therefore, certain rights which must be respected.

Respect for the rights of other people is not only ethically desirable but an essential part of being human. A logical extension of this is the inclusion of a bill of rights for *all* living things. A society upholding such rights will foster the development of a more mature and responsible state of consciousness in the populace to the ultimate benefit of mankind and the biosphere alike. Racism and "speciesism" divide and destroy both society and the biosphere when the rights of others—people, animals, and plants—have a lower priority than the rights of the power elite.

A bill of rights for animals places consideration upon two basic issues: the right of all sentient beings to live and the right to humane treatment when animals are used by man for any purpose.

Killing wild animals for nonsurvival purposes (sport, nonessential luxuries, and so on) is a violation of their rights. "Survival killing" can be defined as killing to protect livestock or to maintain the balance of nature in a well-managed ecosystem. But should the products of such killing be used for nonsurvival purposes? Should the furs be turned into clothing; should the meat be eaten?

The fine line between trapping as an essential part of stewardship/management and trapping for profit and to satisfy human vanity is clear. To ban all trapping is impractical, but the search for more humane alternatives should not be neglected. Similarly, to ban *all* hunting is illogical since some, for management of ecosystems, is essential. Producing a surplus of wildlife that has to be cropped by hunters needs careful ethical appraisal. Such animals are partially or wholly introduced and propagated by man, which places them, in relation to man, closer to our domestic livestock and pets than to wilderness creatures. Most hunters don't have to kill in order to live. Nor do most of those who wear furs need them to survive the cold. Our domesticated plants, animals, and associated industries which have taken over so much of the biosphere should be used instead— on ethical as well as ecological grounds. Man must define more exactly the limits or boundaries of his egosphere in terms of animal rights, humane responsibilities, and ethically objective and rational ecological/environmental considerations.

Under the present systems of animal management—on farms, in laboratories, and zoos—there are obvious economic limitations to setting up more humane seminatural environmental systems. This does not mean that we should not seek other more humane alternatives. Zoo safari parks are a major advance over small city zoos. Some research laboratories have seminatural field stations for raising animals, also an improvement. Farms can readopt the once-widespread free-ranging or semiopen corral or climatic house systems in which the livestock are relatively free to roam and enjoy natural social relationships with each other.

A more open farm system may necessitate destruction of wildlife habitat if present farmland cannot be used more efficiently through crop rotation, diversity of products, and so on. Efficient land use has barely been explored in America. Methods of farm livestock husbandry must balance and even complement wildlife habitat protection, reclamation, and management. Farmers, corporate farm agencies, real estate developers, wildlife and natural resource agencies, and conservationists have differing values and priorities. But the rights of these different interest groups must be weighed against long-term consequences outlined in environmental impact statements and against the rights of wildlife to life and habitat.*

Legally the land a person owns is his property, but morally speaking such land is only his in *trust*, and he should be the responsible steward for all that lives on it.

It is unfortunate that there are still many people who do not see the connection between animal rights, humane stewardship, and the future of their children. They believe that human problems—war, poverty, pollution, and overpopulation—should be rectified first. Animals and nature come last, if at all, in their scheme of things. But it is less a question of priorities than a realization that the problems of man, animal, and nature are all a consequence of our own actions, attitudes, and values. According rights to animals and bringing them within the framework of our moral concern would do much to improve the human condition.

There is still one case in which the rights of the individual—man or animal, group or species—must be overridden. The greater good of the whole—the biosphere—takes precedence over the rights of individuals and species. This may be regarded as an absolute right. That which supports the greater good of the whole is consonant with the concept that the right to a whole and healthy biosphere is the *absolute right* of all life. All other individual and species rights must be secondary to this one absolute right. The rights of individu-

---

* See Norman Myers, *The Sinking Ark* (New York: Pergamon, 1979).

als and of species are therefore relative and must be defined and respected in relation to the holistic and absolute right of the biosphere. The rights of one species or interest group cannot take precedence over the right to life of other species.

Each species has the right to be protected from extinction, the right to be destroyed humanely, if and when destruction is essential, first, for the greater good of the ecosystem and, secondly, only when it is essential for the greater good of humanity (not of some vested interest group) and there is no possible alternative to killing. The right, for example, to kill whales when there are alternative food sources and occupations for those engaged in such killing is superseded by the right of whales to life. In the absence of alternatives and with increasing competition between animals and people for the same resources, the relative rights of animals will become more and more subordinate to the rights of people for food and living space. But within the framework of the natural laws of ecosystems, such human rights must remain subordinate and relative to the greater rights of all species not to become extinct through human-induced annihilation rather than with natural succession. Also, human rights and related claims and actions must not jeopardize the absolute right of all life to a whole and healthy biosphere.

There is a subtle paradox in the organization of life which has been overlooked by those concerned with the relative value of various species. Organization is in the shape of a pyramid, and as we ascend the food-chain pyramid ecologically, we find a numerical decrease in the numbers of individuals—from trillions of microorganisms to billions of invertebrates and finally to only a few million vertebrates (divided into many herbivores, several omnivores, and a few carnivores). If we were to place a value on species on the basis of numerical rarity, we would opt in favor of those few carnivores at the top of the biotic pyramid. This valuation could be justified further with reference to the evolutionary continuum of increasing brain development. It is a fairly accurate generalization that the species higher on the evolutionary scale are also high up in the biotic pyramid and have more highly evolved brains than lower species.

But though numerically more plentiful and seemingly expendable, the lower species are actually far more important to the integrity of the pyramid of life. In fact, humans and some primates and carnivores are expendable in terms of preserving the well-being of the whole. It is the microorganisms and invertebrates that help in the recycling process of life's nutrients, as it is the lowly plant kingdom that locks in energy for all life from the sunlight. At this level of valuation grasses, worms, nitrogen-fixing bacteria, and dung beetles are more important to the totality of life than man or mountain lion, who are essentially energy-using opportunists.

Without the presence of lower plant and animal organisms, the higher organisms could neither have evolved nor exist today. This is because of the way in which the flow of energy through ecosystems has developed, as a gradient of increasing species consciousness with the concomitant decrease in such species numbers. If there were too many mountain lions or wolves, they would soon become extinct by decimating their prey. Negative feedback systems to regulate the numbers of each species have evolved to preserve the balance and diversity of life within ecosystems.

This exquisite system, with its seemingly paradoxical, yet complementary, qualities of decreasing species numbers as species consciousness increases, is a perfect self-regulating system. Perfect, that is, until the advent of a biologically atypical species: man. He is an omnivore. In terms of population numbers he should be a herbivore, but in terms of brain development he should perhaps be a carnivore. The unique consciousness of the human species, coupled with its prodigious population growth, puts it outside the evolved integrity of the biotic pyramid—an evolutionary experiment in species creation that may be a mistake, a tragic error.

As an atypical species we cannot value life by our own yardstick of intelligence since this is not the sole direction of ecology and evolution. The apparent linear pattern of an ascending biotic pyramid is superimposed upon a nonlinear complex series of cycles and subcycles, of delicate feedback systems within and between micro- and macroscopic organisms, which constitutes the macrocosm of the biosphere, a seamless web of interdependence upon which we and other highly evolved species are wholly dependent.

Man, relatively speaking, is an alien as well as an expendable opportunist species. While we may seem to be a freak of nature or a failure in the biological evolution of consciousness, by the same token the uniqueness of our position necessitates certain new adaptations which are not easily available. A primary one is our need for energy, which, because of our enormous requirements, we can no longer draw from the natural resources of the biotic pyramid without destroying it. We must therefore become independent of nature, or else we will destroy it and ourselves in the process. Today's search for energy sources that are safe and ecologically sound is a symptom not of economic necessity, but of mankind evolving into a new dimension, where technology is a closed and balanced system which neither depletes nor pollutes the biosphere. The future of all life on earth may well hinge on what is done within the next few decades to rectify the biological imbalance between man and nature. Evidence of this imbalance is confirmed by the symptoms today of environmental crises, pollution, desertification, overpopulation, and extinction of more and more nonhuman species. If we turn our backs now on nature, ignoring the plight of the animals and the environment, we will share their fate. The door to the future will be closed, and the continuum, that golden pyramid of life, will be destroyed. We will pass forever through the stargate of extinction, and it will not be in a blaze of glory, for enlightenment then would be too late.

10

The Significance of Suffering

I
n the recorded history of our species, one continuous theme
emerges: violence of man against man and increasingly of man
against nature. Violence against humanity is considered a
crime, but so, too, is violence against nature, although it is rarely
punished.

Violence may be defined here as those actions which do not entail
consideration of the intrinsic rights of others (including nonhuman
creatures and objects of natural creation). There are four major
areas of violence:

1. Individual and personal violence. This includes the ways in
   which people use and abuse their bodies with improper
   diets, drugs, and so on. Their thoughts, actions, and beliefs
   can also cause needless suffering. Intrapunitive (self-
   directed) aggression is particularly prevalent. Individual
   violence may erupt from social influences, particularly dis-
   crimination, repression, privation, frustration, and hopeless-
   ness/helplessness.

2. Social and political violence. Groups of people with common values, needs, or beliefs often seek expression and fulfillment irrespective of the rights of others. A lack of ethical

constraint is particularly evident today in the competitive individualism of capitalism and the repression of individual personal freedom in communism.

3. Nature violence. The individual and collective actions of human beings do not always first take into account the intrinsic rights of nonhuman life forms and natural objects of creation. This form of violence includes killing or causing suffering for nonsurvival purposes; destroying and polluting the environment for short-term gain and profit; violating the laws of nature by such actions as using insecticides indiscriminately or conducting biological warfare; allowing unregulated population growth; participating in biocidal actions such as deforestation or draining swampland; introducing alien species or supporting the proliferation of selected others irrespective of ecological consequences and the rights of other resident species; competing with another species for the same niche or resource when there are other options available to us.

4. Corporate and technological violence. This occurs through the unregulated growth of technology that is purely for profit, and the developing global reach of multinational corporations the actions and motives of which are all too often purely self-serving.

These four major areas of violence in mankind reinforce each other, making reform seem impossible. Only when external pressure from concerned groups is exerted on all four areas of violence at once will there be any reform. But this approach is virtually impossible.

There is one alternative—to change and reeducate the mind and heart of humanity, substituting a science of humanity for a science of technology to control and exploit nature. Obviously this is a tall order, but one place to begin is with an understanding of suffering—the result of violence—and its place in our lives.

Suffering is a major and fundamental concern of Christianity. The powerful symbol of the crucifixion, of Christ suffering for humanity, is a constant reminder of mankind's potential for insensitivity and ignorance. It is difficult to "forgive them for what they do" and to uphold one's faith and adhere to the doctrine of loving one's fellows when one is aware of the extent of animal and human suffering in the world today. There is much unavoidable, "natural" suffering for which no one is to blame, such as an animal's being hunted by a predator or starving in the winter or a mother in labor or a child bereaving the loss of a parent or companion animal. But there is perhaps even more *unnatural*, unnecessary, unjustifiable, and avoidable suffering that man brings upon himself and animals alike. The politics of war and famine have been well documented and even justified by some historians and others as necessary "evils"—the price of freedom, natural regulation of human populations, and so on. Even stronger justifications are given for man-induced, unnatural suffering in animals. Economic necessity, scientific knowledge, human health, and other rationalizations deflect even the most carefully worded (and "unemotional") criticisms by humanitarians, who are often put down as ill-informed idealists and sentimentalists.

ANIMALS IN RESEARCH

Much human sickness and suffering are caused by stress, social problems, anxiety, overcrowding, psychosomatic factors, work pressures, family problems, improper diet (too much alcohol, smoking, and so forth), and pollutants and adulterants in food, water, and air. Why, therefore, make animals suffer in biomedical research when most of our ills are self-induced and only need self-correcting?

To produce symptoms of such ailments in animals experimentally, to test new drugs on them, and to *model* the symptoms are standard practices. But are they an adequate science? Why not instead address the causes, and why especially make animals suffer emotionally in psychological tests designed to "model" human emotional problems? For example, Catherine Roberts, in her analysis and critique of the scientific conscience, has the following to say about the prolonged social deprivation studies to which H. Harlow subjected rhesus monkeys in order to understand the basis of love and attachment in man:

> Harlow has been criticized recently for transferring concepts from the field of human psychology to the field of animal behavior because in his experiments the "love or affection" of the infant monkeys for the surrogate mothers could be better explained as imprinting. I believe that criticism of the rhesus experiments should rest on a deeper foundation than ethology: to conduct a scientific investigation of the emotional responses of acutely distressed laboratory animals and call it a "contact with the nature of love" reveals a profound unawareness of the limitations of science. And what is more important in the present context, it provides at the same time an admirable illustration of the basic outlook of modern secular and scientific humanism.

She goes on to observe:

> Modern scientists, with the approbation of modern humanists, are subjecting these animals, in highly artificial environments, to extreme mental torture in the proud delusion that they are thereby doing all in their power to help their fellow men. That these experiments are conducted to attain a knowledge of love makes them not only ludicrous but revealing as well. For in the final analysis they reveal a grave lack of understanding of the subject that is believed to be under investigation.

Since the publication of her critique, even more extreme forms of deprivation have been instigated on primates, and at this time animal psychologists have developed a new "model" of human depression, dubbed "learned helplessness," which develops in dogs and rodents subjected to inescapable shock, drowning, or other acute psychological stress.

Roberts questions the values of humanists who accept such research by stating:

> To condemn the rhesus experiments for what they are—odious examples of cruelty to animals that degrade the humanness of those

who designed and perpetrated them—obviously does not appeal to modern humanists. Besides opposing their aims, condemnation would constitute a barrier to free inquiry and the attainment of truth. Humanists are, of course, no more insensitive to animal suffering than anyone else and probably much more sensitive than most. They are also awake to the dangers of the misuse of applied science and technology. But they cannot rationally object to an experimental science that depends upon animal suffering for its results when they believe that such results will augment human health, happiness, and survival. For these ends, they maintain, are our supreme ends. Secular and scientific humanists, it must be remembered, have no standard of morality whatsoever except the rational.

A much more stringent ethic is needed to constrain and guide the wholesale use of animals for research, educational, and commercial purposes. Animals should not be subjected to physical or psychological suffering unless the results promise to alleviate a comparable or greater (but never a lesser) suffering in humans or other animals. To subject animals to suffering for knowledge's sake (in which there is no conceivable clinical application) or to develop, *post hoc*, an animal "model" of a human emotional disorder is ethically reprehensible. If it is a high-fidelity model, presumably the animal is suffering much as a human being would. Yet in spite of the psychologists' claims to relevance of their animal models, they avoid ethical responsibility by discounting all concerns as being ill-informed and anthropocentric. They remain secure in the consensus of their inhumane and pseudoscientific cult. Such atrocities should be questioned since these kinds of animal experimentation are a travesty of scientific freedom and a blight on the biomedical establishment.

From a psychohistorical perspective, the way in which society (and science) regard and treat living creatures and nature is, to a disturbing degree, closely related to the self-induced afflictions of the human body and spirit and of man, society, and the environment. Thus, without a radical transformation of values, it is unlikely that science and technology will enable us to heal ourselves and the biosphere. The longer we continue to exploit nature and to subject animals to unnecessary suffering and privation, the farther we will be away from the point at which we may begin to harmonize with nature and assume the awesome responsibility for our own continued evolution.

Roberts affirms this view by observing:

> My own opinion is that the further advancement of science—and particularly, biology—if it continues to be as automatic, mindless, and heartless as modern scientism demands, will not accelerate human evolutionary progress but retard it. For the biologist's ultimate goal cannot be different from that of any other human being: to realize his human potential. And ... neither moral apathy nor the objective and automatic nature of current scientific activity offers much promise in the attainment of this end. ...

SCIENTIFIC VALUES AND ANIMAL SUFFERING

What are the values and tenets of science? Both Michael Polanyi, in his book *Personal Knowledge,* and Catherine Roberts, in her book *The Scientific Conscience,* contend that the responsible scientist's attainment of knowledge is based on a union of objectivity with personal motives. While the personal motives may range from pure curiosity to the desire for status or tenure, the motives displayed to the public are essentially altruistic. One accumulates knowledge for the present or future benefit of society or, more specifically, conducts research on animals in order to improve human or animal health and reduce human or animal suffering and disease, as the case may be.

Roberts terms the latter objective humaneness, which justifies suffering (of research animals) for the greater good, as distinct from the subjective humaneness of modern society, a society which needs the National Society for Medical Research in the United States and the Research Defence Society in the United Kingdom to convince it that scientists make animals suffer only when it is unavoidable (because they can find or think of no alternatives) and justifiable or necessary on the grounds of objective humaneness. Good public relations are essential for the contribution of public (tax) support via government grants.

But opposition between, as well as polarization within, the two idealistic camps of objective and subjective humaneness continues. Philosophers and others are adding a new dimension of *animal rights* to these conflicting ideologies: The arete, or supreme creative perfection of any living organism, and its intrinsic nature and worth are quasi-subjective dimensions which objective humaneness rarely addresses and which subjective humaneness often overlooks in the zeal of antivivisectionist judgments of scientists as sadistic Frankensteins.

While it is too early to evaluate or prognosticate the impact of the animal rights movement, it is appropriate to reflect upon the ideological differences between objective and subjective humaneness. How accurate is Catherine Roberts in her pronouncement that "present progress in biological and medical research is often dependent upon means which are retarding the realization of human potentialities and thereby doing mankind more harm than good"?

A major concern that more educators, veterinarians, and animal welfarists are beginning to voice is that many students and scientists alike have little or no formal training in laboratory animal science, behavior, and basic principles of surgery and postoperative care. Animals are often selected for a project on the basis of habit or convenience rather than upon consideration of the three Rs of ethical responsibility in animal research—*replacement, refinement,* and *reduction* (see page 132). Only too often ethical concerns are excluded from the scientist's credo that any means (i.e., unavoidable animal suffering) is justifiable if the goal is for the good of humanity.

Many scientists and laboratory animal veterinarians are now beginning to question this credo. The "divine right" of scientists is being challenged not by ill-informed subjective humanitarians but by members of the scientific community itself.

What is needed is a more detailed analysis of the varieties of human suffering with a view to define which can best be rectified without having to create animal models and to subject animals to all manner of pain, privation, sickness, fear, anxiety, and so on.

Scientists and others might also consider some of the basic principles of Christian and Buddhist thought vis-à-vis the meaning and purpose of suffering and the humanistic/spiritual ways of alleviating many forms of human suffering. Where indeed do *love, compassion* and *empathy* fit today in the research laboratory and in our highly sophisticated medical technology? These are the most potent means of alleviating many forms of human (and animal) suffering and are the essence of subjective humaneness. If they continue to be ignored in the education of doctors and biomedical scientists, Catherine Roberts will be right: Science will retard the realization of human potentialities and thereby do mankind more harm than good.

OBJECTIVITY AND EMPATHY

Subjective humaneness is only too often discounted by "objectivists" on the grounds that one is being emotional. A philosopher friend of mine recently gave a very moving lecture on the question of animal rights and was criticized by his colleagues (all of whom read their papers like robots) for being too emotional. Why do scientists, academics, and others discount emotionality? Because it is subhuman or perhaps because it can bias one's objectivity? Yet objectivists are not without motives, bias, or vested interest, and if they were purely objective, they would actually do nothing but simply observe.

As animal instincts are often demeaned, so, too, in our Western culture human emotions are looked down upon. Educationally this can be crippling since man is not a robot or biocomputer. Worse perhaps, the discounting of emotions in the quest for scientific objectivity can inhibit empathy and responsible compassion toward experimental animals. Student initiates may protest or question the ethics of various classroom exercises on living animals (which are outlawed in both Sweden and the United Kingdom), but eventually most succumb to their academic conditioning and become desensitized. This is perhaps the major concern that Roberts does not quite grasp when she raises the question that science may retard the development of human potentialities.

Mary Midgley emphasizes that our emotionality is part of our nature and that in order to be whole within ourselves and to be able to relate with the rest of nature, we must preserve this wholeness. She states:

> We cannot dismiss our emotions and the rest of our nonintellectual nature, along with the body and the earth it is fitted for, as alien, contingent stuff. We have somehow to operate as a whole, to preserve the continuity of our being.
>
> This means acknowledging our kinship with the rest of the biosphere. If we do not feel perfectly at home here, that may after all have something to do with the way in which we have treated the place. Any home can be made uninhabitable. Our culture has too often talked in terms of conquering nature.

Professor Midgley gives another insight into the reasons behind anthropomorphism—namely, it is part of a general misperception of others (be they animals or people) and a lack of understanding wherein a person projects feelings, thoughts, motives, and so forth onto the other. So we are often guilty of being paedomorphic, gerontomorphic, anthropomorphic, andromorphic, and so on! While it is impossible to know what another animal or person is feeling, sensing, or thinking, we guess with accuracy that improves with experience on the basis of overt behavior and awareness of context and probability. We even make mistakes in identifying our own motives and feeling. Presumably the more "together" a person is in terms of being cognizant of these internal psychological processes, the more "whole" he or she will be and the more effective in interpersonal and interspecies relationships. The less cognizant or "whole," the more the person is likely to project his own subjective state upon others and to see others, as psychologist Abraham Maslow details, in a mode of "dependency" cognition, of satisfying or fulfilling one's positive or negative expectations, needs, and so on.

SUFFERING, SURVIVAL, AND THE EVOLUTION OF ALTRUISM

As has been all too apparent in the preceding chapters, all sentient life has the capacity to suffer physically and, at higher levels of brain development, to suffer psychologically as well. The capacity to suffer increases as mental and social complexity increases. Is there a biological and social value or a natural purpose of suffering, and if there is, should we still attempt to reduce the burden of suffering?

Suffering motivates the individual to attempt to change or avoid stressful stimuli, both physiological and psychological. Given this definition, suffering is in the best interests of the individual and is actually essential for survival. A creature not responding to painful stimuli such as extreme cold or physical injury would not live long. Pain perception and the capacity to suffer can therefore help protect the animal from its physical and social environment. This is why a veterinarian will sometimes not give an analgesic to an animal that is lame because it might cause itself further injury if it felt little or no pain. (Those who give drugs such as "bute" to make lame horses able to race should be disbarred from the veterinary profession.)

As the individual evolves into a more socially dependent species, a significant change occurs in the capacity to suffer. Through identification with kin as a result of early socializing attachment, suffering can be both personal and transpersonal. The individual can vicariously experience or identify with the suffering of another. It empathizes. This is expressed as altruism and is common in many social species of animals. Specific signals, such as the care-soliciting whimpers of young animals, are given by the one in distress to evoke care-giving behavior in another of its kind. Parent-infant behavior sets the patterns for later exchanges. The longer the period of infant dependence, the greater will be this capacity for transpersonal suffering, empathy, and altruism. Such an evolved phenomenon is a highly advantageous survival strategy not only for the individual but for the group or species as a whole. (It may also be used to make another feel guilty and lead to a number of pathologies that parents give to their emotionally bound children.)

The next evolutionary stage in the capacity to suffer is empathy between species. Here sensitivity extends beyond the boundaries of the individual's social group and species to include various other sentient species. This may be first initiated through early socialization as when two different species are raised together or share the same niche or habitat, either naturally or under conditions of domestication. Interspecies empathy may also occur between species that are close on the evolutionary ladder and share similarities in emotional reactions and body and other communication signals and displays.

Altruism or mutual support between species is again of survival value. Only in the human species has this altruism the additional dimension of nonreciprocity. Concern for the welfare and suffering of other sentient creatures (especially those under human dominion or those affected directly or indirectly by human activities) is evolving independent of any reciprocal response from those species that engender our concern. Altruistic concern is not wholly unselfish, for our future survival is connected to the survival of other species and their contribution to a diverse, balanced, whole, and healthy biosphere. Since all living creatures are dependent on whole and healthy ecosystems, our concern should also embrace the well-being of the biosphere—the trees, lakes, oceans, mountains, air, water, and so on.

This newly evolving form of transpersonal altruism is associated with humane stewardship and distinct from human-centered altruism, which equates human survival with economic necessity even at the expense of other species' survival. Under human-centered altruism self-serving actions take precedence over the rights of others. Such a utilitarian view is not compatible with humane ethics since it fosters and condones competitive individualism rather than transpersonal altruism.

Where there is life there is one form of suffering or another. It is an inescapable part of life, and for mankind, greater empathy and sensitivity toward the suffering of others mean being better parents, citizens, healers, husbanders of domestic animals, and stewards of wild creatures. To be insensitive to suffering is unnatural and an unhealthy obstacle to personal fulfillment, survival, and evolution. Insensitivity may be a defense mechanism to avoid being hurt or feeling uncomfortable. Because suffering is unavoidable, some may even consider it justified. Such rationalizations again serve to eliminate the burden of responsibility and empathy for another being.

Defenses and rationalizations are not wholly unnatural since no one likes to suffer even vicariously. But in the final analysis, such self-protective reactions are not in the best interests of the individual or of life in general, for suffering can be reduced only when it is shared and experienced through empathy. Responsible, compassionate intervention may then be assured.

Passive acceptance of one's own or of another's suffering is as bad as denial or defensive rationalizations. The psychoanalyst Viktor E. Frankl was an inmate at a Nazi concentration camp, where he observed that acceptance of one's lot led only to apathy and physical or spiritual death. On the other hand, suffering prevents apathy; one who cannot suffer is dead. Similarly, one who cannot empathize with the suffering of others is also dead. Says Frankl: "Only under the hammer blows of fate, in the white heat of suffering, does life gain shape and form," but he is careful to point out that work is also important for mental health. Gandhi, too, urged that the poor be given not food, but work, since without work, life has little content or meaning. Welfare without gainful employment is a quick way to destroy humanity. But unremitting suffering, such as hunger, can aggravate a lack of content in life, leading to frustration, alienation, then, finally, apathy and psychic death. Any method used to reduce or avoid suffering must address its causes, not merely alleviate the symptoms. Welfare, drugs, escapist distractions, and so on negate the positive aspects of suffering as a personal and social stimulus for reform.

As previously stated, all suffering is connected. The humane movement's concern to alleviate suffering in animals cannot ignore other areas of human-induced suffering. For example, those who are indifferent actually support systems of destruction and suffering through their alienation and insensitivity. There are also those who are hypnotized by false values into a state of conformist complacency with material comfort and with the status quo which accepts all suffering as unavoidable—the price of progress.

The Indian philosopher-psychologist Jiddu Krishnamurti states: "Suffering is but intense clarity of thoughts and feelings which makes you see things as they are." The way to liberation from suffering, therefore, lies in suffering itself through empathy (a Buddhist as well as a Christian view). The Buddha, in his infinite wisdom, saw all life as suffering, and if there was none, there would be death. Empathetically felt suffering of others and the fellowship of suffering through compassion he saw as the golden key to human liberation and world peace. Suffering activates empathy and responsible compassion, but it may be transcended by love and understanding. While there is still suffering in the world, there is still insufficient love and understanding. Altruistic actions must be constrained within a framework of responsibility so as to avoid causing more extensive suffering by upsetting the natural ecological order of all life on earth. The alleviation of all human suffering may not be compatible with ecological harmony and the rights of nonhumans to life.

Today's mobile society destroys a sense of community, of "spirit of place," and concern for the ecological well-being of one's environs. People feel alienated and rootless and void of altruistic motivation. What we are left with is the more restricted concern for ourselves and our families. With the breakdown of the community the survival of the fittest quickly replaces responsible cooperation and reciprocal altruism. Natural controls over antisocial behavior, especially crime and violence, which have evolved over epochs, are weakened. Legislation and law enforcement are not substitutes for reciprocal altruism and responsible community action.

There is a continuum in the development of ethics and of responsible altruism from the person (integrated mind and body), the family, and the community (integrated individuals) and different communities and nations (the integrated nation and world). As a species we seem to be in a transitional phase in our evolution from the era of local or national community spirit and the new age of a global community spirit, which David Spangler discusses in *Towards a Planetary Vision*. Many of the societal ills of today are symptoms of social change and transition. Suffering and altruism are both the consequences and the directives for our own continued evolution.

11
Have Religions Failed?

T he attitudes that people have toward animals, and nature in general, stem not only from utilitarian and other values but also from deeper cultural and religious traditions. Although a reverence for all life may be part of the religious philosophy, it is often lacking in everyday relationships with animals, both domesticated and wild. The utilitarian principle—exploiting animals to satisfy one form of human need or another—generally overrides higher moral and ethical principles. Sometimes religious belief or superstition may even stand in the way of ethical responsibility. For example, the Hindus refuse to kill certain animals even when one may be suffering. Reverence for all life can therefore lead to unnecessary suffering in which responsible action (mercy killing) is considered unethical or sacrilegious. There are paradoxes, therefore, between religious beliefs and the way in which people treat animals (as well as each other).

A comparative study of the major world religions reveals two common omissions in the theology of creation and man's relationships with man, nature, and God. Yet evolution and ecology are the two essential threads which unite all, both the Creator and the created, in time and space. The community of living things in a given place was certainly known by all peoples, but instead of being a starting point for responsible action and stewardship, it became

186

something to be exploited under man's God-given dominion. Evolution is also absent in most religions. Without adequate knowledge of man's biological kinship with all life, the only foundation for the biospiritual ethic of reverence for all life was a shared creator. But this foundation was easily destroyed by the utilitarian principle and the notion of man's God-given supremacy over all. With man's lacking any understanding of evolution and ecology, there was little reason for concern over life other than human life. An anthropocentric and egocentric world view was inevitable. Religions of the past failed to unify man and animal, culture and nature, in spite of the enlightened and often humane teachings of their founders.

Hinduism comes closer to a biospiritual ethic—reverence for life—than other religions in many ways. The Hindu gods Vishnu, Brahma, and Shiva represent the forces of preservation and continuity of life, creation, and destruction. These are the rudiments of an ecological/evolutionary theology. Many nature gods (such as the snake, provider of good crops) are also worshiped in Hinduism, and animistic beliefs are prevalent. In their religious myths, both men and gods depend upon animals as allies—Vishnu is depicted with a snake, Shiva with a bull. The concept of Karma—of cause and effect—also comes close to the scientific view of ecology—of interrelated worlds of cause, effect, and relationship.

Buddha later unified Hinduism into a more existential philosophy, teaching ethical responsibility and the Middle Path of right thought and action as distinct from the "otherworldly" reality-negating religions of the day. In India, however, Buddhism was eventually reassimilated into Hinduism. Where Buddhism exists today, it does little to promote active compassion for animal and human suffering and instead promulgates passive detachment and noninvolvement from this (illusory) world reality. It does, however, still contain the seeds for responsible stewardship; they have yet to find the fertile soil.

Dr. Albert Schweitzer summarized the Buddhist view as follows:

> Buddha's ethic of compassion is, however, incomplete. It is limited by world- and life-negation. Compassion consists in the con-

stant realization of the fact that all creatures are continually subject to suffering. It is an intellectual sympathy rather than an immediate compassion of the heart which carries within itself the
impulse to help. That man, in the thought of Buddha, the preacher
of compassion, should be concerned only with his own salvation
and not with that of all creatures, is a weakness in his teaching.

I would not entirely agree with Schweitzer's analysis; the fault is
more in the present-day interpretations of Buddhist philosophy than
with the original teachings of the Buddha, as emphasized by Professor F. S. C. Northrop and the Reverend J. Austin.

Jainism, an offshoot of Hinduism, is concerned with mankind's
having to kill other living creatures in order to survive. Jains avoid
killing whenever possible, practicing vegetarianism and even avoiding agricultural practices since tilling the soil might cause the death
of small creatures. Monks wear masks to avoid accidentally inhaling
some small insect and killing it. For the same reason Jains also refuse
to drink unfiltered water. Without others to destroy the jungle and
prepare the land for crops, needless to say, the Jains could not survive, and their religion is clearly impractical. As such, it does not
fully resolve the spiritual conflict and biological fact of man's having to kill in order to survive.

Ahimsa is the principle of nonviolent action. It is one of the most
meaningful principles of human conduct in relation to others—animals as well as people. As defined and demonstrated by Mahatma
Gandhi, this important ethic is valid not only for political actions
but for man's actions toward all living creatures. One day, in humanely destroying a hopelessly sick calf in his ashram, Gandhi violated the creed of the Hindus which states that no man must kill a
cow since it is held to be sacred. Fully aware of this and knowing
that he would be vehemently ridiculed, he still demonstrated responsible action through mercy killing. Ahimsa, he taught, is
responsible reverence for life, as distinct from the blind, passive reverence that comes from religious belief or sentimentalism and leads
one to do nothing about another's suffering.

In spite of the power of ahimsa in Hindusim, which is the most
common religion in India, Gandhi once stated: "I hardly think the

fate of animals is so sad in any other country in the world as it is in our own poor India." Simply not killing or hurting by following ahimsa to the letter does not fulfill the need for responsible action and compassion. Only when ahimsa is freed from its original principle of nonactivity does it become a commandment to exercise full compassion. Commenting on Gandhi's refined definition, Schweitzer observed: "It is one of the most important of Gandhi's acts that he compels Indian ethics to come to grips with reality."

Miss Crystal Rogers, longtime director of the Animals' Friend, a humane shelter in New Delhi, summarizes the Indian situation succinctly: "While ahimsa is preached, people are generally apathetic or indifferent towards animals. They often seem to lack the ability to empathize. Something may be missing in childhood education: it is a common sight to see children beating animals with sticks or throwing rocks at them."

Ahimsa is widely preached but practiced in a detached way without full compassion and, therefore, answers only part of the problem of man's relationship with nature. Apathy and indifference to another's suffering (be it animal or man) and the inability to empathize, as discussed earlier, may be nothing more than an adaptive mechanism to protect the psyche from an environment suffused with suffering and the basic problems of survival. The notion of Karma can contribute to this indifference of another's suffering. To be poor, starving, or sick is one's burden, one's fate which is to be borne for this lifetime. If one is devout, there is always the hope of reincarnation on a higher plane the next time around. Personal suffering is endured, and the suffering of others is accepted as natural and unavoidably predetermined. One's fate is not, however, an act of the gods, and it is doubtful if divine intervention can free a man from his personal Karma without an act of will, although people may believe the contrary.

Perhaps because of this, helping others and active compassion are rare in many societies. Taking full responsibility for one's actions, condition, and future is needed, and the social freedom and mobility to transcend Karma can come in countries like India only when the caste system is abolished.

While Western cultures may show a more responsible attitude toward animals, the utilitarian principle often overrides compassion and reverence for life. As I've discussed in previous chapters, nature is viewed as a resource, to be managed and exploited as one chooses. Certainly responsible management is superior to the wholesale destruction of natural habitats occurring in many third-world countries. But management and exploitation still jeopardize wilderness areas. As natural, untouched ecosystems they should be preserved in their pristine state, but in the face of shortsighted national need for raw materials and fossil fuels, their future is far from optimistic.

According to Professor G. M. Teutsch, in the ancient cultures of Egypt, India, and Judea there was a widespread belief in reincarnation or in the transmigration of souls based on a kinship of all living things. This belief demanded humane treatment of animals and slaves and equal status for women. Greek thought was influenced for a long time by the ancient beliefs. Pythagoras in the fifth century B.C. founded a school of Orphic thought, based upon the doctrine of the migration and kinship of souls, which continued right into the fourth century B.C. It was not until the Greco-Roman transition that mankind's relationships and ethical responsibilities toward animals changed. Under Roman law and its class system, slaves, noncitizens, sons, daughters, wives, and animals had no rights. Gradually most people came to acquire legal rights, but animals never did. These past events undoubtedly influenced the contemporary anthropocentric view which gives man dominion over the natural world and ignores the many biblical references to our kinship with all life. (See Paul's Epistle to the Romans, which proclaims that the glory of God's kingdom shall include all creatures.)

It is from the Judeo-Christian misinterpretation of the Scriptures concerning man's dominion over all living things and his God-given freedom to subjugate nature that the utilitarian principle gains acceptance. Dominion is regarded as dominance over all to do as one wishes, rather than as responsible stewardship. Viewing wildlife as a resource for the sole use and benefit of man is a narrow, egocentric assumption, far removed from an attitude of reverence for life and careful stewardship. We progress blindly and arrogantly, using natural resources not to satisfy basic survival needs, but to fuel continuing growth (euphemistically termed progress) and needless consumption. Western man's narrow, self-centered world view puts him outside the realities of life. However, unlike the world-negating detachment of Hinduism which leads to passive indifference, Western man's detachment is far more actively destructive.

Professor Lynn White makes the following statement: "Christianity is the most anthropocentric religion the world has seen. . . . Man shares, in great measure, God's transcendance of nature. Christianity not only established a dualism of man and nature but also insisted that it is God's will that man exploit nature for his proper ends." Philosophers such as Descartes supported this Judeo-Christian teleology by insisting on man and animal as completely separate. Animals were regarded as soulless mechanisms, unconscious, unfeeling automatons existing solely for man's use.

Was nature made nonsacred by Christianity so that we may exploit it without guilt or remorse? It can still be sacred or resanctified and used for the greater good. God and nature need not be separated for our own convenience and to allay our guilt and responsibility.

Our ancestral nomadic pastoralists shared nature resources with other creatures and had man-, nature-, and God-inclusive religions. Later agrarians, with hubristic man-God-centered religions, excluded nature from their moral and mythical, social and mystical activities. These activities became impoverished with humanocentrism and self-deification. (As Dolores La Chapelle describes, early Christians turned the paganists' Pan into the "devil" and turned their priests and priestesses into warlocks and witches.)

If, in this book, I give the impression that I believe that man is God or is to become God, please do not misinterpret this as hubris. It is hubris if the God in question is seen as having "created all things for man's sake" (to quote Calvin). It is not hubris if the God is seen in the Old Testament and pagan way of Maimonides, the Orthodox Jewish philosopher, who observed: "It should not be believed that all beings exist for the sake of the existence of man. On the contrary, all the other beings too, have been intended for their own sakes and not for the sake of something else." The distinctions between a man and nature/God oneness and a man and God oneness which excludes nature on utilitarian grounds are obvious.

"God"-given dominion (of man over nature) not only absolved us but sanctified those actions which under pagan law would be violations of all that which is sacred. John Passmore emphasizes that in Genesis and the rest of the Old Testament it is said that man is or has the right to be master of earth, but that the world exists to glorify God rather than to serve man. Later Greek and Christian theology perverted this into anthropocentric dominionism and a *man-centered* rather than *man-nature-embracing theology.*

In spite of Darwin's evolutionary theory proving man's relatedness to other animals, dualism of man and nature persists in Western thought today. It rationalizes indifference and even cruelty to animals. The utilitarian principle is another justification and stems from the Judeo-Christian belief in dominionism.*

Yet freed from rationalizations, Christianity and Western science contain the essential spiritual and biological elements from which a biospiritual ethic may be formulated. Science teaches us that biologically we are kin with animals—related through evolution and dependence on nature. Christianity teaches that spiritually both man and animal are part of the same creative process. Each living thing is to be revered as part of creation and therefore as a part of the Creator (God), implying that all life is divine. (Righteous people, for example, are urged to show concern for the lives of their animals [Proverbs 12:10].) This belief, together with the evolutionary fact of man's kinship with all creatures, makes it impossible to view wildlife as nothing more than a resource for man's exclusive use.

A negative aspect of evolutionary theory is that it can be interpreted as evidence of the superiority of species, thus giving support to man's supremacy. The dichotomy between man and nature is increased. Schweitzer counters this by arguing:

> What we are doing, when we establish hard and fast gradations in value between living organisms, [is] but judging them in relation to ourselves, by whether they seem to stand closer to us or farther from us. This is a wholly subjective standard. How can we know

* Utilitarian justifications and dominionism also contaminate science and biomedical research, where animal suffering is often accepted as an unavoidable necessity for the well-being of humanity.

what importance other living organisms have in themselves and in terms of the universe? The utilitarian principle where animals are valued in terms of a resource of usefulness to man strengthens further man's separateness from other living things.

Apart from creation, there are other bases for a Judeo-Christian reverence for life. Some passages in the Bible which have been ignored teach that all life is sacred. For example, this beautiful passage from Ecclesiastes (3:18–21):

> I said in my heart with regard to the sons of men that God is testing them to show them they are but beasts. For the fate of the sons of men and the fate of the beasts is the same: as one dies, so the other. They all have the same breath, and man has no advantage over the beast; for all is vanity. All go to one place; all are from the dust, and all turn to dust again. Who knows whether the spirit of man goes upward and the spirit of the beast goes down to earth?

René Dubos urges the development of a "theology of the earth" and states:

> The biblical injunction that man was put in the Garden of Eden to "dress it and keep it" [Genesis 2:15] is an early warning that we are responsible for our environment. To strive for environmental quality must be considered as an eleventh commandment, concerned of course with the external world, but also encompassing the quality of life. An ethical attitude in the scientific study of nature readily leads to a theology of the earth.

But now in the West a new religion—namely, the science of technological progress—is directing and dictating man's attitudes and values. And as we've seen, technology now threatens not only the biosphere but also man's future. Says Dr. Barry Commoner in *The Closing Circle*:

> We have become accustomed to think of separate, singular events, each dependent upon a unique, singular cause. But in the ecosphere every effect is also a cause. . . . Such ecological cycles are hard to fit into human experience in the age of technology. . . . We

have broken out of the circle of life, converting its endless cycles into man-made linear events.

These events, destructive as they are, tend to be justified by human needs and ideals of progress and growth.

The biospiritual ethic of a reverence for all life puts man back in touch with the reality of nature and its cycles. Man's life gains deeper significance. In Schweitzer's words:

> Standing as he does with every other creature, under the law of the will-to-live, with its inner inconsistency, the human being finds himself again and again in the position of being able to preserve his own life and life in general only at the cost of other life. If he is moved by the ethics of reverence for life, he injures or destroys life only under the compulsion of a necessity which he cannot escape, never from thoughtlessness. If he is a free man, he seeks, so far as he has the opportunity, to taste the blessedness of being able to sustain life and of protecting it from pain and annihilation.

He also observes:

> Life outside a person is an extension of the life within him. This compels him to be part of it and accept responsibility for all creatures great and small. Life becomes harder when we live for others, but it also becomes richer and happier.

The attitude of early American Indians toward nature is in sharp contrast with that of their "civilized" conquerors. In 1855 Chief Seathl (Seattle) of the Duwamish tribe in the state of Washington replied to the government's proposal to purchase the tribe's land. His letter to President Franklin Pierce clearly illustrates the views of the "savage" in relation to nature:

> If I decide to accept, I will make one condition. The White man must treat the beasts of this land as his brothers. I am a savage and I do not understand any other way. . . . What is man without beasts? If all the beasts were gone, men would die from great loneliness of spirit, for whatever happens to the beasts also happens to the man. All things are connected. Whatever befalls the earth befalls the son of the earth.

The philosophical and religious views of Amerindians contain certain elements not unlike those of Taoism and Zen Buddhism. Philosophical rather than religious paths, Taoism and Zen Buddhism are undoubtedly closer to a biospiritual world view than any contemporary religion. They merge the objective and the subjective, the "I" and the "me," the observer and the observed, the "I" and the "thou." Unlike Western thought, as D. T. Suzuki and Alan Watts describe, the Taoist and Zen world view is nondualistic. Opposites—such as good and evil, light and dark, life and death—do not contradict but are interdependent, complementary parts of one whole. Life is not personal or impersonal but *trans*personal. One experiences events in *relationship*. This interdependence of all things places Zen in the same scientific framework as ecology, in which the organism and the environment are inseparable.

The artificial Western split between the material (objective, concrete) and the spiritual (subjective, intangible) is resolved in Zen, which unites these polarities and therefore inevitably helps unite man with nature as one. Awareness of this state is called satori, or awakening to man's original and ultimate inseparable union with all of life. The world is seen as a field of patterned activity in which nothing can be separated from the whole or valued more or less than any other thing. This is no mystical state or "supreme" condition, but rather, as Andrew Weil sees it, the normal, integrated, healthy condition of human consciousness. Man is freed from the hypnosis of "otherworldly" religions, egocentric and dualistic perceptions, and materialistic values and dependencies.

The Brihardaranyaka, an ancient Indian manuscript, states: "The inorganic is life that sleeps, the plant is life that feels, the animal is life that knows and man is life that knows that it knows." Man differs qualitatively, but not absolutely. It is a difference only in degree along an unbroken continuum. Our bodies contain the mineral elements of primordial rocks; our very cells share the same historically evolved components as those of grasses and trees, as Lewis Thomas describes in *Lives of a Cell*, and our brains contain the basic neural core of reptile, bird, and fellow mammal.

Zen Buddhism and Taoism are keys to an ecology of the mind in which self and other are united. Since one is a part of all life, to demean or destroy anything of life is to demean or destroy oneself. This change in consciousness means a change in man's relationship with man and nature. Alan Watts states this simply: "What is needed is not a new kind of technique but a new kind of man, for, as an old Taoist text says 'When the wrong man uses the right means, the right means work the wrong way.'"

The teachings of Lao Tzu in the *Tao Te Ching* have great relevance to understanding the deeper significance of conservation, which is the preservation of Tao, of order and balance between such complementary, yet opposing forces as life and death, prey and predator, ecological cycles of succession, degradation and regeneration, and so on. Self-regulation is an intrinsic aspect of natural systems. This is the unmanifest reality, that aspect of Tao which science has yet to grasp. Lao Tzu states: "Where Tao is, equilibrium is." Taoism's emphasis on nonaction, nonintervention is a guiding philosophy for contemporary environmental concerns. "The wise man lets things develop in their natural way and does not venture to act." But let it not lead us to abandon our responsibilities of responsible stewardship, of self-dominion, and the most careful monitoring of our impact upon the biosphere. Tao must be restored and preserved.

Evolution is now in our own hands, as is the future of the biosphere. I do not intend to advocate a return to or adoption of mysticism, primitivism, or authoritarianism. There is no single solution or simple formula; personal panaceas are idealistic and illusory. The reality that we all must face is that while we have biological freedom, we must have responsibility and accountability. As consciousness evolves, so do conscience and the ethical sensitivity and sensibility to constrain and guide human action toward the greater good of all life on earth.

12

Education to Empathy and Communion

The need for a basic change in human consciousness has been the recurrent theme of this book. We know only too well that the ways of past generations spell disaster for future generations. The most effective way of bringing about change is through the children of today, through enlightened education. Yet too often class texts tell the teacher to use a "scientific approach" to instruct children about the ways of animals. Such an approach is exclusively objective and mechanistic. It teaches *how* an animal functions and *what* it is made of but usually neglects *who* the animal is and *why* it exists. The identity of the animal deals with its evolution and relationships with its own and other species. Why it exists is the complex and discomforting question "Why are there frogs, dogs, bugs, birds . . . ?" Such a question is too often left unanswered, yet it deals with some very fundamental aspects of life and creation. These concerns are germane to the young student's emerging awareness of self in relation to the world and the significance of his or her existence. An early encounter with the *purpose* of being also opens up the ecological perspective. The child learns why the frog, dog, bug, or bird has come to be what it is and to occupy a particular place or niche in the "seamless web" of life.

Learning about form and function is balanced by learning also about individual identity, purpose, and relationships. This balance prevents the child from adopting the Cartesian attitude toward animals, viewing them as unfeeling machines. But asking a balanced set of how, what, who, and why questions is only the beginning. The next level of involvement entails a degree of subjectivity, drawing upon and developing the child's empathy and imagination. Long a part of the arts and humanities, subjectivity has not as yet been integrated into biology and the other sciences. Even when imagery, mythos, and subjectivity are allowed to develop early in childhood, they are usually supplanted by more "mature" classroom activities as the child grows up. These are characteristically rational, objective, scientific, and logos-oriented. In the long run, the child may suffer a permanent impairment of the powers of imagination which include subjective rapport and empathy.

There are innumerable learning experiences which help develop the subjective side of the child's consciousness and potential. In many of them a dog or other suitable animal becomes a focus and *catalyst*. In fact, animals, in the right contexts, can be a teacher's best ally, especially in the younger grades. Most young chidren like animals, but not all enjoy schoolwork. They can be motivated to learn when an animal is the focus for reading, creative writing, art, mathematics, history, and so on.

Animals will benefit from their role in the classroom. As children mature, they tend to become more and more influenced by their peers, but between five and eight years of age—the critical period—the child is most open and receptive. There is a recognized correlation between antisocial behavior in adults and indifference or cruelty toward animals earlier in life. Without early, humane contact with animals, the child's later peer relationships may suffer.

The classroom exercises listed below exemplify the ways in which animals can be incorporated into schoolwork. Through them cognitive and social skills can be demonstrated and developed in the students.

1. IDENTIFICATION WITH THE ANIMAL THROUGH A DIRECTED FANTASY GAME. Students relax with eyes closed as the teacher tells them a story about a specific animal. Each lis-

tener imagines that he or she is that animal. The teacher emphasizes sensory experiences—touch, smell, hearing, and so on—and emotional ones as appropriate. This can be reinforced with a creative writing assignment.

2. OBSERVATION. For this, one or more living animals are needed. Gerbils, hamsters, or mice are the usual classroom animals. After careful observation of the animal's behavior, the child *mimics* its actions and sounds in detail. Two or more students interact together (say, like gerbils) and attempt to communicate with each other, using the animal's signals only. Making a clay model of the animal or drawing it will also increase the powers of observation.

3. EMPATHY. Discuss an animal's behavior in different contexts. Like humans, the animal shows fear, anxiety, anger, joy, depression, excitement, and playfulness. Also like humans, some animals, especially cats and dogs, may need to be disciplined for their own good. Realizing this similarity can establish the essential bridge of empathy between child and animal. The class can also discuss what animals do and do not like and how this compares to their own likes and dislikes. They will find a host of similarities. Sensitivity and empathy may be enhanced further by designating suitable environments and using simple equipment to give the child the physical sensory experience of being in the animal's world. A darkened quiet room for listening to recorded whale sounds will simulate the ocean; closing eyes and using only touch will approximate the sensory experience of an anemone; large cardboard ears and a beeper transform the child into a bat, picking up sonar echoes from solid objects. With imagination, the possibilities are unlimited.

4. INTERSPECIES COMMUNICATION. Once the powers of observation, mimicry, and empathy have been developed, a dog or cat (of suitable disposition) might be brought into the

classroom so that the students can attempt to establish one-to-one communication with the animal. Without using human words, they must try to communicate their feelings and intentions in the same way that the animal does. For example, a broad smile, panting sounds, and a raised "paw" in the down-on-all-fours position is a mimic gesture which all dogs recognize as playful.

Identification, observation, mimicry, and communication often take place outside the classroom setting, and students with pets at home should be encouraged to communicate with them. But in a more carefully structured way, in the classroom under a teacher's guidance, these natural aspects of learning how to relate, understand, and appreciate a fellow being, human or nonhuman, could be greatly enhanced. (See *What Is Your Dog Saying?* by the author and W. D. Gates, for example.)

5. TRAINING. Most young children identify well with the fact that a puppy, like a child, has to learn things for its own good and the good of others, whose rights and needs must be respected. Housebreaking, like toilet training and obedience training, especially near traffic, can be appreciated by the child. And with guidance the child can teach the puppy. Such role reversal—child as teacher—is a valuable learning experience in itself.

6. GENERAL CARE. Caring for the pet—giving it the right shelter, food, water, exercise, veterinary treatment ("shots"), grooming, and so on—teaches the child self-care and general principles of health, hygiene, and nutrition. (See *Understanding Your Pet* by the author for more details, especially for classroom menageries.) There is also some role modeling—child as parent—which may be extremely valuable for instilling responsibility and understanding. (Children who care for animals must be supervised by an adult. For if the child neglects the animal, not only will the animal suffer, but so will the child when it experiences guilt

or develops irresponsible, bad habits which may follow it in later years.)

How animals take care of themselves can also be an instructive lesson. Children can observe the animal's habits of self-grooming, its ability to make a den or build a house or fortress (termites) or to protect itself with stingers, claws, or camouflage coloration (praying mantis), and so on.

Animals also care for each other, another valuable lesson for children. A bitch will nurse, groom, and clean her pups, regurgitate food for them, and even defend them from strangers. A visit to a kennel or seeing a suitable film or slides will be enough to teach the child.

OTHER RELATED TOPICS: EXPANDING AWARENESS

Animals can provide a new perspective in other curriculum areas. The dog is an excellent focus for a study of the following subjects:

HISTORY. The dog has played many roles in man's history up to the present day, demonstrating how some animals are man's best friend.

LITERATURE AND CREATIVE WRITING. There are several classic short and long stories about dogs—*Greyfriar's Bobby, Lassie,* and so on. Any child in the class who has a dog at home may be easily motivated to write about some particular experience with the pet.

SOCIAL STUDIES. Examine the various roles of the dog in society, for example, their use as "co-therapists" (as described in Chapter 5) for emotionally disturbed children and adults, chronic invalids of all ages, senior citizens in retirement homes, and so on. Also, the problem of pet overpopulation and its effects is a good topic for study.

SCIENCE AND MATHEMATICS. Experiments involving any *direct* treatment of any animal (surgery, injecting drugs, experimental diets, and so on) should be outlawed in schools. Students can become competent scientists by developing their latent observational abilities instead. What they observe can be recorded, and their analytical skills developed through quantitative analysis of qualitative data such as how often a male dog marks trees and other objects when he goes for a walk, which objects are preferred, when and why he scrapes the ground with his feet after marking.* In mathematics there are many approaches, such as calculating how many relatives a female dog could leave (when she breeds once a year for say six years, has three female pups each litter, each of which has the same reproductive potential as the mother).

HOLISTIC EDUCATION

As previously stated, direct study of animals should include a balanced series of questions: What? How? Who? and Why? The following example will clarify this holistic educational concept.

What is the structure of a frog (or dog or any other creature)?

How does it function and behave?

Who is a frog? Knowing how it functions, one can then empathize and imagine how it feels to be a frog. Mimicry and creative fantasy can be used to enhance this subjective and "zoocentric" mode.

Why are there frogs? Such a question acts as a jolt, a self-reflective shock, helping to detach awareness from either a wholly subjective (zoocentric) or wholly objective (humanocentric) mode. Instead, the two modes of thought are integrated. In consideration of why there are frogs, values can also be explored, and humane ethics considered. Subsequent questions, depending upon the animal that is being studied, can lead in various directions. Evolution and ecology can be focused upon. Or questions of identity and purpose

---

* See Allen W. Stokes, *Animal Behavior in Laboratory and Field* (San Francisco: W. H. Freeman & Co., 1968) and M. W. Fox, *Understanding Your Dog* (New York: Coward-McCann, 1972) and *Understanding Your Cat* (New York: Coward-McCann, 1974) for many topics for classroom use for older students.

can be redirected to the students themselves: Who and why are you? Present and past relationships between man and the animal can be studied. What is the animal's place in the economy and society? Are there public health problems? Has the animal been significant in man's history, art, religion, and mythology.

The encyclopedic coverage becomes more than a factual overview when the student has first learned to empathize with the animal and has reflected on its purpose. As a scientist who has spent many years asking only what and how an animal is and after a lifetime of being educated along this mode of inquiry, I can say only that the shift in perspective generated by the who and why questions has not only expanded my own awareness and improved my scientific abilities but also given me a more balanced and integrated world view and an appreciation of the deeper significance and purpose of all life.

This holistic and humane educational model entails not a radical revision of curriculum content but rather a rigorous appraisal of what, why, and how things are taught. The greatest self-actualizing lesson of all, through discovering and experiencing that a frog is a frog is a frog, is then within the reach of both teacher and student alike.

Other benefits of a balanced approach to understanding and appreciating an animal remain to be evaluated. The child may be better equipped for later creative learning, for *intuition* may be enhanced.

Because of the human capacity for empathy and mimicry and because in many respects the human brain is an aggregate of the reptile, avian, marsupial, and mammalian brains, humans can communicate with other species, especially those that are close to them in evolution (primates and carnivores, such as the cat and dog). While people may never actually *know* what another animal is thinking, it is well within their capacities to know something about an animal's emotional state and intentions, to reciprocate such awareness and to share their own feelings and intentions. Observation, mimic communication, and identification with an animal make us more sensitive, and our relationships, with both humans and nonhumans, will have a deeper significance.

REALITY TEACHING

What we see isn't always what is really happening. Studying pet cats, for example, is one of the best ways to understand this. Their nature leaves gaps in what we know about them, and our minds tend to fill in these gaps with all kinds of unreal myths. Some people associate cats with aloofness, independence, indifference, and untrustworthiness and believe that cats are untrainable, temperamental, unpredictable, vicious, manipulative, parasitic, wild, antisocial. For other people, cats are feminine, agile, cuddly, mysterious, graceful, proud, relaxed, inscrutable, fascinating, sensuous. A cat may be one or all of these in the eyes of the beholder, depending upon what expectations of and attitudes toward cats a person has. In itself, though, the cat is none of these things. Only when a person dismisses all preconceptions about cats, can he or she begin to see the cat for itself.

Unprejudiced observation is a facet of the primary scientific method. In a state of detached objectivity, one simply observes and records without interpretation and without seeking validation of some preconceived notion. Such objectivity, combined with subjective attitudes of empathy, compassion, and reverence for all life, can be the key to communion and, with a little intuition, to a much deeper understanding of the nature of all things.

There are other facets to consider in the relationships between children and animals, especially ideas which children are likely to acquire from others. One of these is the *utilitarian* world view in which plants and animals are valued only if they are useful to man. For example, very quickly children learn that certain plants are considered "weeds" and certain animals "pests," "varmints," and "game." They are given utilitarian values. Yet in their ecological setting these plants and animals are of inestimable value.

When specific topics are selected, the utilitarian and dominionistic attitudes of our culture can be explored and exploded. The child can learn that everything has a place and purpose in the grand scheme of things. Humans are an integral part of this, and the student should be encouraged to identify when, why, and how man disrupts, exploits, and destroys other life forms and their ecosystems. Discuss feasible alternatives which are conducive to a more harmonious relationship between humans and the rest of creation.

Another important facet which greatly influences how one relates to certain animals is emotional conditioning. Most children are quick to decide that certain animals are ugly, slimy, gross, and, therefore, bad. Their decisions usually reflect a parent's view. Animals that are not appealing, cuddly, and endearing do not evoke a protective or nurturing response in the child, which also leads to misconceptions. Just realizing this may help children overcome their misconceptions and fears about a variety of aesthetically and emotionally unappealing creatures.

The best way to learn to appreciate all creatures is to explore beneath the illusory surface of beauty and ugliness and study the creature in question. The child will discover that snakes aren't slimy, that wolves are not bloody killers but affectionate and loving parents (as I show in *The Soul of the Wolf*), and that few spiders are poisonous and most spiders aren't out to bite everyone. More important, the child will realize that ugliness is a value judgment, just as beauty is. The teacher may explore how many "beautiful" animals are aesthetically pleasing because they have evolved for speed, agility, and so on. Similarly the "ugly" can be examined to discover why they have their shapes: humps, bumps, scales, and horns for defense; large, ungainly bodies because they live in water or don't need to move swiftly because of their defensive armor. Knowledge of the true nature of animals will lead to a mature world view in which there are no value judgments.

Some of this learning should take place outside the classroom in the woods or park. There both teacher and students should resist the temptation to be doing something all the time. *Sit quietly, observe, and listen.* One should be quiet in the woods, for example, not only to avoid scaring animals away but because the woods *are* quiet, something to be respected. A quiet but alert human is then less of an intrusion and perhaps may be not an unwelcome guest! The child learns that one can study and enjoy nature in nondestructive ways. Passive contemplation complements active exploration. But children cannot remain passive for long periods, so the two modes must be balanced according to the group's capacity.

Being responsible for an animal in the classroom or at home, and being taught its needs in some detail can help develop a sense of humane stewardship. The child should not be trained cookbook fashion as a mere caretaker, nor should the animal be treated and indulged as a living toy. The humane steward is sensitive to the needs and rights of the animal and is responsible for its well-being. From this orientation, relevant topics such as responsible pet ownership and the pet overpopulation problem might be introduced.

The classroom is also a good setting in which to learn gradually of mankind's role as *co-creator*. This entails understanding the laws of nature and working in harmony with them (as distinct from the dominionistic and utilitarian modes).

Begin with a simple project such as planting some seeds—beans or cress—and observing their germination. The child develops a sense of competence in helping create something. The next project should be a bit more complicated—setting up a vivarium or aquarium "miniecosystem," or estabishing a small organic garden or hydroponic unit. This can be complemented with field trips to study life in the natural setting—a pond, under a log, and so on—and to collect carefully selected specimens for culturing microorganisms from the soil or leaf mold. Collecting and identifying are only the first step. For an aquarium or vivarium to be successfully established and maintained, ecological relationships between the living plants and animals and the nonliving elements in their environment must be studied and understood. On the basis of this experience, older groups can discuss many of the problems and dilemmas of the "real world," in which humans have disturbed the ecological relationships. Discussions of such topics as predator control, protection of endangered species, pollution controls, effects of clear cutting and strip mining follow naturally and train students to begin thinking like humane stewards. Unfortunately such issues are usually dealt with as a separate unit under "environmental studies" or another course name. But they are best approached as outlined above—following a thorough grounding in factual data and an exploration of values and attitudes which underlie many of the problems between man and the rest of creation. Through this gradual approach the perceptions, sensitivity, and values of the child develop as the curriculum evolves. Without a firm base and prior orientation toward humane stewardship, the underlying *causes* may be overlooked, and only the surface symptoms addressed.

Humane education is perhaps the most potent area for changing human consciousness. The humane educator can lead the student away from a restricting anthropocentric world view acquired from parents and culture. Yet many teachers are afraid to take the first step. A teacher of children whose parents hunt and trap animals may feel intimidated and be threatened or dismissed if he or she imposes more humane values upon the children. Even textbooks and other children's books try to avoid creating any controversies. It is little wonder that children become bored with such unstimulating, tasteless pabulum. Their minds are best developed when they explore controversies. The friction of opposing views sparks classroom debate. Teachers need not *impose* their own values but rather have the children explore and discuss their own and others' actions and values, using the Socratic method of question, example, and discussion. They will be guided gently toward humane views, especially when the discussion focuses on ethical issues and dilemmas—such as we must kill to live—and ultimately on the intrinsic rights of other living things and our relationships with and responsibilities toward others.

The self-actualizing process of personal growth can be encouraged by the fostering of empathy toward all life forms. Designing student exercises to facilitate growth is the most important challenge to the humane educator. With a teacher's help, a child can learn gradually to recognize and cope with such feelings as fear, uncertainty, jealousy, revulsion, and the polarities of like/dislike. "Getting in touch" with feelings and with preconceived ideas and expectations can help open the doors of perception so that the child can examine his or her existing values and attitudes and develop more realistic and compassionate ones. Cleansing perception* from emotional and conceptual contaminants is the key to empathy and to a realistic, impartial, and rational regard for others.

Humane educators must also deal with negative feelings that their students have toward those who behave selfishly, are inhumane toward animals, and lack ethical responsibility. One grade-school student was so shocked when first exposed to examples of mankind's inhumanity to animals that she decided that all humans were bad. Such feelings are dangerous and must be carefully examined. Otherwise, they can set up judgmental attitudes which will block any fruitful exchange. Feelings of outrage, condemnation, anger, frustration, humiliation, and pain are an essential part of the learning experience when properly focused. As Gandhi urged, we must learn to hate the deed, not the wrongdoer.

It seems that we have a long way to evolve, and not much time, considering the state of the world—overpopulated and overexploited. Fortunately a change in consciousness doesn't take generations. The human mind is flexible; it can be improved upon.

Education toward empathy and ethical responsibility will hasten the change in human consciousness. But education today focuses primarily upon technological advancement. Ethical progress is not adequately rewarded by a society which places ethics after production and profit. This attitude toward ethics is clearly reflected in college curricula in which ethics is a mere subsection of philosophy and is rarely integrated with other disciplines, such as science, medicine, psychology, law, business administration, economics, or sociology. Technologists and specialists educated in these disciplines without a basis in ethical responsibility, medical practitioners, biomedical researchers, and lawyers fall into the trap of unethical conduct when it is rationalized that the end justifies the means. The growing schism between what is moral or ethical and what is legal should engender the concern of all educators. Keeping faith in the essential goodness of human nature and in the potentials of humane education, we must work to pull out the very roots of our culture

---

* One of the best outlines of this important and highly effective educational process can be found in the writings of Jiddu Krishnamurti. For example, his *Talks and Dialogues* (Berkeley, Calif.: Shambala Publications, 1969).

and examine all our values, beliefs, needs, prejudices, and dependencies. An enlightened and sensitized consciousness, the natural mind, will emerge, at one with the natural world as a whole. Fortunately this problem is beginning to be recognized, as reflected in Sissela Bok's *Lying: Moral Choice in Public and Private Life* and in her report coauthored with Daniel Callahan, director of the Hastings Center (published in the September 1979 issue of *Change* magazine). The report describes the work and conclusions of a nationwide task force's appraisal of the need for teaching ethics at all levels of higher education. Already some 12,000 courses in ethics are currently offered in universities through the United States, although many have been found lacking in content and quality. The preliminary report lists some basic goals in the teaching of ethics:

> Students' moral imagination should be stimulated. This means encouraging students to understand that there is a "moral point of view" and that, while moral conflicts are often inevitable and difficult, the way in which they are resolved results in actual suffering or happiness. A part of this is emphasizing that human beings "live in a web of moral relationships."
>
> Students should be taught to recognize ethical issues. A proper course should teach students to realize that many technical, social, psychological or political problems raise fundamental questions of right and wrong, of human rights and conflicting obligations.
>
> Students' analytical skills should be developed. They should be taught to understand the difference between sound and slipshod arguments in moving from moral principles to their application in the real world.
>
> Students should be made to feel a sense of personal responsibility. Any course in applied ethics should explore the role of personal responsibility in a setting of freedom to make moral choices.

13

The Nature Connection: Animals and Human Fulfillment

Extolling the virtues and beauty of the European countryside, René Dubos senses a "God within" those pastorally manicured enclosures. Yet this "countryside" which he and so many other writers praise is actually a facsimile of nature. It is a tamed and man-shaped artifact, its cultivation reflecting a neat and orderly civilization. Though beautiful it may be to inspire a Wordsworth or a Constable, it is a man-made beauty, not truly natural. It has been shaped by generations of pastoralists into one great patchwork of domesticated fields, plants, and animals, interspersed with old game parks and the wilder remnants of less usable and as yet undrained marshes and moors. Even the woods and forests are tamed, for gone are the wolves, bears, and wild boars. The wilderness is an illusion.

Diversity has been reduced, and an unnatural order has been established and is maintained with good "management." Today even this delicate balance is being threatened by the inexorable pressures of growth and development, pollution and exploitation.

In contrast with the parklike status quo of Europe, we see greater extremes elsewhere—in the intensely husbanded terraced fields of the Andean Indians in South America; in the small cultivated enclosures of Asian countries beside the vast agribusinesses of the United States. And wherever there is wilderness left, it is threatened by mining, logging, and other grand-scale progressive developments. Inexorably the diversity of the world is being reduced, simplified, domesticated.

As we've seen, bigness and lack of diversity stamp modern agribusiness. This system, like the landscape of Europe, mirrors the very organization of our culture. There is bigness and lack of species diversity in our cities and suburban developments. As on the factory farm, there is also alienation, detachment, dehumanization. There can be no real sense of belonging, of kinship, for we are *natural* beings and are nature-deprived. Our kinship with nature goes beyond our own specialist profession and nuclear family into the very roots of our being, into the unconscious of our evolutionary past and ontogenetic future. This connection, which has been broken in the organization of contemporary society, is the *nature connection.* It is an inseparable part of our humanness, and without it we suffer the modern psychic diseases associated with anomies—social vacuums void of morals or ethics. Zoos and sterile parks, mechanized farms, subdued pets, and indoor plants do not satisfy this need for a direct link to nature. Being partially man-made creations, they reflect more of ourselves and satisfy our human-centered needs rather than reflect the deeper otherness of nature. At best they are substitutes for what is natural.

While the human spirit may seek unity with all creation because we all are of the same essence, it is through the diversity of creation that we gain a greater depth of understanding and appreciation for ourselves and all life. As we simplify nature, we impoverish our children of their nature heritage, and we narrow the landscape of our own psyches at the same time. Paul Shepard observes: "If all creatures are possible ideas, relationships, emotions, feelings, the habitat is for us the outward form of the whole space of the mind. Our man-made landscapes are caricatures of the rational mind, the external extension of civilized thought." Surrounded by a natural world which is nothing more than a human artifact, we can see only ourselves. Like Narcissus, we may suffer under the delusion of self-worship and see or value nothing beyond the humanized world that we have created.

During the early years a child shows a natural interest in animals and nature. As Paul Shepard proposes, this may be a normal developmental stage essential for the emergence not only of sensitivity and compassion but of self-awareness. The key to human intelligence rests upon the child's exposure to a richly diverse environment. Self-awareness arises out of socialization, whereby the distinction between self and other is distilled. If the child's social environment is restricted, its awareness of self in relation to others will be shallow. Such cultural deprivation is aggravated further when the child is deprived of contact with nature and nonhuman creatures. On the other hand, a child given an even broader socialization with adults, other children, and animals will have much greater sense of self and other. In this way, animals can make us more human by teaching us what is human and what is not. They can also teach us empathy and understanding through what man and animal share as living beings.

Socialization with a wide variety of nonhuman, nondomesticated species in their natural environments is essential for normal development. Says Paul Shepard:

> . . . the physical reality of animal differences and multiformity are in some way prior to the development of companionship among people, an experience of animals without which strictly human interactions give us crowding rather than fellowship. It is felt as a loss of harmony in the self or within society or among nations, but it has its source in a failure of the primitive sources of energy for bringing a disparate world together.

Anthropocentrism is thus a self-denial rather than a self-world affirmation. Shepard also says:

> Modern technology makes everything a product of man. Order in nature, according to the philosophy of this view, offers no guiding wisdom, no heuristic design, no relationships with hidden analogies to culture. It offers only molecular order to be rearranged for our consumption, species order to be tamed for our amusement, and stellar order to be the arcane playground of mathematical games and spectator rocket sports.

The total domination of nature is civilized man's most dehumanizing and biocidal error.

Socialized today with placid pets, animal picture books and fables, and anthropomorphic Disney types of movies, the modern child has a distorted view of nature's reality. While admittedly keeping animals as pets and being close to nature in childhood can help establish the nature connection essential for the development of human potential, the dangers of creating a false connection are very real. Animals are not little people. But they can and should be significant others in our lives, for nature can be one of our most significant teachers.

The child must be taken beyond the world of domestic pets and farm animals that reflect infantilism, dependence, conformity, obedience, and utilitarianism. These humanized animals dilute the experience of other species. They could even lead to misconceptions of animals and nature in general. Contact with natural ecosystems and the diversity of species therein will deepen the child's experience of otherness and concept of self.

Our ideal vision of the future must include wild animals, for they are culturally indispensable to the development and life of the human mind. It is in the roots of nature that our intelligence evolved, as it is in animal life that we may find our deepest connections and ultimate significance. Our growing alienation from the natural world is a threat to the quality of the human experience. As we impoverish the earth, we impoverish ourselves and our culture. Man, as animal, and nature make one inseparable whole from which we have evolved intelligence and from which we gain self-awareness in a rich and varied cultural perspective.

Life and ecosystems will go on without wolves, whales, lions. Most endangered species are dispensable, for few are ecological necessities, especially since man can help control whatever imbalances might arise from their absence. The real argument for maintaining species diversity*—a whole earth—is a selfish one. We

---

* For some very convincing economic arguments, see Norman Myers, *The Sinking Ark* (New York: Pergamon, 1979).

need it for a whole mind, as an essential part of our growing and being human and perhaps also for a whole spirit of earth.

Effective education and legislation can do much to guide the human consciousness toward a more ethical and responsible relationship to the natural world. Shepard states:

> The only defense of nonhuman life ... is one close to human well-being ... the human mind needs animals in order to develop and work. Human intelligence is bound to the presence of animals. They are the means by which cognition takes its first shape and they are the instruments for imaginary abstract ideas and qualities, therefore giving us consciousness. They are the code images by which language retrieves ideas from memory at will. They are the means to self-identity and self-consciousness as our most human possession, for they enable us to objectify qualities and traits. By presenting us with related-otherness—that diversity of non-self with which we have various things in common—they further, through our lives, a refining and maturing knowledge of personal and human being.

There will be difficult times and much hardship ahead before we reach a steady state and restore ourselves in harmony with nature and each other. The many man-made crises and ethical issues of today are the evolutionary imperatives that can shape or destroy our future. We must honestly and earnestly address them and assume the awesome responsibility for our own continued evolution.

Postscript

Considerable progress has been made in the United States during the past two decades toward equal rights for all people. And for the first time in history, serious consideration is being given to animal and nature rights. Ironically, in the absence of the latter, we can never claim, as a nation, to have equal rights for people since we all are deprived of our right to a whole and healthy environment, abundant with a natural diversity of plants and animals. The rights of nature can be upheld only at some personal cost. By developing moral incentives and ethical guidelines for responsible living, we will be ready to make personal sacrifice when necessary. But our culture today is founded on anthropocentric and economic imperatives. The points of contact between man, animal, and nature have been long neglected. Still, there are promising signs of change. Humane (animal welfare) and conservation movements, working to apply science to the rights of animals and whole ecosystems, have grown and gained strength. Veterinary colleges in the United States now include courses dealing with animal rights. In Britain the RSPCA has endorsed a university chair (professorship) in animal welfare. I could cite many other promising trends in this direction. This is not just a social revolution but the beginning of an ethical transformation of our culture from utilitarianism to responsible living and a reverence for all life.

"The basis of all animal rights should be the Golden Rule: we should treat *them* as we would wish them to treat *us*, were any other species in our dominant position," says Christine Stevens, president of the Animal Welfare Institute. Since the turn of the century more than 50 species of birds and more than 70 mammalian species have become extinct. Today an estimated 200 mammalian and 350 avian species are threatened with extinction, together with 20,000 to 25,-000 species of plants and an uncounted number of insects, reptiles, and amphibians. The rate of extinction is accelerating, and while we may be able to clean and heal the earth, we will never be able to replace any living thing that is extinct. Of all our priorities, the endangered species issue cannot be postponed.

Today is the conservationist's era of preservation of remaining wilderness and wildlife. Tomorrow the task will be restoration of wildlife and wilderness areas. Zoos and wildlife refuges are responsible for maintaining populations of species that face extinction in the wild so that there will be wildlife to restore. Complementing these areas is continued research into wildlife biology and diseases.

Without the cooperation of governments and the change in human consciousness discussed throughout this book, we will have a planet dying faster than at its natural rate. And when this occurs, such accelerated and pathological entropy would break the natural evolutionary continuum. The ultimate purpose and significance of the entire creative process would then be lost—to man and all.

I must emphasize that in this book I am not advocating the abandonment of science and technology. Rather, the systems which serve us must be better controlled for the greater good of all humanity in harmony with the rest of the world. In other words, self-serving interests must not conflict with the interests of all life on earth. When they do, science and technology should help eliminate the conflicts between man and nature. Man must be held accountable for his actions in a much broader framework than ever before, embracing humane ethics, respect for the rights of nonhuman life, and awareness of the ecological principles by which all individuals, societies, and industries must abide. Nor am I saying that man is to become God. Rather, he must be a co-creator, harmonizing ethically, socially, spiritually, and ecologically. This is an essential evolutionary step, part of becoming civilized and fully human. We work in harmony with nature—to steward, conserve, and, wherever possible, preserve the primal state. Nature can be used, even reshaped, to sustain human interests, provided we respect and abide by its laws and rights. We can enhance nature and its potentials, but we may not destroy.

Sources and Further Reading

CHAPTER 1

Ardrey, Robert. *The Territorial Imperative.* New York: Atheneum, 1966.

Darwin, Charles. *The Expression of the Emotions in Man and the Animals.* London: John Murray, 1972.

Fox, Michael W. *The Soul of the Wolf.* Boston: Little, Brown, 1980.

———. *The Dog: Its Domestication and Behavior.* New York: Garland, 1978.

———. *Between Animal and Man.* New York: Coward, McCann & Geoghegan, 1976.

———. *Understanding Your Cat.* New York: Coward-McCann, 1974.

———. *Understanding Your Dog.* New York: Coward-McCann, 1972.

———. *Integrative Development of Brain and Behavior in the Dog.* Chicago: University of Chicago Press, 1971.

Griffin, Donald R. *The Question of Animal Awareness.* New York: Rockefeller University Press, 1977.

Lorenz, Konrad. *On Aggression.* New York: Harcourt Brace, 1963.

MacLean, Paul D. *The Triune Concept of the Brain and Behavior: The Clarence M. Hincks Memorial Lectures, 1969,* D. Campbell and T. J. Boag, eds. Toronto: University of Toronto Press, 1973.

Montagu, Ashley. *Touching: The Human Significance of the Skin.* New York: Harper & Row, 1972.

Morris, Desmond. *The Naked Ape.* London: Jonathan Cape, 1967.

Premack, Ann J. *Why Chimps Can Read.* New York: Harper & Row, 1976.

CHAPTER 2

Connell, John H. "Diversity in Tropical Rain Forests and Coral Reefs," *Science,* 199:1302–10 (1978).

Darwin, Charles. *The Origin of Species.* Rowman, N.Y.: University Library, 1972.

Dubos, René. *A God Within.* New York: Scribner's, 1972.

Eckholm, Erik. *Losing Ground.* Earth Watch Institute, Washington, D.C. New York: W. W. Norton, 1976.

Fox, Michael W. *The Dog: Its Domestication and Behavior.* New York: Garland, 1978.

———. *The Wild Canids.* New York: Van Nostrand, Reinhold, 1975.

———. *Integrative Development of Brain and Behavior in the Dog.* Chicago: University of Chicago Press, 1971.

Frankl, Viktor. *Man's Search for Meaning.* New York: Simon & Schuster, 1975.

Geist, Valerius. *Mountain Sheep and Man.* Ithaca, N.Y.: Cornell University Press, 1975.

Kruuk, Hans. *The Spotted Hyena.* Chicago: University of Chicago Press, 1972.

La Chapelle, Dolores. *Earth Wisdom.* Los Angeles: International University Press, 1978.

Lee, Richard B., and Irvin DeVore. *Man the Hunter.* Chicago: Aldine, 1968.

McHarg, Ian. *Design with Nature.* Garden City, N.Y.: Natural History Press, 1969.

Mech, L. David. *The Wolf.* Garden City, N.Y.: Natural History Press, 1970.

Murchie, Guy. *The Seven Mysteries of Life.* Boston: Houghton Mifflin, 1978.

Neihardt, John C. *Black Elk Speaks.* New York: Simon & Schuster, 1972.

Odum, Eugene P. *Fundamentals of Ecology.* Philadelphia: W. B. Saunders, 1971.

Schaller, George B. *The Serengeti Lion.* Chicago: University of Chicago Press, 1972.

Schweitzer, Albert. *The Teaching of Reverence for Life.* New York: Holt, Rinehart and Winston, 1965.

Shepard, Paul. *Thinking Animals.* New York: Viking Press, 1978.

Smith, Richard L., *The Ecology of Man: An Ecosystems Approach.* New York: Harper & Row, 1976.

Thomas, Lewis. *The Lives of a Cell.* New York: Viking Press, 1974.

Thoreau, Henry David. *Walden.* New York: Macmillan, 1966.

CHAPTER 3

Brown, Lester. *The Twenty-ninth Day: Accommodating Human Needs and Numbers to the Earth's Resources.* New York: W. W. Norton, 1978.

Lee, Richard B., and Irvin De Vore. *Man the Hunter.* Chicago: Aldine, 1968.

Schwabe, Calvin W. *Cattle, Priests and Progress in Medicine.* Minneapolis: University of Minnesota Press, 1978.

Spangler, David. *Toward a Planetary Vision.* Forres, Scotland: Findhorn Foundation, 1977.

Teilhard de Chardin, Pierre. *Man's Place in Nature.* New York: Harper & Row, 1978.

Zeuner, Frederick E. *A History of Domesticated Animals.* New York: Harper & Row, 1963.

CHAPTER 4

Bosch, Robert van den. *The Pesticide Conspiracy.* New York: Doubleday and Company, 1978.

Domalain, Jean-Yves. *The Animal Connection.* New York: William Morrow, 1977.

Fox, Michael W. *Understanding Your Pet.* New York: Coward, McCann & Geoghegan, 1978.

Graham, Alistair. *The Gardeners of Eden.* New York: Rowman, 1974.

Graham, Alistair, and Peter Beard. *Eyelids of Morning: The Mingled Destinies of Crocodiles and Men.* New York: New York Geographic Service, 1973.

Kellert, Steven R. "Perceptions of Animals in American Society," *The National Association for the Advancement of Humane Education Journal,* 4:2–10 (1977).

Olsen, John. *Slaughter the Animals, Poison the Earth.* New York: Simon & Schuster, 1971.

Regenstein, Lewis. *The Politics of Extinction.* New York: Macmillan, 1975.

Roots, Clive. *Animal Invaders.* New York: Universe Books, 1976.

Ryden, Hope. *God's Dog,* 2nd ed. New York: Viking Press and Penguin Books, 1979.

Scheffer, Viktor B. *A Voice for Wildlife.* New York: Scribner's, 1974.

Smith, R. L. *The Ecology of Man: An Ecosystem Approach.* New York: Harper & Row, 1976.

Watson, Lyall. *Gifts of Unknown Things.* New York: Simon & Schuster, 1977.

CHAPTER 5

Allen, Robert, and William Westbrook. *Handbook of Animal Welfare.* New York: Garland, 1978.

Beck, Alan. *The Ecology of Stray Dogs.* Baltimore: York Press, 1973.

Benning, Lee E. *The Pet Profiteers.* New York: Quadrangle, 1976.

Boone, John A. *Kinship with All Life.* New York: Harper & Row, 1954.

Corson, Samuel A., Elizabeth O'Leary Corson, and Paul D. Gwynne. "Pet-Facilitated Psychotherapy," in *Pet Animals and Society,* R. S. Anderson, ed. London: Bailliere Tindall, 1975.

Fox, Michael W. *How to Be Your Pet's Best Friend.* New York: Coward, McCann & Geoghegan, 1980.

———. *Between Animal and Man.* New York: Coward-McCann, 1976.

———. *Understanding Your Dog.* New York: Coward-McCann, 1972.

Levinson, Boris M. *Pets and Human Development.* Springfield, Ill.: C. C. Thomas, 1972.

Maslow, Abraham H. *Toward a Psychology of Being.* New York: Van Nostrand, 1968.

Nowell, Iris. *The Dog Crisis.* New York: St. Martin's Press, 1978.

Szasz, Kathleen. *Petishism: Pets and Their People in the Western World.* New York: Holt, Rinehart and Winston, 1968.

CHAPTER 6

Berry, Wendell. *The Unsettling of America: Culture and Agriculture.* San Francisco: Sierra Club Books, 1977.

Britton, David K., and Berkeley Hill. *Size and Efficiency in Farming.* Farnborough, England: Saxon House, 1975.

Fox, Michael W. *Humane Concerns of Factory Farming.* Washington, D.C.: Institute for the Study of Animal Problems Report, 1979.

Harris, Marvin. *Cannibals and Kings. The Origins of Cultures.* New York: Random House, 1977.

Harrison, Ruth. *Animal Machines.* London: Vincent Stuart, 1964.

Hightower, John. *Eat Your Heart Out.* New York: Random House, 1976.

Kiley-Worthington, Marthe. *Behavioral Problems of Farm Animals.* London: Oriel Press, 1977.

Singer, Peter. *Animal Liberation.* New York: Random House, 1975.

Teutsch, Gotthard M. "The Ethical Aspects of Farm Animal Management," in *The Ethology and Ethics of Farm Animal Production,* D. W. Folsch, ed. Stuttgart: Brinkhäuser, 1978.

CHAPTER 7

Ames, B. N. *National Society for Medical Research* 28:6 (June 1977).
Diner, Jeff. *Physical and Mental Suffering of Experimental Animals.* Washington, D.C.: Animal Welfare Institute, 1979.
Fox, Michael W. *Laboratory Animal Science, Ethology and Ethics.* Ms. in preparation, 1980.
Pratt, Dallas. *Painful Experiments on Animals.* New York: Argus Archives, 1976.
Roberts, Catherine. *The Scientific Conscience: Reflections on the Modern Biologist and Humanism.* New York: Braziller, 1967.
Rowan, Andrew N., ed. *The Use of Alternatives in the Discovery, Development and Testing of Therapeutic Products.* London: Macmillan Ltd., 1980.
————. "Primate Testing: Adequate Alternatives," *Science,* 199:934 (1978).
Russell, William M. S., and Richard L. Burch. *The Principles of Humane Experimental Technique.* London: Methuen and Company, 1959.
Ryder, Richard. *Victims of Science.* London: Davis-Poynter, 1975.

CHAPTER 8

Berry, Wendell. *The Unsettling of America: Culture and Agriculture.* San Francisco: Sierra Club Books, 1977.
Ferkiss, Victor. *The Future of Technological Civilization.* New York: Braziller, 1974.
Illich, Ivan. *Medical Nemesis.* New York: Random House, 1976.
Leiss, William. *The Domination of Nature.* New York: Braziller, 1972.
Leopold, Aldo. *A Sand County Almanac.* New York: Oxford University Press, 1949.
Passmore, John. *Man's Responsibility for Nature.* New York: Scribner's, 1974.
Schumacher, Ernest F. *Small Is Beautiful: Economics as If People Mattered.* New York: Harper & Row, 1975.

CHAPTER 9

Fox, Michael W. *One Earth, One Mind.* New York: Coward, McCann & Geoghegan, 1980.

————. *Between Animal and Man.* New York: Coward-McCann, 1976.

Fromm, Erich. *The Anatomy of Human Destructiveness.* New York: Holt, Rinehart and Winston, 1973.

Hume, C. W. *The Status of Animals in the Christian Religion.* London: The Universities Federation for Animal Welfare, 1962.

Keniston, Kenneth. *The Uncommitted.* New York: Dell, 1965.

Lévi-Strauss, Claude. *Structural Anthropology.* New York: Doubleday, 1967.

Linzey, Andrew. *Animal Rights.* London: SCM Press, 1976.

Lowen, Alexander. *Depression and the Body.* New York: Coward-McCann, 1972.

Rogers, Carl. *On Becoming a Person.* Boston: Houghton Mifflin, 1971.

Roszak, Theodore. *Unfinished Animal.* New York: Harper & Row, 1975.

Schweitzer, Albert. *The Teaching of Reverence for Life.* New York: Holt, Rinehart and Winston, 1965.

Singer, Peter. *Animal Liberation.* New York: Random House, 1975.

For additional material on animal and nature rights, see:

Clark, Stephen R. L. *The Moral Status of Animals.* Oxford: Clarendon Press, 1977.

Goldovitch, S. R., and J. Harris, eds. *Animals, Men and Morals: An Enquiry into the Maltreatment of Animals.* New York: Taplinger, 1972.

Morris, Richard K., and Michael W. Fox, eds. *On the Fifth Day: Animal Rights and Human Ethics.* Washington, D.C.: Acropolis Press, 1978.

Paterson, D., and R. D. Ryder. *Animals' Rights—A Symposium.* London: Centaur Press, 1979.

Regan, T., and P. Singer, eds. *Animal Rights and Human Obligations.* Englewood Cliffs, N.J.: Prentice-Hall, 1976.

Stone, Christopher D. *Should Trees Have Standing? Towards Legal Rights for Natural Objects.* Los Altos, Calif.: Wm. Kaufman, 1974.

CHAPTER 10

Frankl, Viktor. *Man's Search for Meaning.* New York: Simon & Schuster, 1975.

Gandhi, Mohandas. *Selected Writings,* R. Duncan, ed. New York: Harper & Row, 1971.

Krishnamurti, Jiddu. *Talks and Dialogues.* Berkeley, Calif.: Shambala Publications, 1969.

Midgley, Mary. *Beast and Man: The Roots of Human Nature.* Ithaca, N.Y.: Cornell University Press, 1978.

Polyani, Michael. *Personal Knowledge.* Chicago: University of Chicago Press, 1974.

Roberts, Catherine. *The Scientific Conscience: Reflections on the Modern Biologist and Humanism.* New York: Braziller, 1967.

Spangler, David. *Towards a Planetary Vision.* Forres, Scotland: Findhorn Foundation, 1977.

CHAPTER 11

Austin, Jack. "Buddhist Attitudes Towards Animal Life," in *Animals' Rights—A Symposium,* David Paterson and Richard D. Ryder, eds. London: Centaur Press, 1979.

Bok, Sissela. *Lying: Moral Choice in Public and Private Life.* New York: Pantheon, 1978.

Commoner, Barry. *The Closing Circle.* New York: Alfred Knopf, 1971.

Dubos, René. *A God Within.* New York: Scribner's, 1972.

Gandhi, Mohandas. *Selected Writings,* R. Duncan, ed. New York: Harper & Row, 1971.

La Chapelle, Dolores. *Earth Wisdom.* Los Angeles: International University Press, 1978.

Lao Tzu. *Tao Te Ching,* Ch'u Ta-Kao, trans. New York: Samuel Weisner, 1973.

Northrop, F. S. C. "Naturalistic Realism and Animate Compassion," in *On the Fifth Day: Animal Rights and Human Ethics,* R. K. Morris and Michael W. Fox, eds. Washington, D.C.: Acropolis, 1978.

Passmore, John. *Man's Responsibility for Nature.* New York: Scribner's, 1974.

Schweitzer, Albert. *The Teaching of Reverence for Life.* New York: Holt, Rinehart and Winston, 1965.

Suzuki, Daisetz. *What Is Zen?* New York: Harper & Row, 1971.

Teutsch, Gotthard M. "The Ethical Aspects of Farm Animal Management," in *The Ethology and Ethics of Farm Animal Production,* Delbert W. Folsch, ed. Stuttgart: Brinkhäuser, 1978.

Watts, Alan. *This Is It.* New York: Vantage Books, 1973.

Weil, Andrew. *The Natural Mind.* Boston: Houghton Mifflin, 1972.

White, Lynn. "The Historical Roots of Our Ecological Crisis," *Science,* 155:1203–07 (1967).

CHAPTER 12

Bok, Sissela. *Lying: Moral Choice in Public and Private Life.* New York: Pantheon, 1978.

Fox, Michael W. *The Soul of the Wolf.* Boston: Little, Brown, 1980.

————. *Understanding Your Pet.* New York: Coward, McCann & Geoghegan, 1978.

————, and W. D. Gates. *What Is Your Dog Saying?* New York: Coward, McCann & Geoghegan, 1977.

CHAPTER 13

Dubos, René. *A God Within.* New York: Scribner's, 1972.

Shepard, Paul. *Thinking Animals.* New York: Viking Press, 1978.

APPENDICES
Humane Alternatives

(Notes for a more humane and ecologically balanced lifestyle)*

We unknowingly support and encourage many inhumane and unethical uses of animals. To be humane entails constant vigilance, a recognition of our blind spots, unthinking actions, and selfish needs. It also means discovering alternatives in our lives to reduce needless waste and suffering of our animal kin. The following notes may help you broaden your awareness and the extent of your moral concern and thus increase your effectiveness as a humane being in the war against inhumanity.

THE FOOD WE EAT

Many modern intensive factory farming systems are inhumane, especially for veal calves and to a slightly lesser extent for pigs, poultry, and battery egg-laying hens. Eat *no* veal or calf liver, and eat *less* pork, bacon, chicken, and eggs (unless they are guaranteed from free-range hens). Then there will be less suffering. Balance your diet, and improve your health with high-protein vegetables—lentils, beans, soya—and more fresh vegetables, grains, and fruits in season. Cheese, yogurt, and other dairy products are generally ac-

* Adapted from M. W. Fox, *Understanding Your Pet* (New York: Coward, McCann & Geoghegan, 1978).

ceptable since most dairy herds are not kept under inhumane, intensive conditions. The decision to eat fish as an alternative to many intensive farm products is also a valid option for some people.

Also, avoid tuna until the fishing industry does more to reduce the destruction of dolphins, and eat no imported goose liver (pâté de foie) or turtle because the geese are inhumanely force-fed and turtles are becoming endangered through overharvesting.

While these dietary decisions are personal, vegetarianism for some may seem too difficult. I would advocate nonvegetarians at least to become "conscientious omnivores," aware of what and whom they eat, and to experiment with some vegetarian cookbooks.

THE PRODUCTS WE CONSUME

Stick to old (tested) brands, especially of toiletries, household cleaning agents, and nonprescription drugs (particularly eye- and mouth-washes). "New and improved" products and product development to capture the consumer market with a novel but nonessential innovation involve countless animal lives and often unjustifiable pain and suffering in the course of running safety tests for the consumer. Sticking to the old brands will help reduce industry's incentive to use and abuse more animals in researching and developing further new and nonessential products.

The perfumes you use should contain no musk (from wild civet cats and other mammals) or ambergris (from whales), and all cosmetics should be labeled as being of vegetable origin. They will then not contain the oil of turtle, whale, or other animal extracts, which the label on the bottle will not usually disclose. Look out also for whale-oil lubricants and mink-oil products.

THE CLOTHES WE WEAR

The smaller your wardrobe is, the less energy you will have consumed. Cotton and wool are more economical than synthetic (polyester) materials. Kapok and the synthetic fibers are more "humane" insulators of parkas than duck and goose down. Wear no furs of wild animals (even if not on the endangered list) since these are inhumanely caught and their use for personal decoration alone is ethically untenable. On the basis of this latter point, all ranch-raised furs should be avoided also. (To keep warm, use woolen sweaters and Kapok-filled jackets and parkas!)

THE OBJECTS WE LIKE

Art objects, personal accouterments, and the like may be made of wild animal products that we should avoid since to purchase such objects is to support the needless killing of animals for nonessential purposes. Avoid art objects and other things made of butterflies, birds' feathers, snake and other animal skins, such as alligator and ostrich, seal-skin toys, elephant and walrus ivory, and turtle shell (statues, chess sets, jewelry, and so on). Alternatives to such nonessentials are abundant.

THE SHOWS AND SPORTS WE ENJOY

Look out for television and screen films and adult and children's books that abuse or demean our animal kin. Voice complaints to the television networks and their sponsors, local movie houses, bookstores, and public and school libraries. Media materials that create or perpetuate false or negative myths and attitudes toward animals and that detract from the humane ethic of animal rights should be vetoed. Dog- and cockfight "entertainments," greased-pig catching, bullfights, raccoon baiting of dogs, and fox hunting are inhumane and should be boycotted and protested. Also, because conditions are such that animal abuses are frequent and often unavoidable, horse racing and greyhound racing (which in many states involves prior training with live rabbits and cats) are ethically unacceptable. Other "sports" such as trophy and big-game hunting, hunting with bow and arrow, and trophy (deep-sea) fishing are to be condemned. Hunting as a nonsubsistence activity is often ethically and ecologi- cally untenable. Roadside zoos, some municipal zoos, and circuses with various animal acts require rigorous scrutiny. Alternatives and substitutes are many: spectator sports (soccer, baseball, football) for the voyeur; nature photography and natural history study for the hunter/killer; and roulette or backgammon for the gambler!

HOUSE AND GARDEN ACTIVITIES

Avoid using nonselective pesticides and herbicides; they will kill in- nocent creatures as well as pests and weeds and may kill you or your children. Lights off on the patio will keep bugs away, as will bug repellent on you. Don't use bug sprays or electic bug "roasters"; only a few of the millions you kill would have bitten you. If you have a big lawn, let some of it grow to seed and create a meadow for butterflies and other insects, for birds and reptiles, and there will be seeds for the birds and small rodents for the winter. Also, the more energy you can conserve, the fewer material goods you buy, and the less meat you use, the more energy there will be available for the rest of the world—for other people who are less affluent and for the wildlife the existence of which is threatened by strip mining, oil spills, deforestation, hydroelectric dam construction, and pollution.

THE ANIMALS WE ENJOY

Before you obtain a pet—be it a dog, cat, gerbil, parakeet, or what- ever—be sure to read up first on how to care for it. Your life-style may not be compatible with keeping a dog, or your home not right for a new cat or other pet. (Several helpful pamphlets are available from the Humane Society of the United States.*)

* For specific information and pamphlets on these topics, write to the Hu- mane Society of the United States, 2100 L Street NW, Washington, D.C. 20037, and for a detailed, practical, and philosophical review, see M. W. Fox *Between Animal and Man* (New York: Coward, McCann and Geoghegan, 1976).

So far as wild creatures are concerned, purchase none in a pet store, even those that have been imported or raised in captivity. To sell wild animals as "pets" is a gross misrepresentation. Any life form taken from the wild for study or enjoyment should be returned as soon as possible to the same place in the same (or better) condition in which it was found.

It is a long way, as I see it, before humans will cease to exploit, manipulate, and control others, be they wild or domestic animals, people, or pristine wilderness and ocean. The weakness of humanity is our blindness, a cultural blind spot which some call ignorance, in which a selfish and immature ego claims the world as ours and prevents us from seeing ourselves as a part of the world. Kinship with all life is a biological (evolutionary) fact, but our culture, our ways of doing, perceiving, and relating blind us to this reality.

Animal Welfare Laws

This report was prepared by the Humane Society of the United States in August 1979. It summarizes the major federal legislation and lists sources for information on state and local legislation.

FEDERAL LAWS

The name of each act is followed by its congressional number and information on the history of its passage and any amendments which have been made.

THE ANIMAL WELFARE ACT (7 U.S.C. §2131 et seq.; passed 1966, amended 1970 and 1976). The Animal Welfare Act established a sweeping regulatory system to protect dogs, cats and many species of wild animals from abuse and represents the direct involvement of the federal government, to the maximum extent of its constitutional power, in the cause of animal welfare. This statute regulates individuals and establishments which buy or sell animals for research or exhibition purposes and to a limited extent the pet trade. Animal dealers, research laboratories, pet stores offering wild animals for sale, animal auctions, zoos, circuses and animal trainers are required by law to provide humane care, treatment and handling for the animals they house. The Act is administered by the U.S. Department of Agriculture (USDA).

The U.S. Department of Agriculture enforces regulations which set minimum husbandry standards for feeding and watering, cage size, sanitation, temperature range, veterinary care and euthanasia. Dealers and most exhibitors are required to be licensed and pay fees based on a sliding schedule. Others such as laboratories are required to register but do not pay fees. Common carriers (airlines, railroads, trucking companies, etc.) must register and adhere to standards developed to assure humane transportation.

Birds, reptiles, rodents, and farm animals are not covered by the Animal Welfare Act. In June 1979 USDA issued regulations covering the care, treatment, and handling of marine mammals in captivity, offering protection to them for the first time.

The 1966 Animal Welfare Act was motivated largely by Congressional concern about the theft of pet animals for sale to research labs. Animals now must be held five days by dealers and exhibitors before sale. Records of purchases or sales and animals on hand must be kept. Both requirements are designed to facilitate the tracing of stolen animals.

Although research laboratories are required to adhere to the USDA standards for humane treatment, in boarding their animals, the actual conduct of any experiment is expressly exempted. Researchers are directed to use appropriate analgesics, anesthetics, tranquilizers and painkillers, but this requirement is automatically lifted if, according to the researcher, the use of one of these substances would interfere with the action of the experiment. The animal care veterinarian of the institution is responsible for the fulfillment of this requirement.

The 1976 amendments included provisions to make animal fighting a federal offense. Animal fighting ventures are illegal under this statute whenever interstate or foreign commerce is involved. This law makes it illegal for anyone to sponsor an animal in any animal fighting venture, to sell, buy, transport or deliver any animal for this purpose and to use the mails to promote an animal fighting venture. All dog fighting is covered under this statute, but cockfighting is only punishable under the Animal Welfare Act in states where it is not legal. Although the USDA, through its Office of Investigations, is immediately responsible for administration of this law, the department may obtain the assistance of the FBI, the Department of the Treasury or other law enforcement agencies on the federal, state, or local levels. Search and seizure warrants can be issued and civil and criminal penalties can be levied against violators.

For violations other than the animal fighting sections, cease and desist orders may be issued against violators and licenses may be suspended. Civil and criminal penalties are another legal recourse against violations of the Act.

Animal and Plant Health Inspection Service (APHIS) has regional inspectors and veterinarians who conduct periodic inspections and investigate any violations. Part-time inspectors and private veterinarians who work on a fee basis also conduct inspections.

The USDA has come under fire for poor enforcement of the Act. Violations have continued without correction or legal action. Strong enforcement has been lacking. Funding has been insufficient and the federal inspectors and veterinarians spend only five per cent of their time on Animal Welfare Act issues. Most of the time, they work on livestock disease eradication. For questions, complaints, or information, write to:

> Administrator
> Animal and Plant Health Inspection Service
> USDA
> Washington, D.C. 20250

MARINE MAMMAL PROTECTION ACT OF 1972 (16 U.S.C. §§ 1361–1407; passed 1972, amended 1973 and 1976). In the Marine Mammal Protection Act (MMPA), Congress set forth a national policy to maintain marine mammal populations at optimum sustainable levels (OSP), while maintaining the health and stability of the marine ecosystem. This law established a moratorium of indefinite duration during which no marine mammals could be taken (killed, harassed, etc.) by any person subject to the jurisdiction of the United States. Nor, during the moratorium, can any imports be made of marine mammals or products from them.

Certain exceptions to the moratorium are allowed. The public display industry (marinelands, zoos, etc.) and the scientific community can apply for a permit to obtain marine mammals. Generally, they are granted. Natives in Alaska are also allowed to continue taking marine mammals for subsistence. The tuna fishing industry was given a two-year "grace" period for the purpose of developing technology in order to stop killing porpoises incidentally in the course of fishing. (Two years was not enough and after three more years of court cases and Congressional hearings, the tuna industry is now under a strict regulatory regime forcing them to reduce porpoise mortality and serious injury rate to near zero.)

In addition to the moratorium, the Act bans importation of any marine mammal or product if the animal was taken in an inhumane manner, or if it was nursing, or less than eight months old at the time it was taken. This provision effectively bans import of the Canadian white baby harp seal skins.

A mechanism is available to "waive" the moratorium both for importing and taking marine mammals. If the applicant can prove that the taking is humane, that the stocks are at OSP, and that a management scheme is in place which will maintain the stocks at the OSP level and is consistent with the Act, then a waiver may be granted.

One waiver of the moratorium has been granted to allow walrus to be killed in Alaska. A waiver to allow the import of South African seal skins was voided by the Courts because the seal pups were nursing, and were less than eight months old when killed. Also, the State of Alaska has applied for a waiver for eight of its marine mammal species which would effectively reopen sport hunting of many of these mammals. Their application is pending.

The administration of the MMPA is split between the Department of Commerce (National Marine Fisheries Service) for whales, dolphins, porpoise and seals; and, the Department of the Interior (Fish and Wildlife Service) for manatees, dugongs, sea otters, polar bears and walrus.

The Act also created a third arm called the Marine Mammal Commission which is an independent scientific advisory body charged with reviewing policies and actions of the federal agencies and making recommendations to further the objectives of the Act.

Civil and criminal penalties are available under the Act.

A 1978 amendment to the law makes it illegal to conduct commercial whaling in waters subject to the jurisdiction of the U.S.

For any questions, complaints, or information, you can write to the appropriate agency:

> Director
> National Marine Fisheries Service
> U.S. Department of Commerce
> Washington, D.C. 20235

> Director
> Fish and Wildlife Service
> Department of the Interior
> Washington, D.C. 20240

THE HUMANE METHODS OF SLAUGHTER ACT (7 U.S.C. 1901 et seq., P.L. 95–445; passed 1958, amended 1978). These statutes require that livestock must be stunned by humane methods prior to slaughter. The 1958 law defined these methods as those which render livestock insensible to pain by a single blow or gunshot or electrical or chemical means that are rapid and effective before being shackled, hoisted, thrown, cast, or cut. Slaughter in accordance with the ritual requirements of a religious faith is exempted, provided that the prescribed method causes the animal to suffer loss of consciousness by anemia of the brain caused by the simultaneous and instanteous severance of the carotoid [*sic*] arteries.

From 1958 until October 1979, when the 1978 law takes effect, only slaughterhouses selling meat to the federal government were covered by the humane law. The U.S. Department of Agriculture administered the law and maintained lists of slaughterhouses stating which plants used humane, non-humane, or ritual methods. It was the responsibility of federal purchasing agents to assure that the meat purchased was from slaughterhouses employing humane methods. Plants not adhering to humane standards were technically ineligible for federal contracts, however, enforcement appears to have been non-existent. No record of a plant being denied a federal contract exists. Nor is it know whether any federal purchasing agent ever checked slaughter methods. The 1958 law will be superceded [*sic*] by the new law (P.L. 95–445) although the same provisions delineating what is a humane method will be incorporated into the new law.

The 1978 Humane Methods of Slaughter Act amended the Federal Meat Inspection Act by incorporating humane slaughter standards into federal meat inspection standards, and making plants violating these standards subject to strong penalties. Administration of the Act remained with the U.S. Department of Agriculture.

As a result of the enactment of the P.L. 95–445, all slaughterhouses engaged in interstate or foreign commerce and all plants in states which do not maintain a separate state meat inspection system for interstate plants, will be monitored for compliance with this law by federal meat inspectors. The inspectors will be able to take a range of actions to prevent the inhumane slaugher of livestock, including "withholding inspection" which is tantamount to closing down plant operations.

Slaughterhouses, which only do business within their own state and are located in states which have separate state meat inspection programs, will eventually have to adopt humane slaughter methods. Integral to the Federal Meat Inspection Act is a requirement that any state meat inspection system's standards are at least equal to the federal. As a result, the states which do not have humane slaughter statutes and are not totally under federal inspection, will have to enact new legislation or issue new regulations. These states are being granted additional time for compliance to allow them to pass new laws.

In addition, the new law will require that foreign slaughterhouses exporting meat to the United States will have to comply with the humane standards just as they currently have to comply with health standards in the Federal Meat Inspection Act.

Also as a result of the 1978 law, federal meat inspectors will check that livestock are being humanely treated from the time that they arrive at the slaughterhouse until slaughter. The Senate Committee Report on the 1978 law stated that preslaughter handling as cited in the original law should be interpreted to begin when the livestock comes into custody of the slaughterhouse. Previously, in-spectors had no authority to prevent abuse of the livestock by slaughterhouse personnel. Regulations will be issued defining stan-dards for humane preslaughter handling.

For further information on this statute contact:

Administrator
Food Safety and Quality Service
U.S. Department of Agriculture
Washington, D.C. 20250

THE HORSE PROTECTION ACT (15 U.S.C. §§ 1821 et seq.; passed 1970, amended 1976). This law prohibits exhibition or transportation in commerce for show or exhibition of any horse which has been sored for the purpose of affecting its natural gait. The Act also prohibits the use of chains, boots, and other devices which may reasonably be expected to cause physical pain or distress to a horse. The manage-ment of horse shows are required to disqualify any "sored" horse. The United States Department of Agriculture through the regional inspection system of the Animal and Plant Health Inspection Ser-vice, enforces this law. The Department also relies on self-policing activities by the industry. Civil and criminal penalties may be levied against offenders. For further information, contact:

Administrator
Animal and Plant Health Inspection Service
USDA
Washington, D.C. 20250

TULE ELK PRESERVATION ACT (P.L. 94–389; passed 1976). This statute directs a Federal/State cooperative program for the preservation and enhancement of Tule Elk, an animal native to California. The Secretary of the Interior is directed to make an annual report to Congress in March of each year on activities carried out under the Act.

BALD EAGLE PROTECTION ACT (16 U.S.C. § 668 et seq.; passed in 1940, amended 1959, 1962, and 1972). This law provides protection for the bald eagle (the national emblem) and the golden eagle by prohibiting except under certain specified conditions, the capture, killing, or possession of and commerce in such birds. The Department of the Interior administers this law.

LACEY ACT (18 U.S.C. § 42–44; passed 1900, amended 1948, 1949, 1960, and 1969). The Lacey Act prohibits importation of wild vertebrates and other animals declared by the Secretary of the Interior to be injurious to man, agriculture, forestry, and wildlife resources except under certain circumstances such as zoological, educational, medical, and scientific purposes. It also prohibits the transportation in interstate or foreign commerce of wildlife or their parts or products taken or possessed in violation of federal, state, or foreign laws or regulations issued pursuant to those laws. The Department of the Interior took over enforcement of this law from the Department of Agriculture in 1939. To date, there has been only uneven enforcement of this law.

For further information on the Lacey Act, Tule Elk Preservation Act, and Bald Eagle Protection Act, write to:

Director
Fish and Wildlife Service
Department of the Interior
Washington, D.C. 20240

EXPORT OF HORSES BY SEA (P.L. 95–52). The Export Administration Amendments of 1977 contain a provision forbidding the export of horses by sea for slaughter. The Department of Commerce is responsible for administering this law.

For further information, contact:

Secretary of Commerce
Commerce Building
14th Street and Constitution Avenue, NW
Washington, D.C. 20230

THE WILD, FREE-ROAMING HORSES AND BURROS ACT (16 U.S.C., §§ 1331–1430 and 95–514; passed 1971, amended 1978). The original

1971 statute protected wild horses and burros on federal lands administered by the Bureau of Land Management (BLM), Department of the Interior and the U.S. Forest Service (USFS), Department of Agriculture. Congress determined that these animals were "living symbols of the historic and pioneer spirit of the West." This recognition of the value of these animals simply existing and roaming free for their own sake formed the policy basis of the Act. Wild horses and burros were given co-equal status on public lands with livestock, wildlife, and other uses. Prior to 1971, the animals had no legal status and were subject to wholesale exploitation by meat and glue processing interests, with acquiescence and often the encouragement of state and local authorities.

The 1971 law required BLM and USFS to manage the herds only at the minimally necessary levels, the premise being that these animals should be left alone and interfered with only when they encroach upon other legitimate uses of the public lands. Criminal sanctions for capturing or harrassing [sic] these animals included imprisonment. In order to eliminate the profit motive, the sale of any captured horse or any commercial use of the animals' remains was prohibited. Most significantly for the HSUS, the Act mandated the humane treatment for captured animals. Old, lame, or diseased animals were permitted to be destroyed in the most humane manner possible. The adopted animals were also to be assured humane conditions. Capture and removal operations were to be done under federal supervision. Captured animals were placed with private individuals under adoption contracts whereby the federal government retained title to the animals and the adopter agreed to care for the animals properly. Adopted horses could be transferred only with government consent. This scheme was designed to prevent horses from being laundered through owners into slaughterhouses.

This Act seemed adequate to protect the animals. Unfortunately, BLM has favored livestock interests for decades and did not properly enforce the Act. Lawsuits agains BLM were required to obtain minimal compliance. BLM alleged that there was continual overpopulation of the ranges by wild horses and argued for the annual removal of the horses. However, the population statistics cited by the agency have been shown to be inadequate and unreliable.

The adoption program was mismanaged by BLM. Captured horses were frequently corralled for long periods because BLM's recruitment of adopters was inefficient. Prospective adopters sometimes waited for up to two years. BLM's enforcement of the humane clause of the adoption contract has also been lax. Horses have been abused both in the corrals and by adopters.

Congress accepted BLM's arguments against the horses and in 1978 passed legislation and strengthened BLM's authority to deal with the alleged overpopulation of the herds. BLM is now directed to remove any animals determined to be "excess" and dispose of the excess either by adoption or "humane and cost-efficient" destruction.

To dispose of more horses through adoption, an incentive was provided. After one year under adoption contracts, full ownership will be granted to the adopter. The horses then would no longer be protected federally.

The 1978 amendments limit to four, except under special written authorization, the number of animals any individual can adopt in one year, and require that BLM determine that the individual has properly cared for the animals during the one-year adopting period before title passes. Also, it remains unlawful to sell any horse or burro, or its remains, for processing into commercial products.

Finally, the 1978 amendments require BLM to maintain a current inventory of horses and burros on public lands and provide for a research study under the aegis of the National Academy of Sciences to supply needed, scientifically gathered information on the herds and their relation to the habitat. Congress intended this information to determine the extent of range overpopulation, and form the basis for more rational management of the herds in the future.

For further information, contact:

Division of Range
Bureau of Land Management
Department of the Interior
Washington, D.C. 20240

Range Management
U.S. Forest Service
Department of Agriculture
Washington, D.C. 20013

THE MIGRATORY BIRD TREATY ACT (16 U.S.C. § 701 et seq.; passed 1918 and amended 1960 and 1969). This statute, administered by the Fish and Wildlife Service (Department of the Interior), protects various species of migratory birds by federal regulation from all forms of capture, harrassment [*sic*], or death, including sport hunting. The original Act was passed in 1918 to effectuate the treaty concluded in 1916 between the British Crown (on behalf of Canada) and the United States for the purposes of "saving from indiscriminate slaughter" and "insuring the preservation of" specific species of migratory birds. Treaty Conventions, Preamble, 39 Stat. 1702. Later, similar treaties with Mexico (1936) and with Japan (1972) were also given effect by the MBTA. The treaties essentially proclaimed that hunting of migratory game birds would be restricted to a three and one-half month period of each year, to occur between September 1 and March 10.

The heart of the MBTA consists of two sections: 16 U.S.C. § 703 is a sweeping *prohibition* of the killing, taking, hunting, capture, etc., of any migratory bird species included in the treaty conventions; 16 U.S.C. § 704 is a broad grant of discretion to the Secretary of the Interior to *allow* the killing, taking, hunting, capture, etc., of such migratory birds when and to the extent, if at all, such acts are compatible with the purposes and terms of the treaty conventions, and in so determining, the Secretary is explicitly charged by the Act to have "due regard to the zones of temperature and to the distribution, abundance, economic value, breeding habits, and times and lines of migratory flight" of migratory bird species.

The purpose of the MBTA is clearly to protect and ensure the preservation of *species* of migratory birds, as distinct from individual birds of even large numbers of birds within a species. This legally permits the hunting and slaughter of literally millions of individuals within a particular species of bird so long as the population of that species is not critically depressed.

For further information, contact:

Office of Migratory Bird Management
U.S. Fish and Wildlife Service
Department of the Interior
Washington, D.C. 20240

THE TWENTY-EIGHT HOUR LAW (45 U.S.C § 71 et seq.; passed 1906). This statute was the first federal anti-cruelty law in the United States. The current law was enacted in 1906 and was a revision of a law passed in 1877.

The law applies to livestock in interstate transportation and prohibits railroads from confining livestock in boxcars for more than twenty-eight hours without unloading, resting, feeding, and watering the animals for at least five consecutive hours. Owners of a particular shipment, upon written request, may be granted an extension allowing a total of thirty-six hours for confinement without rest. Violators of this law are subject to fines of up to $500. The United States Department of Agriculture enforces this law.

For further information, contact:

Secretary of Agriculture
Washington, D.C. 20250

THE ENDANGERED SPECIES ACT (7 U.S.C. § 136, 16 U.S.C. § 1531 et seq., P.L. 95–632; passed 1969, amended 1973 and 1978). The Endangered Species Act protects those species of plants and animals which are endangered or threatened with extinction over all or a significant portion of their habitats. The Act regulates the taking of species, restricts trade of such species and their by-products through a permit system, and, through regulations, protects species habitat from significant environmental modification or degradation. It also provides for the acquisition of habitat needed for the survival of a species and requires that all federal agencies avoid making adverse impacts which may threaten the survival of a species.

The type of restriction on the taking of or trade in a particular species and its by-products depends on whether it is listed as "threatened" or "endangered." Endangered species are closer to extinction than threatened species; therefore, endangered species have a higher degree of protection. Species are often listed as threatened if they are a likely candidate for endangered status because of trade or habitat encroachment pressure. Through the Endangered Species Act, international wildlife treaties are implemented. There are two important exemptions to the Endangered Species Act: (1) animals which were held in captivity prior to passage of the 1973 amendments; (2) Alaskan natives are allowed to hunt species if their hunting is primarily to supply subsistence needs. There are both civil and criminal penalties to punish violators of this law. The United States Department of the Interior, Fish and Wildlife Service, administers this law.

The Endangered Species Act also authorizes establishment of cooperative agreements and grants-in-aid to states with adequate conservation programs for endangered and threatened species.

The 1978 amendments significantly weakened the protective provisions, particularly for non-vertebrates. A cabinet level committee was established for the purpose of resolving conflicts between species and federal projects such as a dam. By a vote of 5 out of 7, the committee can order the extinction of a species in favor of a development project. The committee has been mandated to take economic data under consideration when deciding on an exemption application.

For further information, contact:

> Director
> U.S. Fish and Wildlife Service
> Department of Interior
> Washington, D.C. 20240

SELECTED TREATIES

Coding and ratification information follow the name of each treaty.

AGREEMENT ON THE CONSERVATION OF POLAR BEARS (I.L.M. 13:13–18, Jan. 1974). This 1973 agreement between the governments of Canada, Denmark, Norway, USSR, and the United States recognizes the responsibilities of the circumpolar countries for coordination of actions to protect polar bears. Except under certain specified conditions, taking of polar bears is prohibited. The agreement was signed by the United States on November 15, 1973, and ratified September 30, 1976. Agreement entered into force November 1, 1976, with ratification by three countries. Public Law 92–522, the Marine Mammal Protection Act of 1972 (16 U.S.C. 1361 et seq.; 86 Stat. 1027) provides authority for the United States to implement the agreement.

CONVENTION ON INTERNATIONAL TRADE IN ENDANGERED SPECIES OF WILD FAUNA AND FLORA (T.I.A.S. 8249). Establishes a system of import/export regulations to prevent the commercial overexploitation of plants and animals listed in three appendices to the Convention. Different levels of trade regulations are provided depending on the threatened status of the listed species and the contribution trade makes to that condition. Procedures are provided for periodic amendments to the appendices. The Convention was signed by 80 nations in Washington, D.C., on March 3, 1973. United States ratification occurred on September 13, 1973, with documents submitted to the depository government (Switzerland), January 14, 1974. The Convention entered into force 90 days after ratification by the tenth nation, July 1, 1975. Implementing legislation for the United States was provided by enactment of Public Law 93–205, the Endangered Species Act of 1973 (16 U.S.C. 1531–1543; 87 Stat. 884). Designation of scientific and management authorities to represent the United States in convention matters was achieved on April 13, 1976, by Executive Order 11911.

INTERIM CONVENTION ON THE CONSERVATION OF NORTH PACIFIC FUR SEALS (U.S.T. 2283; T.I.A.S. 3948, Feb. 9, 1957; amended Oct. 8, 1963, Sept. 3, 1969, and May 7, 1976). The practice of harvesting seals by shooting them while they are at sea is called pelagic sealing. This method is cruel and wasteful and caused the near extinction of the Northern fur seal. A treaty was signed in 1911 to end pelagic sealing and begin controlled harvests on land. This did allow the population to recover.

The treaty was renewed four times since 1957. Canada, Japan, the Soviet Union, and the United States are parties. The treaty calls for population research, and for the United States to conduct a controlled harvest on the Pribilof Islands giving fifteen per cent of the gross value of the skins to Canada and fifteen per cent to Japan. The Soviet Union also conducts a harvest and gives fifteen per cent each to Canada and Japan.

In a later treaty the method of kill was considered and tests were run on humaneness of clubbing, shooting, electrocution, and certain drugs. Clubbing remains as the method of kill.

In 1976 attempts were made to change the treaty to a more conservation, protection mode with little success. The United States did set aside one area where no killing takes place as part of a scientific inquiry into effects on unharvested populations.

This treaty will probably remain in force unless some way to protect seals from pelagic sealing is found.

INTERNATIONAL WHALING CONVENTION (62 Stat. 1716). This Convention entered into force November 10, 1948. It recognized the need to safeguard whale stocks for future generations by setting quotas and other regulations to limit whaling. The goals include making the orderly development of the whaling industry possible. Sixteen nations signed the original Convention including the United States. Present membership is twenty-three nations but not all the original signatories remain. The Convention set up an International Whaling Commission which meets annually in the summer to set quotas for the next whaling season. Attempts to adopt a ten-year moratorium on all commerical whaling were defeated in 1972, 1973, and 1974. In 1974, a New Management Procedure was adopted to allow total protection of whale stocks falling below a certain population level. Several whale species are considered endangered and are totally protected by IWC nations. Currently, not all nations engaged in whaling are members. In 1979, a ban on factory ships except to kill minke whales was adopted. This greatly reduced the number of sperm whales killed. Also adopted was a moratorium on all commercial whaling in the Indian Ocean.

MIGRATORY BIRD TREATIES (39 Stat. 1702; 50 Stat. 1311; 25 U.S.T. 3329). These three treaties involving the United States, Canada, Mexico, and Japan form the basis of the Migratory Bird Treaty Act. Both the treaty and the Act are thoroughly described in the "Federal Laws" section, *supra*.

CODE OF FEDERAL REGULATIONS. The Code of Federal Regulations (C.F.R.) contains the rules and regulations issued by administrative agencies to implement federal statutory law. The C.F.R. is divided into fifty titles which represent broad areas subject to federal regulation. Each title is divided into chapters, which usually bear the name of the administrating agency. The titles and chapters of interest to animal welfare organizations are listed below. The C.F.R. is sold by the Superintendent of Documents, U.S. Government Printing Office, Washington, D.C. 20402. The price ranges from $3.50 to $7.75 per volume.

Title 7—Agriculture
Chapter III   Animal and Plant Health Inspection Service
Chapter V   Agricultural Research Service

Title 9—Animals and Animal Products
Chapter I   Animal and Plant Health Inspection Service
Chapter II   Packers and Stockyards Administration
Chapter III Animal and Plant Health Inspection Service (Meat & Poultry Products Inspection)
Chapter IV   Agricultural Research Service

Title 15—Commerce and Foreign Trade
Chapter IX   National Oceanic and Atmospheric Administration

Title 36—Parks, Forests, and Public Property
Chapter I   National Park Service
Chapter II   Forest Service

Title 40—Protection of Environment
Chapter I   Environmental Protection Agency

Title 43—Public Lands: Interior
Subtitle A—Office of the Secretary of the Interior
Subtitle B—Regulations Relating to Public Lands
Chapter II   Bureau of Land Management

Title 50—Wildlife and Fisheries
Chapter I   U.S. Fish & Wildlife Service, Dept. of Interior
Chapter II National Marine Fisheries Service, Nat. Oceanic & Atmospheric Admin., Dept. of Commerce
Chapter III International Regulatory Agencies (Fishing and Whaling)
Chapter V   Marine Mammal Commission

STATE LAWS

It is impossible in a brief report to summarize each of the animal welfare laws of the fifty states; however, we have attempted to list the provisions most commonly contained in state codes relating to animal welfare. By using the Humane Society list in reviewing your state code, you should be able to determine which laws are applicable in your state. Copies of existing statutes can be obtained from the state law libraries or other reference agencies for a nominal fee. When requesting a copy of a statute, either a precise description of the statute, or, more preferably, a code citation (title and section number) should be provided. The library or other reference agency is usually able to respond within ten days to two weeks.

Provisions Often Found in State Laws Relating to Animal Welfare: cruelty; transportation; fighting, baiting and racing; animal experimentation; powers of humane agents; disposal of animals; licensing and regulation of pets, spay and neuter, strays, license fees; licensing, registration, and regulation of facilities handling animals (pet stores, kennels, shelters, riding stables, breeders, and dealers); use of animals as commercial lures; sale of infirmed or injured animals; poisoning or disfigurement; abandonment of animals; sale of chicks, ducklings, and rabbits; malicious destruction of animals; humane education; endangered species; trapping; hunting; parks and refuges; humane slaughter.

A thorough check should be made of the codes relating to Agriculture, Health, Education and Fish and Game.

STATE LAW LIBRARIES

ALABAMA
Supreme Court Library
Judicial Building
Montgomery 36104
205/832-6410

ALASKA
Court System
941 Fourth Avenue
Anchorage 99501

ARIZONA
Division of Library & Archives
Department of Administration
State Capitol
Phoenix 85007
602/271-5031

ARKANSAS
Supreme Court
Justice Building
Little Rock 72201
501/374-2512

CALIFORNIA
Law Library
State Library
Box 2037
Sacramento 95809
916/445-8833

COLORADO
Supreme Court
220 State Capitol
Denver 80203
303/892-2064

CONNECTICUT
Public Service Division
State Library
231 Capitol Avenue
Hartford 06115
203/566-4301

DELAWARE
State Law Library
Box 635
Dover 19901
302/678-4749

DISTRICT OF COLUMBIA
Library of Congress
First Street between E. Capitol
Street and Independence Avenue,
SE
Washington
202/426-5000

FLORIDA
Supreme Court Library
Supreme Court Building
Tallahassee 32304
904/488-8919

GEORGIA
State Library
40 Capitol Square
Atlanta 30334
404/656-3468

HAWAII
Supreme Court
Box 779
Honolulu 96808
808/548-7432

IDAHO
Supreme Court
451 W. State Street
Boise 83720
208/384-3317

ILLINOIS
Supreme Court Library
Supreme Court Building
Springfield 62706
217/782-2424

INDIANA
Judiciary Department
State House
Indianapolis 46204
317/633-4640

IOWA
Law Library
State Capitol
Des Moines 50319
515/281-5124

KANSAS
Supreme Court Law Library
Supreme Court Building
Topeka 66612
913/296-3257

KENTUCKY
State Law Library
State Capitol
Frankfort 40601
502/564-7417

LOUISIANA
Law Library
301 Loyola Avenue
New Orleans 70160
504/527-8268

MAINE
State Law & Legislative Ref. Lib.
State House
Augusta 04330
207/289-2754

MARYLAND
Dept. of Legislative Ref. Lib.
Box 348
Annapolis 21404
301/267-5561

MASSACHUSETTS
State Library
State House
Boston 02133
617/727-2590

MICHIGAN
Law Library
Law Building
Lansing 48904
517/373-0630

MINNESOTA
Law Library
117 University Avenue
St. Paul 55155
612/296-2775

MISSISSIPPI
State Library
219 Gartin Building
Jackson 39205
601/354-7113

MISSOURI
Law Library
Box 387
Jefferson City 65101
314/751-4214

MONTANA
312 State Capitol
Helena 59601
406/449-2471

NEBRASKA
State Law Library
1420 P Street
Lincoln 68508
402/432-2922

NEVADA
Supreme Court Library
Supreme Court Building
Carson City 89701
702/885-5140

NEW HAMPSHIRE
State Library
Supreme Court Building
Concord 03301
603/271-3777

NEW JERSEY
Law Library Bureau
Div. of State Lib., Archives & History
Dept. of Education
185 W. State Street
Trenton 08608
609/292-6209

NEW MEXICO
Supreme Court Law Library
Supreme Court Building
Santa Fe 87501
505/827-2515

NEW YORK
State Library
Education Department
Education Building Annex
Albany 12224
518/474-5957

NORTH CAROLINA
Supreme Court
Justice Building
Raleigh 27602
919/829-3425

NORTH DAKOTA
Supreme Court
State Capitol
Bismarck 58505
701/224-2227

OHIO
Supreme Court
30 E. Broad Street
Columbus 43215
614/466-2044

OKLAHOMA
Governmental Service Branch
Department of Libraries
Library Building
Oklahoma City 73105
405/521-2502

OREGON
Supreme Court Library
1147 State Street
Salem 97310
503/378-6030

PENNSYLVANIA
State Library
116 Education Building
Harrisburg 17120
717/787-7343

RHODE ISLAND
State Law Library
Providence County Court House
Providence 02903
401/331-0131

SOUTH CAROLINA
Supreme Court Library
1231 Gervais Street
Columbia 29201
803/252-3373

SOUTH DAKOTA
Supreme Court
State Capitol
Pierre 57501
605/224-3256

TENNESSEE
Supreme Court Law Library
Supreme Court Building
Nashville 37219
615/741-2016

TEXAS
State Law Library
Supreme Court Building
Austin 78711
512/475-3807

UTAH
Supreme Court
332 State Capitol
Salt Lake City 84114
801/533-5071

VERMONT
State Law Library
Department of Libraries
111 State Street
Montpelier 05602
802/828-3268

VIRGINIA
Supreme Court
Supreme Court Building
Richmond 23219
804/770-2075

WASHINGTON
Law Library
Temple of Justice
Olympia 98504
206/753-6526

WEST VIRGINIA
Law Library
East State Capitol
Charleston 25305
304/348-2607

WISCONSIN
State Library
303–316 E. Capitol
Madison 53702
608/266-1424

WYOMING
State Library
Supreme Court Building
Cheyenne 82002
307/777-7281

AMERICAN SAMOA
State Law Librarians
Government House
Pago Pago 96799
633-4116

GUAM
Law Library
Department of Law
Agana 96910

VIRGIN ISLANDS
District Court
St. Thomas 00801
809/774-0640

In addition, any private law office or your local county or city attorney's office will have copies of all up-to-date state statutes.

MUNICIPAL LAWS

City and county ordinances are even more varied than state laws. In general municipal ordinances are confined to animal control and taxation measures. Some communities do, however, make provision for the care and treatment of animals in their ordinances. The Humane Society would suggest that the interested individual or humane society official obtain a copy of his local laws from the appropriate municipal agency in your [sic] community.

Federal Committees, Departments, and Agencies

L isted here are the major groups within the federal government which are charged with considering, framing, or implementing environmental and natural resource information. Animal welfare is among their concerns.

UNITED STATES SENATE

COMMITTEE ON AGRICULTURE, NUTRITION AND FORESTRY (Room 322, Russell Building, Washington, D.C. 20510; telephone [202]224-2035). Chairman: Herman E. Talmadge. Concerned with agriculture and agricultural commodities; inspection of livestock, meat and agricultural products; animal industry and diseases of animals; pests and pesticides; agricultural extension services and experiment stations; forestry, forest reserves, and wilderness areas other than those created from the public domain; agricultural economics and research; human nutrition; home economics; extension of farm credit and farm security; rural development, rural electrification and watersheds; agricultural production and marketing and stabilization of prices of agricultural products; crop insurance and soil conservation; school nutrition programs; food stamp programs; food from fresh waters. The committee shall also study and review, on a comprehensive basis, matters relating to food, nutrition and hunger, both in the United States and in foreign countries, and rural affairs and report thereon from time to time.

COMMITTEE ON ENERGY AND NATURAL RESOURCES (Room 3106, Dirksen Building, Washington, D.C. 20510; telephone [202]224-4971). Chairman: Henry M. Jackson. Concerned with energy policy; energy regulation and conservation; energy research and development; solar energy systems; nonmilitary development of nuclear energy; naval petroleum reserves in Alaska; oil and gas production and distribution; extraction of minerals from oceans and outer continental shelf lands; energy related aspects of deepwater ports; hydroelectric power, irrigation and reclamation; coal production, distribution, and utilization; public lands and forests, including farming and grazing thereon, and mineral extraction therefrom; national parks, recreation areas, wilderness areas, wild and scenic rivers, historical sites, military parks, and battlefields; and, on the public domain, preservation of prehistoric ruins and objects of interest; mining, mineral lands, mining claims and mineral conservation; mining education and research; territorial possessions of the United States, including trusteeships.

COMMITTEE ON ENVIRONMENT AND PUBLIC WORKS (Room 4204, Dirksen Building, Washington, D.C. 20510; telephone [202]224-6176). Chairman: Jennings Randolph. Concerned with environmental policy; environmental research and development; ocean dumping; fisheries and wildlife; environmental aspects of outer continental shelf lands; solid waste disposal and recycling; environmental effects of toxic substances, other than pesticides; water resources; flood control and improvements of rivers and harbors, including environmental aspects of deepwater ports; public works, bridges, and dams; water pollution; air pollution; noise pollution; nonmilitary environmental regulation and control of nuclear energy; regional economic development; construction and maintenance of highways; public buildings and improved grounds of the United States generally, including federal buildings in the District of Columbia. The committee shall also study and review, on a comprehensive basis, matters relating to environmental protection and resource utilization and conservation, and report thereon from time to time.

HOUSE OF REPRESENTATIVES

COMMITTEE ON AGRICULTURE (Room 1301, Longworth House Office Building, Washington, D.C. 20515; telephone [202]225-2171). Chairman: Thomas S. Foley. Concerned with adulteration of seeds, insect pests, and protection of birds and animals in forest reserves; agriculture generally; agricultural and industrial chemistry; agricultural colleges and experiment stations; agricultural economics and research; agricultural education extension services; agricultural production and marketing and stabilization of prices of agricultural products; animal industry and diseases of animals; crop insurance and soil conservation; dairy industry; entomology and plant quarantine; extension of farm credit and farm security; forestry in general, and forest reserves other than those created from the public domain; human nutrition and home economics; inspection of livestock and meat products; plant industry, soils, and agricultural engineering; rural electrification.

COMMITTEE ON INTERIOR AND INSULAR AFFAIRS (Room 1324, Longworth House Office Building, Washington, D.C. 20515; telephone [202]225-2761). Chairman: Morris K. Udall. Concerned with forest reserves and national parks created from the public domain; forfeiture of land grants and alien ownership, including alien ownership of mineral lands; geological survey; interstate compacts relating to apportionment of waters for irrigation purposes; irrigation and reclamation, including water supply for reclamation projects, and easements of public lands for irrigation projects, and acquisition of private lands when necessary to complete irrigation projects; measures relating to the care and management of Indians, including the care and allotment of Indian lands and general and special measures relating to claims which are paid out of Indian funds; measures relating generally to the insular possessions of the United States, except matters affecting their revenue and appropriations; military parks and battlefields; national cemeteries administered by the secretary of the interior; and parks within the District of Columbia; mineral land laws and claims and entries thereunder; mineral resources of the public lands; mining interests generally; mining schools and experimental stations; petroleum conservation on the public lands and conservation of the radium supply in the United States; preservation of prehistoric ruins and objects of interest on the public domain; public lands generally, including entry, easements, and grazing thereon; relations of the United States with the Indians and the Indian tribes; regulation of the domestic nuclear energy industry, including regulation of research and development reactors and nuclear regulatory research; also special oversight functions with respect to all programs affecting Indians and nonmilitary nuclear energy and research and development including the disposal of nuclear waste.

COMMITTEE ON INTERSTATE AND FOREIGN COMMERCE (Room 2125, Rayburn House Office Building, Washington, D.C. 20515; telephone [202]225-2927). Chairman: Harley O. Staggers. Concerned with interstate and foreign commerce generally; inland waterways; interstate oil compacts and petroleum and natural gas; except on the public lands, nuclear energy facilities regulation; railroads, including railroad labor, railroad retirement, and unemployment, except revenue measures related thereto; interstate and foreign communications; interstate transmission of power, except the installation of connections between government waterpower projects; securities and exchanges; consumer affairs and consumer protection; travel and tourism; public health and quarantine; health and health facilities, except health care supported by payroll deductions; biomedical research and development; war claims.

COMMITTEE ON MERCHANT MARINE AND FISHERIES (Room 1334, Longworth House Office Building, Washington, D.C. 20515; telephone [202]225-4047). Chairman: John M. Murphy. Concerned with merchant marine generally; oceanography and marine affairs, including coastal zone management; Coast Guard, including lifesaving service, lighthouses, lightships, and ocean derelicts; fisheries and wildlife, including research, restoration, refuges, and conservation; measures relating to the regulation of common carriers by water (except matters subject to the jurisdiction of the Interstate Commerce Commission) and to the inspection of merchant marine vessels, lights and signals, lifesaving equipment, and fire protection on such vessels; merchant marine officers and seamen; navigation and the laws relating thereto, including pilotage; Panama Canal and the maintenance and operation of the Panama Canal, including the administration, sanitation, and government of the Canal area; and interoceanic canals generally; registering and licensing of vessels and small boats; rules and international arrangements to prevent collisions at sea; United States Coast Guard and Merchant Marine academies, and state maritime academies; international fishing agreements.

EXECUTIVE BRANCH

DEPARTMENT OF AGRICULTURE (Fourteenth Street and Jefferson Drive, S.W., Washington, D.C. 20250; telephone [202]44-plus extension; information [202]655-4000). Secretary: Bob Bergland (Ext. 73631).

ANIMAL AND PLANT HEALTH INSPECTION SERVICE (Washington, D.C. 20250; telephone [202]44-plus extension; information [202]447-3977). Administrator: Dr. Francis J. Mulhern (Ext. 73668).

DEPARTMENT OF COMMERCE. National Oceanic and Atmospheric Administration (Washington, D.C. 20230; telephone [202]443-8910). To improve man's comprehension and uses of the physical environment and its oceanic life. Components of the NOAA: National Ocean Survey; National Marine Fisheries Service; National Weather Service; Environmental Data Information Service; National Environmental Satellite Service; Environmental Research Laboratories; Office of Coastal Zone Management; Office of Sea

Grant; Office of Ocean Management; and, NOAA Corps. Created: 1970. Administrator: Richard A. Frank ([202]377-3567).

NATIONAL MARINE FISHERIES SERVICE (Washington, D.C. 20235; telephone [202]634-plus extension). A component of the National Oceanic and Atmospheric Administration. Promotes the protection and rational use of living marine resources for their aesthetic, economic, and recreational value to the American people. Administers programs to determine the consequences of the naturally varying environment and man's activities on living marine resources, to provide knowledge and services to foster their efficient international management, use and protection of living marine resources. Assistant Administrator for Fisheries: Terry L. Leitzell (Ext. 7283).

DEPARTMENT OF HEALTH, EDUCATION, AND WELFARE. Food and Drug Administration (5600 Fishers Lane, Rockville, Maryland 20857; telephone [301]443-plus extension; information Ext. 1544). Protects the health of American consumers by enforcing federal law which requires that foods must be safe, pure, and wholesome; that drugs and therapeutic devices must be safe and effective; that cosmetics must be harmless; and that all these products must be honestly and informatively labeled and packaged. Commissioner: Donald Kennedy (Ext. 2410).

U.S. OFFICE OF EDUCATION (Washington, D.C. 20202). Director, Office of Environmental Education: Walter J. Bogan, Jr. (telephone [202]245-9231).

DEPARTMENT OF THE INTERIOR (Interior Building, C Street between Eighteenth and Nineteenth, NW, Washington, D.C. 20240; telephone [202]343-plus extension; information Ext. 1100). Secretary: Cecil D. Andrus (Ext. 7351). United States Fish and Wildlife Service (Washington, D.C. 20240; telephone [202]343-plus extension). An act of Congress, April 22, 1974, renamed the Bureau of Sport Fisheries and Wildlife the United States Fish and Wildlife Service under the assistant secretary for fish and wildlife and parks. The service aids in conservation of the nation's migratory birds, certain mammals, and sport fishes. This includes application of research findings in the development and management of a system of national wildlife refuges for migratory birds and endangered species; operation of a system of fish hatcheries; management of populations of migratory game birds through regulation of the time, degree, and manner of taking; acquisition and application of technical knowledge necessary for the perpetuation and enhancement of fish and wildlife resources; biological monitoring of development projects; enforcement of several laws, including the Endangered Species Act, the Lacey Act, the Marine Mammals Protection Act, and the Migratory Bird Treaty Act. The service administers federal aid to state governments; provides technical assistance to state and foreign governments; serves as lead federal agency in international conventions on wildlife conservation; and operates a program of public affairs and environmental education to inform the public of the status of America's fish and wildlife resources. Director: Lynn A. Greenwalt (Ext. 4717).

DEPARTMENT OF STATE. Bureau of Oceans and International Environmental and Scientific Affairs (New State Building, 2201 C Street, NW, Washington, D.C. 20520). Has principal responsibility for formulating and implementing policies and proposals for the scientific and technological aspects of United States relations with other governmental and international organizations and for dealing with a broad range of foreign policy issues relating to oceans, fisheries, environment, population, nuclear energy, new energy technology, space, and other fields of advanced technology. Assistant Secretary-Designate: Thomas R. Pickering (telephone [202]632-1554).

INDEPENDENT AGENCIES

ENDANGERED SPECIES SCIENTIFIC AUTHORITY (Eighteenth and C Streets, NW, Washington, D.C. 20240; telephone [202]653-5948). Established in 1976 by Executive Order 11911 to ensure the scientific soundness of governmental decisions concerning trade in wild animals and plants and international wildlife conservation in general. The ESSA's primary responsibility is as the United States Scientific Authority for the Convention on International Trade in Endangered Species of Wild Fauna and Flora. Members: Harold O'Connor, chairman (Department of the Interior); Dr. Robert L. Williamson (Department of Agriculture); Dr. R. V. Miller (Department of Commerce); Dr. Joe R. Held (Department of Health, Education, and Welfare); William Sievers (National Science Foundation); Ms. Jane Yarn (Council on Environmental Quality); Dr. David Challinor (Smithsonian Institution). Executive Secretary: Dr. William Y. Brown.

ENVIRONMENTAL PROTECTION AGENCY (401 M Street, SW, Washington, D.C. 20460; telephone [202]755-2673). Charged with mounting a coordinated attack on the environmental problems of air and water pollution, solid wastes management, pesticides, toxic substances, radiation, and noise. It places under one roof some fifteen programs which had been scattered throughout several agencies of the federal government. Functions include: setting and enforcing environmental standards; conducting research on the causes, effects, and control of environmental problems; assisting states and local governments. Administrator: Douglas M. Costle ([202]755-2700).

INTERNATIONAL WHALING COMMISSION (The Red House, Station Road, Histon, Cambridge CB4 4NP, England; telephone 022-023-3971). Established under the International Convention for the Regulation of Whaling, 1946, to provide for the conservation, development and optimum utilization of whale resources. Member nations: United States, Argentina, Australia, Brazil, Canada, Denmark, France, Iceland, Japan, Mexico, Netherlands, New Zealand, Norway, Panama, South Africa, USSR, and United Kingdom. Chairman: T. Asgeirsson, Iceland. Vice-Chairman: M. C. Mercer, Canada. Secretary: Dr. R. Gambell (at Cambridge address). Executive Officer: M. Harvey (at Cambridge address). U.S. Commissioner: Richard A. Frank, Administrator, NOAA, U.S. Department of Commerce, Rockville, Maryland 20852. Publications: annual reports of the commission; reports of the scientific committee; and special issues of scientific reports. Editor: Dr. R. Gambell.

MARINE MAMMAL COMMISSION (1625 I Street, NW, Washington, D.C. 20006; telephone [202]653-6237). Established by the Marine Mammal Protection Act of 1972, P.L. 92-522, in consultation with the Committee of Scientific Advisors on Marine Mammals, to review periodically the status of marine mammal populations; to manage a research program concerned with their conservation; and to develop, review, and make recommendations on federal activities and policies which affect the protection and conservation of marine mammals. Commissioners: Dr. Douglas G. Chapman, Chairman, Seattle, Washington; Dr. Donald B. Siniff, Minneapolis, Minnesota; Dr. Richard A. Cooley, Santa Cruz, California.

PRIVATE ORGANIZATIONS

There are many hundreds of international, national, and interstate organizations concerned with aspects of environmental protection, conservation, and animal welfare. I have listed those which I consider the most effective ones concerned with animals' rights.

AFRICAN WILDLIFE LEADERSHIP FOUNDATION, INC. (1717 Massachusetts Avenue, NW, Washington, D.C. 20036; telephone [202]265-8394). Provides scholarships for wildlife management training at colleges of wildlife management in Africa; finances and operates wildlife conservation projects in Africa in cooperation with African governmental ministries; maintains an international office in Nairobi which includes wildlife management, scientific, and conservation experts; assists in development of national parks and reserve areas and carries out ecological and game ranching programs. Chairman of the Board of Trustees: Kermit Roosevelt. President: Richard M. Jackson. Executive Vice President: Robinson McIlvaine. Secretary-Treasurer: Peter Conners Andrews.

ANIMAL WELFARE INSTITUTE (P.O. Box 3650, Washington, D.C. 20007; telephone [202]337-2333). Active in improvement of conditions for laboratory animals, protection of endangered species, and humane education. Albert Schweitzer Award is presented annually for outstanding contributions to animal welfare. Membership: 4,-500. Founded: 1951. President: Christine Stevens ([202]337-2332). Publication: *Information Report* (quarterly).

CENTER FOR LAW AND SOCIAL POLICY: THE INTERNATIONAL PROJECT (1751 N Street, NW, Washington, D.C. 20036; telephone [202]876-0670). A foundation-funded, public interest law firm that specializes in representing heretofore-unrepresented public groups with respect to significant foreign affairs issues, in economic, environmental, human rights, and social areas. Represents consumers in foreign trade matters; is involved in law of the sea issues which include law of the sea treaty negotiations, marine pollution, deep-sea mining, and protection of endangered species; has participated extensively in proceedings involving nuclear exports and is engaged in issues involving international human rights and the activities of U.S. corporations abroad. The project collaborates closely with foreign interest groups, both with regard to the above issues and to international agreements of common concern.

DEFENDERS OF WILDLIFE (1244 Nineteenth Street, NW, Washington, D.C. 20036; telephone [202]659-9510). A national nonprofit educational organization, dedicated to the preservation of all forms of wildlife. Promotes, through education and research, protection and humane treatment of all mammals, birds, fish, and other wildlife and the elimination of painful methods of trapping, capturing, and killing wildlife. President: Jocelyn A. Alexander. Publication: *Defenders*.

ENVIRONMENTAL ACTION, INC. (Room 731, 1346 Connecticut Avenue, NW, Washington, D.C. 20036; telephone [202]833-1845). A nonprofit, but not tax-deductible, action organization, which grew out of the Environmental Teach-In. Orientation is toward political and social change in a broad range of environmental issues, including solid waste, transportation, electric utilities, water, and others. Established: 1970. Principal Staff: Peter Harnik, Dennis Bass, Philip Michael, Pamela Devel, Ana Crapsey, A. Blakeman Early, Joanne Slaboch, Suzette Tapper. Publication: *Environmental Action*.

ENVIRONMENTAL DEFENSE FUND, INC. (475 Park Avenue South, New York, New York 10016; telephone [212]686-4191. 1525 Eighteenth Street, NW, Washington, D.C. 20036; telephone [202]833-1484. 2827 Durant Avenue, Berkeley, California 94704; telephone [415]548-8906. 1657 Pennsylvania Street, Denver, Colorado 80203; telephone [303]831-7559). A national organization of lawyers and scientists which serves as the legal action arm for the scientific community. Public membership of 46,000 and a 700-member Scientists Advisory Committee and a Legal Advisory Committee. Currently has approximately seventy cases in varying stages of litigation dealing with the following areas: pest control, water resources, water quality, land use, energy, transportation, noise, wildlife. Incorporated in New York State in 1967 as a tax-exempt, nonprofit organization. Chairman, Board of Trustees: Dr. John Firor. Publication: *EDF Letter.*

ENVIRONMENTAL POLICY CENTER (317 Pennsylvania Avenue, SE, Washington, D.C. 20003; telephone [202]547-6500). Works to influence congressional and executive branch decisions about national environmental issues, specializing in national energy policy, water resources, oil, gas, coal, nuclear, synthetic, and alternative energy sources and energy conservation; develops information needed for informed public participation in environmental decisions; and serves as a Washington base for local and regional citizens' groups. Founded: 1972. President: Carolyn Anderson. Publication: *Washington Resource Report.*

FAUNA PRESERVATION SOCIETY (care of Zoological Society of London, Regent's Park, London NW1 4RY, England; telephone 01-586-0872). To conserve wildlife throughout the world. Membership: 3,500; Founded: 1903. Patron: H.M. The Queen. President: Professor Lord Zuckerman. Membership Secretary: Mrs. K. Gordon. Publication: *Oryx.*

FRIENDS OF THE EARTH (124 Spear Street, San Francisco, California 94105; telephone: [415]495-4770). Committed to the preservation, restoration, and rational use of the earth. Affiliated Friends of the

Earth organizations are active in France, Germany, the United Kingdom, Thailand, Sweden, the Netherlands, Australia, Ireland, New Zealand, Canada, Belgium, Yugoslavia, El Salvador, Switzerland, Italy, Mexico, and Spain. Membership: 23,000; Founded: 1969. President: David R. Brower.

THE HUMANE SOCIETY OF THE UNITED STATES (National Headquarters, 2100 L Street NW, Washington, D.C. 20037; telephone [202]452-1100). Committed to the prevention of cruelty to animals. HSUS major goals include reducing the overbreeding of cats and dogs; opposing sports hunting and trapping; educating people to respect all living things; eliminating animal abuse in entertainment; correcting inhumane conditions in zoos and other exhibitions; stopping cruelty in the handling and transporting of food animals; providing technical assistance to local humane groups; ending cruelty in biomedical research and testing; strengthening anticruelty laws and their enforcement; extending animal protection into areas where there is none; monitoring federal laws to protect animals. Incorporated: November 1954. President: John A. Hoyt. Publications: *The Humane Society News, Close-Up Report, Humane Education, Shelter Sense, KIND.* Regional Offices:

> Great Lakes Region (Indiana, Illinois, Ohio, Michigan)
> 725 Haskins Street, Bowling Green, Ohio 43402
> Director: Sandy Rowland ([419]352-8543)

> Gulf States Region (Arkansas, Louisiana, Oklahoma, Texas)
> 5333 Everhart Road, Building A, Suite 209, Corpus Christi, Texas 78411
> Director: William R. Meade III ([512]854-3142)

> New England Region (Connecticut, Massachusetts, Maine, New Hampshire, Rhode Island, Vermont)
> 630 Oakwood Avenue, Suite 213, West Hartford, Connecticut 06110
> Director: John Inman, Jr. ([203]522-4908)

> Southeast Region (Alabama, Florida, Georgia, Mississippi)
> 3165 McCrory Place, Suite 215, Orlando, Florida 32803
> Director: Donald Coburn ([305]898-1592)

West Coast Region (California, Idaho, Oregon, Nevada, Washington)
1713 J Street, Suite 4, Sacramento, California 95814
Director: Charlene Drennon ([916]447-3295)

New Jersey Branch
1139 East Jersey Street, Room 601, Elizabeth, New Jersey 07201
Director: Nina Austenberg ([201]351-2475)

NAAHE / Norma Terris Humane Education Center
P.O. Box 98, East Haddam, Connecticut 06423
Director: John Dommers ([203]434-8666)

Rocky Mountain Region (Colorado, Utah, Wyoming, Arizona, New Mexico)
1780 South Bellaire Street, Suite 103, Denver, Colorado 80222
Director: Douglas Scott ([303]759-8880)

THE INSTITUTE FOR THE STUDY OF ANIMAL PROBLEMS (2100 L Street, NW, Washington, D.C. 20037; telephone [202]452-1148). Established as a scientific organization to explore the various relationships between man and animals. Areas of investigation include: the potential for balancing the farm animal's environmental requirements and efficient production and slaughter; the reduction in number of laboratory animals and in the stress involved in housing and experimentation; humane and practical methods of birth control for companion animals to reduce the problem of dog and cat overpopulation; wildlife management practices and the maintenance of captive wild animals; animals as an educational resource; the practicality of some of the legal and moral aspects of animal rights. Director: Michael W. Fox. Publication: *The International Journal for the Study of Animal Problems.*

INTERNATIONAL SOCIETY FOR THE PROTECTION OF ANIMALS (29 Perkins Street, Boston, Massachusetts 02130; telephone [617]522-7000). Functions to conserve and protect animals, both domestic and wild. Field staff are deployed to aid animals and advise animal welfare societies throughout the world. Maintains offices in London and Boston. In addition to individual members, 139 animal protection/conservation organizations in fifty countries have membership with ISPA. Incorporated: 1959. President: David S. Claflin. Publication: *ISPA News.*

INTERNATIONAL UNION FOR CONSERVATION OF NATURE AND NATURAL RESOURCES (IUCN, 1110 Morges, Switzerland; telephone 021-71-44-01; telegrams Unicorn, Morges). An independent nongovernmental body founded in 1948 to promote scientifically based action for the conservation of wild living resources. Has 427 voting members in 103 countries; 51 states, 106 government agencies, and 267 nongovernmental organizations. Maintains a global network of more than 700 scientists and professionals organized into six commissions. President: Mohammed Kassas, Egypt. Vice-presidents: Robert E. Boote, U.K.; A. M. Borodin, USSR; Russell E. Train, U.S.A. Chairman of the Bureau: Maurice F. Strong, Canada. Treasurer: D. F. McMichael, Australia. Director General: David A. Munro. Director of Programs: Adrian Phillips. Director of Administration: Richard Herring. Head, Environmental Law Centre, Bonn, FRG: Françoise Burhenne-Guilmin.

LEAGUE OF CONSERVATION VOTERS (317 Pennsylvania Avenue, SE, Washington, D.C. 20003; telephone [202]547-7200). A nonpartisan, national political campaign committee to promote the election of public officials who will work for a healthy environment. Also evaluates environmental records of congressmen, senators and presidential candidates. Researches and publishes congressional voting records on important environmental legislation. Publications: *How Congress Voted on Critical Environmental Issues* and *How Senators Voted on Critical Environmental Issues.*

NATURAL RESOURCES COUNCIL OF AMERICA (Box 20, Tracys Landing, Maryland 20869; telephone [301]261-5277). A society of major national and regional organizations. Exists to advance sound management of natural resources in the public interest by providing its member organizations with information on actions by Congress and the executive branch, by making available to them scientific data on conservation problems, and by providing a medium of cooperation.

It is not itself an action organization, nor does it represent or attempt to control the policies and actions of its member organizations. Membership: forty-seven national and regional conservation and technical societies and organizations.

NATURAL RESOURCES DEFENSE COUNCIL, INC. (122 East Forty-second Street, New York, New York 10017; telephone [212]949-0049. 917 Fifteenth Street, NW, Washington, D.C. 20005; telephone [202]737-5000. 2345 Yale Street, Palo Alto, California 94306; telephone [415]327-1080). Nonprofit membership organization dedicated to protecting America's endangered natural resources and improving the quality of the human environment. Combines monitoring of governmental agencies, scientific research, litigation and citizen education. Areas of concentration: air and water pollution, nuclear safety, land use, transportation, environmental carcinogens, resource management, international environment, Alaska. Membership: 40,000. Founded: 1970. Executive Director: John H. Adams. Publications: *Land Use Controls in the United States: A Handbook on the Legal Rights of Citizens.* A full list of publications is available upon request.

THE NATURE CONSERVANCY (Suite 800, 1800 North Kent Street, Arlington, Virginia 22209; telephone [703]841-5300). Nonprofit membership corporation dedicated to preservation of natural areas for present and future generations; cooperates with colleges, universities, public and private conservation organizations to acquire lands for scientific and educational purposes. Organized: 1946. Chairman of the Board: John E. Andrus, III. President: Patrick F. Noonan.

SIERRA CLUB (530 Bush Street, San Francisco, California 94108; telephone [415]981-8634). To protect and conserve the natural resources of the Sierra Nevada, the United States, and the world; to undertake and publish scientific and educational studies concerning all aspects of man's environment and the natural ecosystems of the world; and to educate the people of the United States and the world to the need to preserve and restore the quality of that environment and the integrity of these ecosystems. With fifty chapters coast to coast, the club's nonprofit program includes wilderness outings, white-water trips, skiing, mountaineering, knapsacking, films, exhibits, conferences, fourteen huts and lodges, a library, and publishing. Founded: 1892 by John Muir. President Ted Snyder. Publication: *Sierra.*

WORLD WILDLIFE FUND (1601 Connecticut Avenue, NW, Suite 800, Washington, D.C. 20009; telephone [202]387-0805). Largest private international conservation organization supporting programs to save threatened and endangered wildlife and habitats as well as scientific ecological research based predominately upon the IUCN (International Union for Conservation of Nature and Natural Resources) World Conservation Strategy. WWF includes national affiliates, with international headquarters located in Morges, Switzerland. Supporters: 70,000. Established: 1961. President: Russell E. Train.

Index